BY
DESIGN

BY DESIGN

THE WORLD'S BEST CONTEMPORARY INTERIOR DESIGNERS

DESIGNERS

A

10 A Work of Substance
14 JJ Acuna / Bespoke Studio
18 Apartment 48
20 ASH

B

22 Batiik Studio
24 Kelly Behun
28 BENSLEY
32 Sig Bergamin
36 Deborah Berke Partners
38 Nate Berkus Associates
42 Linda Boronkay
46 Martin Brudnizki Design Studio
48 Martyn Lawrence Bullard

C

50 Rafael de Cárdenas
52 Darryl Carter
54 Cristina Celestino
56 Champalimaud Design
60 CHZON
64 Commune Design

D

66 Vincenzo De Cotiis
68 Design Research Studio
72 Dimorestudio
76 Joseph Dirand
78 dix design+architecture
80 Doherty Design Studio
82 Sophie Dries Architect
86 Bernard Dubois Architects

F

88 André Fu Studio
90 Ken Fulk

G

92 Fawn Galli
96 GOLDEN
98 Grisanti & Cussen
100 Luca Guadagnino

H

102 Halden Interiors
104 Hare + Klein
108 Hecker Guthrie
112 Shawn Henderson
116 Beata Heuman
120 Fran Hickman
122 Laura Hodges Studio
126 Suzy Hoodless
130 Young Huh Interior Design
132 Humbert & Poyet

J

136 Tamsin Johnson

K

140 Kit Kemp
144 Rita Konig
146 Kråkvik & D'Orazio

L

148 Joanna Laajisto
150 LH.Designs
152 Linehouse
154 Isabel López-Quesada
156 Fiona Lynch

M

160 Maison Vincent Darré
162 Mlinaric, Henry and Zervudachi

N

164 Greg Natale
168 Paola Navone / Studio OTTO
172 Neri&Hu
174 David Netto Design
176 Norm Architects
178 Note Design Studio

O

182 Marie-Anne Oudejans

P

184 Stéphane Parmentier
186 Ben Pentreath
188 Perspective Studio
190 Emmanuel Picault

R

192 Reath Design
194 Redd Kaihoi
198 Retrouvius
202 Richards Stanisich
204 Right Meets Left Interior Design
206 Rockwell Group
210 Roman and Williams
212 Romanek Design Studio
216 Daniel Romualdez
218 RP Miller

S

222 Achille Salvagni
224 Tom Scheerer
226 Glenn Sestig Architects
228 SevilPeach
232 SheltonMindel
236 Space Copenhagen
240 The Stella Collective
242 Robert Stilin

244 Studio Ashby
248 Studio Daminato
250 Studio Jacques Garcia
252 Studio KO
254 Studio Mumbai
256 Studio Peregalli
258 Studio Shamshiri
262 Studio Sofield
264 Studioilse

T

268 Takenouchi Webb
270 David Thulstrup
274 Faye Toogood
278 Virginia Tupker Interiors

V

280 Vincent Van Duysen
284 Gert Voorjans

W

288 Joyce Wang
292 Kelly Wearstler
296 Bunny Williams
298 Woodson & Rummerfield's
    House of Design

Y

302 Yabu Pushelberg
306 Teo Yang Studio
308 Pierre Yovanovitch

NOMINATORS

Ingrid Abramovitch
Executive Editor, *Elle Decor*
New York

Eleanor Acquavella
Director and Co-owner,
Acquavella Galleries
New York

Mark Adams (and the
Vitsœ team)
Managing Director, Vitsœ
Royal Leamington Spa, UK

Jaime Aguilera
CEO and Founder, The-Collective
Santiago, Chile

Sarah Andelman
Founder and Creative Director,
Just An Idea
Paris

Spencer Bailey
Editor-at-Large, Phaidon
New York

Helen Barrett
Deputy Editor, *FT Wealth*
London

Brian Bolke
Founder, The Conservatory;
Co-founder, Forty Five Ten
Dallas and New York

Billy Bolton
Photographer
London

Graeme Brooker
Professor and Head of Interior
Design, Royal College of Art
London

Laura Lee Brown and
Steve Wilson
Founders, 21c Museum Hotels
Louisville, Kentucky

John Clifford Burns
Editor-in-chief, *Kinfolk*
Copenhagen

Felix Burrichter
Creative Director, Curator, and
Editor; Founder, *PIN–UP*
New York

Hatta Byng
Editor, *House & Garden*
London

Anders Byriel
CEO, Kvadrat
Ebeltoft, Denmark

Richard Caring
Owner and Chairman, Caprice
Holdings, The Ivy Collection, and
The Birley Clubs
London

Kissa Castañeda
Regional Editor, Travel and
Design, *Tatler Asia*
Singapore

Tony Chambers
Creative Director, Design
Consultant, and Editor
London

Aric Chen
Independent Curator
Shanghai

Juthatham Bo Chirathivat
Vice President, Central Pattana
Bangkok, Thailand

Yoko Choy Wai-ching
China Editor, *Wallpaper**;
Co-founder, Collective
Contemporist
Hong Kong and Amsterdam

Julie Cirelli
Editorial Director, Harvard
Graduate School of Design
Cambridge, Massachusetts

Lucy Cleland
Editorial Director,
Country & Town House
London

Edie Cohen
Deputy Editor, *Interior Design*
Santa Monica, California

Alicia Colby-Sy
Former Executive Editor,
Town & Country Philippines
Quezon City, Philippines

Amy Fine Collins
Author; Editor at Large, *Air Mail*;
Special Correspondent,
Vanity Fair
New York

Francisco Costa
Founder, Costa Brazil
New York

Sarah Douglas
Editor-in-Chief, *Wallpaper**
London

Jessica Doyle
Design and Interiors Editor,
The Telegraph
London

Ronnie Fieg
CEO and Founder, Kith
New York

Miguel Flores-Vianna
Author and Photographer
London

Yvonne Force Villareal
Founding Partner, Culture Corps;
Co-founder, Art Production Fund
New York

Amy Frearson
Architecture and Design Writer;
Editor-at-Large, *Dezeen*
London

Anthony Barzilay Freund
Editorial Director, 1stDibs
New York

Beatrice Galilee
Curator, Writer, Critic, Consultant,
and Lecturer
New York

Rob Giampietro
Senior UX Manager, Google;
Former Director of Design,
Museum of Modern Art
New York

Matt Gibberd and Albert Hill
Co-founders, The Modern House
London

Jenny Gibbs OBE
Principal, KLC School of Design
London

Marc Glimcher
President and CEO, Pace Gallery
New York; London; Hong Kong;
Seoul, South Korea; Geneva; and
Palo Alto, California

Marianne Goebl
Managing Director, Artek
Berlin

Laila Gohar
Food Artist and Designer
New York

Berto González Montaner
Professor of Architecture, FADU,
Universidad de Buenos Aires;
Editor, *ARQ*, *Clarín*
Buenos Aires

Nikolai Haas
Co-founder, The Haas Brothers
Los Angeles

Mieke ten Have
Interiors Stylist, Consultant, and
Design Writer
New York

Gert Jonkers and
Jop van Bennekom
Founders, *Fantastic Man*
London

Pamela Joyner
Businesswoman and
Philanthropist
San Francisco

Marie Kalt
Editor-in-Chief,
Architectural Digest France
Paris

Peter Koepke
Director, The Design Library
Hudson Valley, New York,
and London

Catherine Lazure-Guinard
Founder and Chief Editor,
Nordic Design
Montreal

Cordelia Lembo
Head of Design, Phillips
New York

Pablo León de la Barra
Curator-at-Large, Latin America,
Guggenheim Museum and
Foundation, New York
Mexico City

James Lohan
Founder and Chief Creative
Officer, Mr & Mrs Smith
London

Trickie Lopa
Co-founder, Art Fair Philippines,
Art in the Park, and
The Nonesuch Fair; Adviser,
PHx Fashion Conference
Makati City, Philippines

Marian McEvoy
Author and Artisan
Wappingers Falls, New York

Tim McKeough
Design Journalist,
The New York Times
New York

Michael Maharam
Former CEO, Maharam
New York

Joseph Mains
Creative Director and Writer
Portland, Oregon

Catie Marron
Writer
New York

Ambra Medda
Founder, Ambra Medda Office
London

Brooke Metcalfe
Author, Editor, and Entrepreneur
London

Sarah Miller
Founding Editor-in-Chief,
Condé Nast Traveller UK;
CEO, Sarah Miller and Partners
London

Martina Mondadori
Founder and Editor-in-Chief,
Cabana
London

Michael Moran
Photographer
Brooklyn

Lorena Mosquera
Managing Director, Zara Home
A Coruña, Spain

Ravi Naidoo
Founder, Design Indaba
Cape Town

Michelle Ogundehin
Author, Design Consultant,
and TV Presenter
Brighton, UK

Rosa Park
Founding Editor-in-Chief,
Cereal and *Cereal City Guides*;
Director, Francis Gallery
Bath, UK

Danielle Rago and Honora Shea
Founders, THIS X THAT
Los Angeles

Zeynep Rekkali Iskov Jensen
Gallery Director and Sales
Manager, Etage Projects
Copenhagen

Joanna Saltz
Editorial Director,
House Beautiful
New York

Matthieu Salvaing
Photographer
Paris

Carla Sozzani
Founder, 10 Corso Como
Milan

David Stark
Designer, Event Planner, and
Chief Creative Officer, David Stark
Design and Production
Brooklyn

Joa Studholme
Color Curator, Farrow & Ball
London

Jacqueline Terrebonne
Editor-in-Chief, *Galerie*
New York

Dana Thomas
Author and Cultural
Correspondent
Paris

Martha Thorne
Dean, IE School of Architecture
and Design, Madrid;
Executive Director, Pritzker
Architecture Prize
Madrid

Stephen Todd
Design Editor,
Australian Financial Review
Sydney

Stefano Tonchi
Global Chief Creative Officer,
L'Officiel
New York

Sally and Anna Tonkin
Co-founders,
Green and Mustard
Portsmouth, UK

Ana Torrejón
Journalist and Teacher;
Editorial Director,
L'Officiel Argentina
Buenos Aires

Simon Upton
Photographer
London

Bronson van Wyck
Founder, Van Wyck & Van Wyck
New York

Marco Velardi
Partner, Apartamento Publishing
and Apartamento Studios
Barcelona

Pilar Viladas
Journalist and Editor
New York

Ben Watson
Chief Creative Officer,
Herman Miller
Zeeland, Michigan

Kate Watson-Smyth
Founder, Mad About The House
London

Teng Wee
Managing Partner,
The Lo & Behold Group
Singapore

Daven Wu
Singapore Editor, *Wallpaper**
Singapore

Hanya Yanagihara
Editor-in-Chief, *T: The New York
Times Style Magazine*
New York

Rachel Zoe
CEO, Creative Director,
Philanthropist, Author,
and TV Personality
Los Angeles

The Interior Experience

William Norwich

At the risk of sounding reductive, having just read the entries in this wonderful, encyclopedic book, my takeaway is that the priority of the most innovative and desirable interior design of the twenty-first century, at least so far, is *experience*. Meaning, unlike decades ago, when the guiding principles for interior design were too often static and entrenched with worries about suitability and materialist display, designers today are most concerned about how their spaces will affect their inhabitants. In other words, how spaces are experienced; how they affect, much more than just how they are perceived critically. Designers are designing for people, not their peers and not their critics.

From the exuberance of a Maximalist such as Sig Bergamin in the colorful, highly textured tropical house he designed in São Paolo, Brazil, to Neri&Hu and their Suzhou Chapel—a white plaster cube perched on a foundation of reclaimed bricks, wrapped in perforated and pleated metal in eastern China— here are more than one hundred designers who are like alchemists, or impresarios, filmmakers, and producers. They are also storytellers who work to create environments of warmth, interest, scholarship, personality, and craft. More than ever before, they design in the context for where their work lives: location, environment, sustainability, and also dreams and aspirations.

Of course, interior design, whether residential or commercial, doesn't walk the same path as other design disciplines. Even when it's quiet it's loud, proud, and out there. Here is a veritable cornucopia of ideas and inspiration for you, whether you are about to commission a designer for your home or business or looking for ideas you can adapt yourself.

With the spring 2019 release of Phaidon's inaugural interior design book, *Interiors: The Greatest Rooms of the Century*, the idea of *By Design: The World's Best Contemporary Interior Designers*, spotlighting work done within the past five to ten years, presented itself as the next logical step. To help with the difficult task of choosing the best of today's interior designers, Phaidon approached an esteemed, international jury—of writers, editors,

curators, designers, stylists, photographers, restaurateurs, hoteliers, and industry influencers— who were invited to nominate individuals and studios that are making exceptional, innovative, and ground- breaking contributions to the field. The ninety plus nominators include: founder of *PIN–UP* magazine, Felix Burrichter; independent curator Aric Chen; creative director and designer Francisco Costa; CEO and founder of Kith, Ronnie Fieg; food artist Laila Gohar; artist Niki Haas; and founders of *Fantastic Man*, Gert Jonkers and Jop van Bennekom.

The criteria for nominations was broad: designers featured had to be working today and have made work since 2015, but they could work in any style, across any sector of interior design, anywhere in the world, and be at any stage in their career. What resulted was a collection of designers and their works that is as diverse as it is dynamic, as surprising as it is affirmative. Reflecting back on the rigorous selection process, I wondered, what is it that these experts talk about when they talk about interior design and decoration, and how did they made their choices?

Great taste and style were important to the New York-based arbiter and art world leader Eleanor Acquavella, but she found the upmost criterion to be a designer's "ability to decorate homes without making it look like *their* home," explaining that the homes should look like they belong to their clients and that no two homes look the same.

The design writer and editor Spencer Bailey had different reasons for each of the several nominations he made but, on the whole, his guiding principles had to do with a mix of design approach, refinement, attention to detail, subtlety, tactility, and, for some, playfulness. He selected designers who don't take themselves too seriously but really "let it fly" out of their comfort zones, which usually suggests they had good clients behind them who wanted their designers to really push their capabilities. To him, designers who can work at broad scales are the most impressive, explaining, "Sometimes, it's really about paying attention to, say, a bathroom sink; other times, it's about a sort of *mise-en-scène*—capturing the entire essence of a room through a combination of material,

furniture, lighting, art, form, and scale." He also responded to projects that have spirit, personality, and a sense of soul. "I appreciate a *wabi-sabi* touch— an appreciation of imperfection, an engagement with the sense of touch, an acceptance to let things be as they are, to intentionally design for use, for wear and tear, for rings on the coffee table." For Bailey, a good interior is one that has been designed for enjoying, using, and, in the case of a home, living in.

For Helen Barrett, who covers the arts, archi- tecture, design, and gardens for *FT Wealth*, foremost in her criteria is an "intelligent response to the sustainability challenge." She is primarily interested in designers who are repurposing architectural salvage and restyling collectables and antiques, which strike her "as obviously good ideas."

The shopping and retail impresario Brian Bolke, director of the Conservatory, looked for originality. For designers in today's digital world, referencing has become increasingly easier and with the proliferation of imagery available, he is concerned about the homog- enization of aesthetics. Bolke therefore looked for original thinkers "who can take in those references and put them back out in an identifiable, signature style." However, he wasn't looking for just the same style, repeated over and over, but "a style that boldly moves forward, yet keeps the innate DNA of the designer. It's a balancing act, and the more effortless it can look, the better. I also think fearlessness is the special sauce that makes it all come together," Bolke says.

In the case of Graeme Brooker, the head of the interior design program at the Royal College of Art, London, he considered three criteria. The first relates to the impact current events are having on our planet, becoming so overwhelming "that design just has to respond. To ignore the climate emergency, social justice, and our rights as humans is a neglect that we cannot afford." Brooker therefore selected some practices that work with existing objects and reuse spaces, thereby helping "to slow the further depletion of our resources by abstaining from demolition and starting again." The second consideration was to look at practices that were less well-known but that had diverse approaches and deserved publicity, even if sustainability of resources wasn't a main priority in their work. Brooker also selected practices and designers who were simply "super-creative" and provided innovative approaches to interior design in response to space, use, and their clients.

Amy Fine Collins, the award-winning journalist and fashion critic, looked for scholarship and sophistication when making her selections. She considered if the designers' works have been influential, asking herself, "are they themselves pacesetters, who may have even founded a kind of school of design taste?" She chose not to include designers whose works seemed too derivative of other designers and contemplated if their interiors reflect a true knowledge of the decorative arts and their history. She also questioned if the designers were knowledgeable in other areas, such as the fine arts, fashion, literature, and music.

All of these disciplines affect how a designer creates an environment, Collins says, before continuing with her list of criteria:

Is the designer's sensibility unmistakable? Is it so distinct that you recognize his or her handiwork right away, or is it generic, part of a trend rather than a unique projection of taste and training? Do they have a real sense of quality, of craftsmanship, of fantasy? How well do they work with color, texture, proportion? Are their environments suitable for the lives of the people who occupy them, or are they put together more as show places, which photograph well or create an instant impression? And does their work age or date well?

These are all essential questions in building a knowledge, and appreciation, of interior design, past, present, and future.

As a journalist, Marie Kalt, the highly regarded editor-in-chief of *Architectural Digest France*, has learned to put her personal tastes aside when appreciating current design and its creators. She responds to news, to the "designers who have a personal vision and who try to consistently express it." In her opinion, these designers are the ones that typically set the trends widely followed by others. They are the ones that will "leave their mark."

As well as thinking about designs that would age well, the esteemed author and scholar Marian McEvoy looked for confident interiors without a hint of self-conscious; celebratory designs that demonstrate a skilled use of high contrast and real color. She also appreciates a design outlook "that embraces historical excellence as well as a sense of contemporary knowhow and adventure. And in the end," she added, "I like brave rooms with good manners."

Brooke Metcalfe, a former *Vogue* interiors editor, explained that she looked for a certain welcome in the work of the designers she admires and is "drawn to design that consistently feels like 'home,'" which she describes as being "a reflection of ordered chaos and beauty, an emotionally familiar, relatable place." She respects designers who champion "a monastic, pared-down aesthetic," but she equally approves of

those who "celebrate the hyper contemporary and cutting edge" and who consider sustainable materials. For Metcalfe, design should translate life into a livable physical space.

In making her nominations, the esteemed architectural and design writer Pilar Viladas included those whose work is informed by the past but that also pushes design forward, and she contemplated the different ways in which designers approach their work. "Some are adept at making art an integral part of their rooms," she suggests, "while others are creating their own art for their interiors." Irrespective of their process, however, Viladas selected designers that "all share a certain level of sophistication [and an understanding of] how texture and nuance help make a room feel comfortable."

For Hanya Yanagihara, the novelist and editor-in-chief of *T: The New York Times Style Magazine*, the designers she chose all differ aesthetically, but one thing they do have in common is that they create intuitive spaces. "Practicality may not sound like such a sexy quality," Yanagihara explains, "but ... when designers know how to make a room that answers all its inhabitants' needs ... they're then free to experiment with color, form, and dimensions in a way that would be jarring, even assaultive, in a less well-considered space." The designers she nominated made Yanagihara question her own definition of a good space as well as what that space should do: "Is it meant to make us feel relaxed? Or is it meant to stimulate us?"

She paused, then proceeded to sum up not only her own criteria but perhaps spoke for most of the nominators here. "All of these magicians are able to do both at the same time; the eye is excited even as the body rests."

Among the more than one hundred entries in *By Design* we see that ASH, a firm based in New York and Los Angeles, devotes its practice to adaptive reuse and revitalization; Batiik Studio in Paris is guided by curiosity, mixing genres, balancing the aesthetic and the rational; and Kelly Behun chooses objects for their emotive impact, not their provenance. The hospitality designer Dorothée Meilichzon creates immersive, storied approaches for hotels and restaurants; a hotel in Spain isn't just a luxurious lodging, it's imagined as an artist's residence. Nate Berkus, in the United States, rejects design trends and uses vintage pieces to compose contemporary tableaux. Darryl Carter, who studied law in his youth before becoming one of the leading designers based in Washington, D.C., inspired by the higher ideals of the U.S. capitol, brings a "meta-level" of history to his projects.

André Fu in Hong Kong is hailed for his mesmeric treatment of light and scale at the hotels and restaurants he has designed. "Comfort" is the experience that Hare + Klein chase for their clients in Sydney. A plush pink sofa is chosen by GOLDEN designers Alicia McKimm and Kylie Dorotic in Melbourne to "inject joy" into a nineteenth-century residence in Melbourne, while Beata Heuman, a protégé of the design legend Nicky Haslam, was inspired by Wes

Anderson's pastel-hued movie *The Grand Budapest Hotel* when she designed the Farm Girl Cafe in London.

David Netto, working mostly in the United States, believes the highest level of design experience results when the people living in his spaces prioritize the personal instead of trends or status. French-born designer Emmanuel Picault is partial to the avant-garde but infuses his interiors with warmth, humor, and soul. With an approach that favors the participatory instead of the reflective, Belgian designer Gert Voorjans was able to transform a drafty medieval castle in Bavaria into a comfortable family home.

Surprise and solace, that is the promise of great, contemporary interior design; the essential practice of the best designers, both new and established; and it's the message of this book. In other words, *experience*. Sounds obvious? Perhaps, but it is also a relatively new idea.

In 1947, the Museum of Modern Art in New York presented an exhibition called *Modern Rooms of the Last Fifty Years*. It reflected modern design from the first half of the twentieth century, which "was born of the turmoil of the Industrial Revolution," to quote from exhibition materials. That, after many thousands of years of manual drudgery, when machines took over people's work, a new way of designing was required. The utility of things, and interiors, the status of owning innovations, exceeded aesthetic and environmental pleasure.

Maybe for us in the twenty-first century, it's the psychological deprivations engendered by the industrial and the postindustrial age—the time away from nature, the social conformities, combined with the exhausting distractions of the computer age—that make us want more. To not go within, within the depths of the possibilities of our interior spaces, is to go without.

Plus, we now contend with the awareness of an endangering carbon footprint, along with the COVID-19 pandemic that has restricted many to more time at home. Combine these with a long period of political unrest, and, as such, we have come to realize that not just the function of our interiors, but the promise of them, has expanded. What people want now in interiors are comfort and stimulation, permission and diversity, good orderly direction and high function—surprises and *experience*.

If we are modern, then we are awake, we are told. Awake to the fact that we are spiritual beings having a human experience, a human experience that will always require, and desire, shelter and hospitality. Why not make these spaces the best spaces they can be? *By Design* shows us the way.

A Work of Substance

Hong Kong; Paris, France;
Bali, Indonesia

1. Osteria Marzia
Restaurant, Bar
Hong Kong
2017

2. Osteria Marzia
Restaurant
Hong Kong
2017

3. The Fleming
Hotel, Guest Bathroom
Hong Kong
2017

4. The Fleming
Hotel, Guest Room
Hong Kong
2017

5. The Ocean
Restaurant
Hong Kong
2015
[overleaf]

3

4

Multinational and multidisciplinary, A Work of Substance is a dynamic award-winning design agency covering interior design, advertising, branding, and product design. Founded in 2010 by Hong Kong-based Maxime Dautresme and Paris-based Florian Michaux, the agency has grown to include Bali-based Marcus Foley and a sizable team of creatives across its three international offices. Together, they design inventive interiors and visual concepts for their expanding portfolio of penthouses, restaurants, bars, and retail spaces.

Clients, including the luxury goods company Hermès and Rosewood Hotels, come to the agency for fresh creative ways to present brand identities and for its diverse team, which can take care of every detail: from a restaurant's architecture and lighting to its menus, napkins, and takeout boxes. At the Fleming, for example, a boutique hotel in Hong Kong with interiors reflecting the city's nautical context, the team designed the space throughout, right down to a custom line of bathroom amenities and scents inspired by Chinese apothecary.

At the Italian restaurant below, Osteria Marzia, shimmering coral-blue tiles, white bamboo panels, and lamps resembling fishing nets bring the magic of the southern Italian coast to the heart of bustling Hong Kong. An inspired customized storage system holds bowls of lemons, thyme, rosemary, and basil to perfume the foyer and bar with the scent of the Aeolian Islands.

In the private room at the Ocean, a Minimalist glass-walled bar with panoramic views of Hong Kong's Repulse Bay, diners become divers in a spectacular underwater-like space. Soft lighting and a deep-blue theme complement the custom aquarium walls, allowing guests to dine amid hundreds of jellyfish.

Across all disciplines the team has a clear aim: to produce vibrant, visual stories inspired by the people and cultures that inhabit each project location. Their designs are immersive and sensory, considering not only the sights but also the sounds, smells, and emotional responses experienced by the user.

JJ Acuna / Bespoke Studio

Hong Kong;
Manila, Philippines

1. Tate Dining Room
Restaurant
Hong Kong
2017

2. Miss Lee
Restaurant
Hong Kong
2019

3. Honbo at The Mills
Restaurant
Hong Kong
2019

4. Nha Trang Vietnamese Canteen
Restaurant
Hong Kong
2017
[overleaf]

2

3

When James Acuna launched his practice, JJ Acuna / Bespoke Studio, in 2015, he simply had to turn to his Rolodex to let people know he was available. By day, Acuna was working in corporate architecture for blue-chip companies, but he'd also spent years forging his lifestyle credentials as the person behind the design site theWanderlister+.

An architecture graduate of Cornell and Columbia universities, the Filipino designer has capitalized on his international background to create a mobile practice in Southeast Asia. Based between Manila and Hong Kong, Acuna's projects range from a dessert food hall in Myanmar's former capital of Yangon to a boutique in the Taiwanese city of Taichung.

In 2017, the Michelin-star Tate Dining Room was reopened at a new location in a fashionable Hong Kong neighborhood. Collaborating closely with chef and owner Vicky Lau, Acuna created an ultrafeminine interior in bleached timber and pastel hues. Overhead, sculptural lighting adds sparkle to the rounded chairs in shades of pale peach and blush that line the steel tables.

At a more casual Hong Kong eatery, Acuna has used a vibrant color palette to foster a sense of fun. For Miss Lee—a vegan restaurant that references Cantonese flavors—its local heritage was reimagined in a boldly contemporary way. The bar's canopy was painted in a shade of teal that pays tribute to the iconic Star Ferry, a double-decker boat that has transported passengers across Victoria Harbour for the past century; rattan chairs in the same hue nod to the island's British colonial past. Even the national obsession with documenting one's meal has been considered: Acuna designed warm lighting perfect for photography.

Acuna has described his Instagram-worthy style as one that turns lifestyle spaces into an extension of the domestic sphere. It's a design ethos that works: his numerous accolades include being crowned *Design Anthology's* Interior Designer of the Year.

Apartment 48

New York City,
New York, USA

1. Flatiron Loft
Private Residence,
Living/Dining Room
New York City, New York, USA
2015

2. Noho Residence
Private Residence, Lounge
New York City, New York, USA
2019

3. Saddle River Residence
Private Residence, Living Room
Saddle River, New Jersey, USA
2016

New York design studio Apartment 48 was born in 1994 when founder Rayman Boozer, then a graduate and aspiring interior designer, had an ingenious high-concept idea: he would open a home furnishings store designed just like an apartment, separated into stylish roomlike zones. The enterprising Manhattan-based venture turned out to be a considerable success, introducing customers and would-be clients to Boozer's aesthetic and Boozer to the world of interior design. Within a few years, the Indiana-raised designer was taking commissions for real apartments.

In the decades since, Apartment 48 has grown in both size and scale. The studio now takes on a wide range of commercial and residential projects across the United States, from tailored private homes and modern lofts to offices, development projects, television studios, and retail showrooms.

In Manhattan's fashionable NoHo district, for example, Apartment 48 transformed a large industrial loft into a colorful, exotically patterned haven. The internal brick walls were painted a rich shade of deep gray and adorned with bright abstract art as well as black-and-white photography. Graphic prints, metallics, and geometric shapes pop against the exposed brick and sit comfortably among carefully sourced vintage and contemporary furniture. The space is upbeat, high impact, and full of personality.

With vibrant blue walls and brightly upholstered furniture, the team turned an expansive warehouse-style apartment in Manhattan's Flatiron District into a feast for the eyes. Embracing their characteristically bold and optimistic style, Apartment 48 livened up the building's angular lines with rich magenta velvets, printed rugs, huge gilded mirrors, and oversize copper lighting.

Known for its storied approach and vibrant palette—Boozer was declared the "go-to designer for color consulting" by New York's *Time Out* magazine—Apartment 48 are industry experts with the experience and vision to deliver joyful, relaxed interiors no matter the context.

1. Upper East Side Residence
Private Residence, Living Room
New York City, New York, USA
2019

2. Candy Bar, The Siren Hotel
Hotel, Bar
Detroit, Michigan, USA
2018

3. The Siren Hotel
Hotel, Lobby
Detroit, Michigan, USA
2018

ASH

New York City, New York, and Los Angeles, California, USA

1

For contemporary property staging, luxury real estate clients are turning to the multidisciplinary design firm ASH. Specializing in the fields of interior and product design, and hotel and residential development, the New York- and Los Angeles-based company has drawn praise for its collection of adaptive reuse and revitalization projects located in Providence, Rhode Island; Detroit, Michigan; and New Orleans. These strategic works have featured in *Forbes* magazine, *Harper's Bazaar*, and *Architectural Digest* (the latter labeled ASH an AD100 firm in 2018).

ASH's bi-coastal and growing operations are lead by the firm's partners: CEO Ari Heckman, CFO Jonathan Minkoff, CCO Will Cooper, and head of staging Andrew Bowen. Together, the business savvy collective offers memorable experiences through contemplative design.

One example is the Siren Hotel in Detroit. The original 1926 Renaissance Revival building belonged to the Rudolph Wurlitzer Company and was home to everything music—from piano makers to vinyl—until its closing in 1982. ASH had their own renaissance at the Siren in 2018, turning the dormant building into a unique hospitality attraction that offers dining, retail, a panoramic rooftop, and 106 boutique guest rooms. The Siren's Candy Bar is a nod to Detroit's jazz era with a discotheque twist. The plushly furnished cocktail lounge, which includes a marble-top bar, was covered from floor to ceiling in bubblegum pink—all magically spotlighted by an original Les Bains disco ball. Retro luxe continues in the lobby with oranges, reds, and greens conveying warmth and romance. The levity of a *Downton Abbey* aesthetic comes together with nineteenth-century fringed lamps and early twentieth-century drapery.

With such enterprise and capacity to expand, the future is bright for ASH, a firm with a multifaceted approach to interior design that moves past premeditation toward the present moment.

Batiik Studio

Paris, France

1. Divine
Bar
Paris, France
2019

2. Divine
Bar
Paris, France
2019

3. Amélie Maison d'art
Gallery
Paris, France
2018

2

3

Color, curiosity, and experimentation unify Rebecca Benichou's playful, contemporary interiors. The Paris-based architect and interior designer, who founded her practice, Batiik Studio, in 2014, describes her approach as a careful balance between the aesthetic and the rational.

Looking to both the past and future, Batiik Studio's residential and commercial interiors blend simplicity of form and tone with functionality, tailoring, and soft pastel hues. Taking inspiration from Modernist architect Luis Barragán and his splashes of rich color, the firm's joyful interiors tend to have a postmodern twist, resulting in multilayered eclectic designs that mix genres and styles.

Arched doorways, large cuts of terrazzo, and lively colors greet guests at Divine, a stylish Parisian cocktail bar. Seeking to achieve an interior that was sophisticated but not intimidating, Batiik Studio looked to the 1980s and juxtaposed glass pendant lighting and splashes of dusty pink and coral against raw and polished concrete walls.

The gallery it designed for Paris-based curator Amélie du Chalard takes its cues from Dimore Gallery in Milan and Salon 94 in New York City by displaying art in a space that looks and feels like a private home. Batiik Studio gutted and renovated the townhouse, removing walls and linking the two floors with a staircase wrapped in a curvilinear oak railing. It laid a striking terrazzo floor, scattered with irregular fragments of pastel-hued marble, and added curved internal windows with wooden frames to delineate the dining and sleeping areas and flood the space with natural light.

Although an architect by trade—she spent five years at French architectural practice ChartierDalix before founding Batiik Studio—Benichou prefers to focus on interior projects. She is motivated by the opportunity to improve well-being and happiness through smart design, and is gaining industry recognition as she does so.

1. Hamptons Home
Private Residence, Library
The Hamptons, New York, USA
2019

2. Long Island Home
Private Residence, Family Room
Southampton, New York, USA
2013

3. Long Island Home
Private Residence, Library
Southampton, New York, USA
2013

Kelly Behun

New York City,
New York, USA

1

Designer Kelly Behun lives among the clouds in a Manhattan high-rise, and there's an airy, ethereal quality to the spaces she designs. After arriving in New York with a business degree, Behun entered the design world by working in an in-house studio for Ian Schrager Hotels, collaborating with Andrée Putman and Philippe Starck, among others. She launched Kelly Behun Studio in 2001 to design interiors, as well as accessories and furniture. It is steered by Behun's elegant but practical approach: objects are chosen for their affective possibilities instead of pedigree or price. Behun builds environments for contemplation—and she isn't afraid of a white wall.

In 2017 Behun designed her first model apartment, which happens to be inside the Matchstick Building, the Manhattan skyscraper at 432 Park Avenue that's one of the tallest buildings in the world. It's no exaggeration to say that Matchstick dwellers are living in the sky. Accordingly, Behun designed an aerie from which to observe the world below. For the apartment's light-drenched main room, she collaborated with surfaces specialists Callidus Guild to create a wall that features a motif based on a sketch by Behun, etched by artisans into the plaster. A cozy library space holds ceramics by the artist Cody Hoyt, which seem to both absorb and emanate light.

It is a testament to Behun's craft that she can adapt this celestial, luminous aesthetic to earthbound spaces —such as her family getaway on Long Island, New York, a gorgeous, Minimalist beach house. Vintage and custom-made pieces personalize the space, from a walnut-slab bar in the kitchen and a bleached-walnut bed in the main bedroom to a statement braided couch by the Campana Brothers near a glass wall in the family room, a cloud-soft spot from which to watch the tides arrive and depart in seaside sunlight. Wherever she works, Behun invites the light.

4

5

4. Long Island Home
Private Residence, Kitchen
Southampton, New York, USA
2013

5. Midtown Penthouse
Private Residence, Living Room
New York City, New York, USA
2017

6. Midtown Penthouse
Private Residence, Library
New York City, New York, USA
2017

BENSLEY

Bangkok, Thailand;
Bali, Indonesia

Luxury design go-to Bill Bensley has been creating extraordinary hotels and resorts since 1989. With more than 200 completed projects and a 150-strong team—which he heads with his partner Jirachai Rengthong—Bensley has created one-of-a-kind spaces in India, Southeast Asia, and the Americas for major hoteliers, including Rosewood and One&Only.

The prolific U.S.-born, Bangkok, Thailand-based architect, who has lived and worked in Asia since his Harvard University days, boasts a highly original oeuvre. His otherworldly spaces include an edible golf course, a Malaysian sultan's royal palace, the world's longest, largest swimming pool, a thrilling zip-line ride over one of Asia's most beautiful ecosystems, and his personal favorites: a boutique hotel and tented camp, created in collaboration with the Shinta Mani Hotel Group.

Although his portfolio is exclusive, Bensley's architectural approach is inclusive. Underpinned by conservation and a genuine interest in the communities where he works, Bensley's magical environments respect their locations' heritage and protect their natural landscape. The studio regularly collaborates with local and international artisans and is a dedicated supporter of the Shinta Mani Foundation, part of the Shinta Mani Hotel Group, which opened a hospitality school in Siem Reap, Cambodia, in 2004.

Paying homage to Indonesia's cultural heritage, Bensley handpicked regional artifacts, paintings, and furniture for his explorer-inspired interiors at Bali's Capella Ubud, interspersing them with treasured pieces from his personal collection. The flamboyant, richly textured interiors conjure up the spirit of adventure; private spaces reflect this inspiration with names such as Captain and Cartographer. Bali's tropical charm and architectural history is celebrated throughout, with furniture crafted in local woods and Balinese carvings on many of the hotel's arched doors.

Bensley's sensitivity to place and provenance has given him a unique understanding of the nuanced touches that elevate a resort from luxurious to exceptional. His ability to create spaces that are daring and lavish, but never excessive or incongruous, has cemented his place on global top 100 designer lists and earned him such titles as "the king of exotic luxury resorts."

1. Shinta Mani Siem Reap,
BENSLEY Collection
Hotel, Butlers' Lounge
Siem Reap, Cambodia
2017

2. Shinta Mani Siem Reap,
BENSLEY Collection
Hotel, Pool Villa
Siem Reap, Cambodia
2017

3. Capella Ubud
Hotel, One Bedroom Rainforest Tent
Keliki, Bali, Indonesia
2018

4. Hotel de la Coupole, MGallery
Hotel, Lobby
Sapa, Vietnam
2018
[overleaf]

Sig Bergamin

São Paulo, Brazil

Sig Bergamin is a self-professed Maximalist, an iconic Brazilian designer with a loyal, jet-setting clientele, a consummate professional with a degree in architecture and a taste for animal print and styles inspired by Asian traditions—in a word, an exuberant maestro. That's two words, but excess seems appropriate. There's no combination of patterns, hues, or materials that Bergamin won't combine in his residential and commercial projects, transcending mere eclecticism and ushering in a kind of playful abundance. His designs suggest bountiful humor, too: isn't it a little funny, and a little wonderful, that these beautiful objects should exist?

Bergamin's knack for bringing beautiful things together lends unimpeachable poise to spaces, such as the Iporanga beach house, a 2019 project in Brazil's Guarujá municipality, where the client's art collection is complemented by graceful mid-century furniture. In the living room, Bergamin's beloved vibrant colors are relegated to the walls, while teal and white seating above a checkered carpet offer space for elegant repose, all the better to take in the collection. For a private São Paulo residence, also designed in 2019, Bergamin turns the house into a concentrated expression of the environment. A vivid tropical mural decorates the front interior wall, linking the real tropics outside with the interior's artful wildness. In the living room, an entryway is flanked by paintings of women in lingerie against green–gray backgrounds, and dusky yellow upholstery adds to an atmosphere of low-key cool, the shadows beneath a tropical canopy. In a sitting room where arched doors open to the outside, Bergamin turns the volume up again with floral- and zebra-print seating, trees in containers, and a geometric design running just beneath the ceiling and extending the room upward, toward an imagined canopy of trees.

Fellow designers have long praised Bergamin's fearlessness. His rooms remain models of ingenuity—at least until he decides to redo them.

1. Tropical House
Private Residence, Living Room
São Paulo, Brazil
2019

2. Tropical House
Private Residence, Entryway
São Paulo, Brazil
2019

3. Tropical House
Private Residence, Living Room
São Paulo, Brazil
2019

4. Iporanga Beach House
Private Residence, Living Room
Guarujá, Brazil
2019
[overleaf]

Sig Bergamin

Deborah Berke Partners

New York City,
New York, USA

When sketching her Queens neighborhood in New York City at fourteen years old, Deborah Berke decided to become an architect—and her architectural and design practice has since developed to be as resolute as her younger self. Berke's values place human-centered experience at the foreground of her work, accounting for it in the environmental, social, and geographic considerations of each project. At Deborah Berke Partners, Berke's firm of more than thirty years, her diverse team creates commercial and residential designs, as well as spaces dedicated to art and education. In 2016 Berke's commitment to pedagogy saw her become dean of the Yale School of Architecture.

The firm's intrinsic relationship to art and design is evident in its adaptive reuse projects. In 2016 Deborah Berke Partners transformed a historic Ford Motor Company plant in Oklahoma City into a 21c Museum Hotel, creating a boutique attraction for contemporary art and hospitality. Similarly, NXTHVN, a not-for-profit arts and community space in New Haven, Connecticut, completed in 2020, sees former factory buildings revitalized into a place for arts activity.

The same sensitivity to context is apparent in the firm's residential projects. In an Upper East Side town-house in Manhattan, for example, a richly decorated family home features the client's collection of postwar Italian decor and furnishings. Minimalism is one of Berke's visual calling cards, but her interior design team are equally unafraid of luxury and warmth; here, the clean Modernist aesthetics are equalized with rich tones and inviting, sociable arrangements. Similarly, in a Chelsea apartment in New York City, a contemporary art collection is juxtaposed against traditional furnishings, creating a room designed to live with art, not simply to exhibit it.

Deborah Berke Partners' trademark for elegant contemporary design is affirmed by such beautiful spaces—and cherished when paired with a socially conscious design ethos.

1. West Chelsea Apartment
Private Residence, Living Room
New York City, New York, USA
2017

2. Upper East Side Townhouse
Private Residence, Living Room
New York City, New York, USA
2018

3. 432 Park Avenue
Private Residence,
Living/Dining Room
New York City, New York, USA
2015

2

3

Nate Berkus Associates

Chicago, Illinois, USA

1. West Hollywood Residence
Private Residence,
Living Room and Terrace
West Hollywood, California, USA
2020

2. Chicago Townhouse
Private Residence, Dressing Room
Chicago, Illinois, USA
2017

3. Greenwich Village Penthouse
Private Residence, Living Room
New York City, New York, USA
2015

Nate Berkus is ubiquitous. Since opening his own Chicago-based firm, Nate Berkus Associates, in 1995, he's been a font of design wisdom, inspiration, and products, appearing on television, in magazines, and in department stores (via lines of home goods and decor). He did have a head start: like Lauren Buxbaum Gordon, who recently became Berkus's partner in the firm, Berkus is a design heir. His mother is a designer; Buxbaum Gordon's parents are antiques dealers; and Berkus is now also married to another designer, Jeremiah Brent. It can seem challenging to describe the foundations of the firm's cozily elegant style, but that's only because it's everywhere—and has been for a while.

Berkus might say that this is a good problem to have. He's outspoken in his rejection of design trends, valuing pieces that are truly beloved and will stay with people over time, acquiring new meaning. The residential spaces his firm has designed usually contain a majority of vintage and antique pieces. A client's home in Seattle, for example, provides lovely validation of the idea that vintage pieces can compose a contemporary tableaux: a beaded chandelier is a burst of celebration above an inventive stacked plywood Impression Chair by Julian Mayor. Buxbaum Gordon shares this sensibility; her Chicago town-house features a dressing room with an Empire chandelier illuminating shelves of carefully selected, color-coded footwear.

An admirer of Brancusi and a pragmatist himself, Berkus has always lived with objects that look timeless and prove functional. The checkered marble floor in his Los Angeles home dates back to the seventeenth century; the kitchen cabinets in his Greenwich Village, New York, penthouse are painted a neat, dirt-disappearing black. He goes for wood and neutrals, highly personalized spaces, and long happy relationships with clients. And with Nate Berkus Associates behind these harmonious designs, who wouldn't want the same?

4. Greenwich Village Penthouse
Private Residence, Kitchen
New York City, New York, USA
2015

5. Seattle Home
Private Residence,
Entrance to Main Bedroom
Medina, Washington, USA
2015

Linda Boronkay

London, UK

1. Soho House Mumbai
Private Members' Club, Bar
Mumbai, Maharashtra, India
2018

2. Cecconi's, Soho House Amsterdam
Private Members' Club, Restaurant
Amsterdam, the Netherlands
2018

3. Little Beach House Barcelona
Private Members' Club, Lounge
Garraf, Spain
2018

4. Soho House Hong Kong
Private Members' Club, Pool Bar
Hong Kong
2019
[overleaf]

As former design director at Soho House, an international group of exclusive private members' clubs, Linda Boronkay has created designs enjoyed by patrons around the world. With projects completed across four continents, Boronkay has proven herself a versatile visionary with a talent for translating the brand into highly localized contexts.

Born in Budapest to an architect father and an antiques dealer mother, Boronkay's childhood was spent being dragged around vintage markets. A degree in fashion design in Paris was followed by a modeling career, an experience that Boronkay credits with her chameleon-like ability to understand the nuances of different cultures. After relocating to London, Boronkay gained experience in studios that include Martin Brudnizki and Tom Dixon. She joined Soho House in 2016, making her imprint on clubhouses from Amsterdam to Mumbai before setting up her own firm in 2020, specializing in product and interior design.

At Little Beach House Barcelona, a Soho House property, Boronkay transformed the small hotel into a relaxed coastal escape. The array of natural textures—think rattan chairs, burlap upholstery, and an abundance of indoor plants—evoke European beach resorts of yesteryear. It continues in the cheerfully decorated bedrooms, featuring patterned tiled flooring and lamps from a local ceramicist.

A different approach was required at Soho House Mumbai, an imposing neoclassical property in an area known as the "Beverly Hills of Bollywood." Intended to reflect India's rich and colorful heritage, local craftsmanship takes center stage at the vividly patterned clubhouse. Block-printed fabrics from Rajasthan are scattered throughout, lampshades are fashioned from antique saris, and works by regional artists adorn the walls.

As time goes on, Boronkay has seen her formerly Minimalist tastes evolve into something bolder. It seems fitting for a career that draws upon a wealth of global travel to craft distinctly individual interiors.

2

3

Martin Brudnizki
Design Studio

London, UK; New York City,
New York, USA

Scandinavia may be known for Minimalism, but Swedish native Martin Brudnizki has built a glittering career on his extravagant approach to design. The genius behind some of the world's most lavish interiors, Brudnizki embraces bold colors, vintage furniture, and luxuriant fabrics to craft intricately detailed spaces.

Born to a stylist mother and an engineer father, Brudnizki credits his exacting eye to their confluent influences. After studying interior architecture, stints followed at renowned design firms until the establishment of his own studio in 2000. His award-winning work for luxury clients has established himself as a luminary of contemporary interior design.

Annabel's, a private members' club in central London, has long played second home to the wealthy. When Brudnizki was commissioned to redesign the four-story, eighteenth-century Georgian townhouse, he wanted to convey a spirit of English eccentricity—so it was decided that each floor would tell its own wildly flamboyant tale. From the hand-painted flamingo murals and ornately tasseled chairs in the Rose Room, to a blush-colored women's powder room with a ceiling bedecked in silk flowers, every corner begs to be discovered.

Brudnizki brought this same reverence for period properties to the Beekman, a hotel in a former nineteenth-century brick office building in Manhattan's Financial District. Determined to complement the building's rich architectural history, Brudnizki converted the cavernous glass atrium into the hotel's central hub. Its grandeur is amplified with walls in rich shades of marbled green and mid-century furnishings. In the dining room this richly layered approach continues with exposed brickwork, leather banquettes upholstered in mohair velvet, and a spectacular series of stained-glass windows.

Brudnizki shies away from being labeled a Maximalist, but he will concede his fondness for high-octane glamour. As he confided in a 2018 interview with *Architectural Digest*, "You can do whatever you want as long as you have a strong point of view."

Martyn Lawrence Bullard

Los Angeles, California, USA

A star of popular television design shows, including *Million Dollar Decorators* and *Hollywood Me*, Martyn Lawrence Bullard has appeared on the small screen in living rooms across the United States, but the rooms he designs for his clients retain a particular, glamorous allure. For his residential and hospitality projects, Bullard operates with the tenet that comfort *is* luxury. He takes care to learn his clients' preferences—favorite colors, restaurants, features of previous homes—and puts his energetic talents to work creating restful spaces, often filled with plush seating and a judicious application of color to brighten monochrome interiors.

Bullard's own home, the Villa Grigio in Palm Springs, California, is a testament to the designer's willingness to adapt. The Villa was built in the 1960s by James McNaughton, one of the Modernist houses that sprang up in the desert for celebrities seeking a retreat. Bullard retained this ethos, but reimagined it as something far removed from the house where Hugh Hefner once (reportedly) partied. The Villa is all about relaxation. A circular conversation pit with fuchsia couches enlivens the living room, while the playful indoor/outdoor aesthetic of the room, which features a bow window overlooking a swimming pool, is extended through an exquisite colonnade. The Villa's library has become a media room, filled with custom-made de Sede Terrazza sofas—a giddy artifact of 1970s design, with layers of leather cushions stacked on a base in a decadent geological formation. A touch of New York cool adds an edge: the living room's zebra-skin rugs once carpeted Andy Warhol's Factory, and the yellow background of a Jean-Michel Basquiat painting draws the eye in the black-and-white main bedroom.

Bullard's reach continues to expand, through his Los Angeles atelier store and lines of furniture, textiles, and home decor. Yet the designer strikes a balance across his ventures—he may be ubiquitous, but with a personal touch.

2

3

1. Villa Grigio
Private Residence, Living Room
Palm Springs, California, USA
2018

2. Villa Grigio
Private Residence, Media Room
Palm Springs, California, USA
2018

3. Villa Grigio
Private Residence, Main Bedroom
Palm Springs, California, USA
2018

Rafael de Cárdenas

New York City,
New York, USA

Rafael de Cárdenas established his eponymous studio in New York City's Chinatown in 2006, and has since forged his path in the design world with all the dynamism and bravado associated with the city's downtown neighborhood. Before founding his practice, de Cárdenas studied fashion at the Rhode Island School of Design and architecture at the University of California, Los Angeles (UCLA), and his designs reflect this dual training. Solid surfaces acquire an emphatic edge; walls and fixtures suddenly have the exciting, confrontational potential of high fashion. Inside the London boutique of jeweler Delfina Delettrez in 2015, de Cárdenas installed a green, malachite-like wall, giving the impression that visitors are stepping inside a gemstone instead of browsing to buy one.

De Cárdenas is an adroit adapter, bringing his lively aesthetic to residential projects, interiors, furniture, and integrated objects. In a two-story penthouse in New York's Greenwich Village, for example, a muted, creamy color palette throughout allows for targeted whimsy: a hand-painted, swirling ceiling in the living room and a contemporary, three-dimensional, assemblage artwork hanging in a bedroom. For an opulent Parisian townhouse, de Cárdenas uses custom-made furniture and cabinetry to create a link between the house's nineteenth-century Hausmann-era architecture and the owner's collection of contemporary Chinese art.

Like his downtown predecessors, the poets of the New York School, de Cárdenas is inspired by Pop culture, and his visions can range from playful to serious. His firm's design for a bathing pavilion on an English country estate includes a fiberglass-and-resin slide that's somehow entirely in concert with the pavilion's deluxe marble changing rooms. In 2017, for a five-story house on New York's West 11th Street, de Cárdenas employed a modulated palette, with warmer colors downstairs and a cooler, more peaceful penthouse. The house's subtle aesthetic progression is a testament to de Cárdenas' talent for using color to define space.

1. Greenwich Village Residence
Private Residence, Living Room
New York City, New York, USA
2013

2. West Eleventh Street Residence
Private Residence, Dining Room
New York City, New York, USA
2017

3. Greenwich Village Residence
Private Residence, Main Bedroom
New York City, New York, USA
2013

Darryl Carter

Washington, D.C., USA

1. Ampeer
Long-term Residence, Mezzanine
Washington, D.C., USA
2018

2. Bethesda Residence
Private Residence, Living Room
Washington, D.C., USA
2016

3. Bethesda Residence
Private Residence,
Hall and Staircase
Washington, D.C., USA
2016

With interior designer Darryl Carter having spent much of his life in Washington, D.C., it's no surprise that the neoclassicism associated with the capital city has influenced his work. Like the architects who planned D.C., he prefers white walls, minimal decoration, and austere lines and forms. However, Carter chooses furnishings that juxtapose these rooms, cleverly combining the sinuously curved brown wood of American or eighteenth-century European antiques with the clean, sharp lines of radiantly contemporary pieces. There's no grandiosity or bombast to his spaces. Their custom touches evince a sure hand, and the contrast of old and new bespeaks a welcoming, wry humor.

Carter works on a range of residential and commercial projects; in 2018, for example, he designed the interior public spaces of the Ampeer, a D.C. landmark and the only building in the city by the architect Stanford White. The 1903 mansion is now a long-term residence for visiting professionals, a hotel-meets-luxury dorm. Carter's vision for Ampeer's communal areas keeps their historic interiors intact, from the plasterwork to the floors. Their new life comes from the custom pieces Carter installed, including a Sputnik-style chandelier and low, beckoning white seating.

For private residences, such as a Bethesda mansion in Maryland overlooking the Potomac River, Carter works his customary magic by being selective with adornment so that each object has space to resonate. The windows of a breakfast-nook rotunda are bare, letting in the view and light. A modernist sculpture greets visitors in the foyer, echoing the curving double staircases rising on each side of the entryway. There's a metalevel sense of history here; the recently built mansion's architecture echoes that of another ancestral home of the client's. Carter previously studied and practiced law, and as a designer he continues to employ judicial restraint— retaining the best of the past and ushering it into modern life.

Cristina Celestino

Milan, Italy

1. Back Home, Milan Design Week
Furniture Collection and Exhibition
Milan, Italy
2019

2. Back Home, Milan Design Week
Furniture Collection and Exhibition
Milan, Italy
2019

3. Experimental Cocktail Club
Bar
Venice, Italy
2019

Few designers can add a tram to their project portfolio, but Milan-based Cristina Celestino is one of them. To mark the city's design week in 2018, she transformed a 1928 streetcar into a dreamlike "traveling salon," fitting it out with raspberry-hued textiles, lush pastel carpets, and custom-made seating from which guests could experience a cinematic view of the city. Celestino's work pays strong attention to craftsmanship and design history (she is an avid collector herself) and often displays a wry sense of humor. She has transformed restaurants, boutiques, bars, and private houses across the world; and clients include Fendi, Sergio Rossi, and Fujifilm.

Her interiors are characterized by pure geometry, unexpected color combinations, a subversive approach to ideas of "masculine" and "feminine" shapes, and sensuous materials, including brass, onyx, leather, feathers, and suede. Her own furniture designs, produced under the label Attico Design, surprise and delight with subtly surrealist pieces in the tradition of Meret Oppenheim. A coffee table resembles an oversize cuff link; an ottoman, a vintage ring box.

At Milan Design Week 2019 she created the Back Home furniture range for Fendi and Fendi Casa, inspired by Karl Lagerfeld's legendary Pequin stripe of 1983, bringing it into her own sugared-almond color palette and using it to create pieces with curvaceous, inventive forms. The Tivoli sofa back is cloud-shaped; coffee tables take on the form of roses; plush armchairs open like flowers to welcome the human body.

Celestino's treatment of a cocktail bar for the Dorothée Meilichzon-designed Il Palazzo Experimental in Venice takes many cues from the city's distinctive architecture, such as the polychrome marble on the bar counter and its torchon pillars. Wall panels in Marmorino (a lustrous stucco containing crushed marble) with black metal frames pay homage to Carlo Scarpa's Olivetti showroom in Venice. Tones of coral pink, violet, teal, and gold creates a postmodern "eighties-meets-Deco" feel. Her vision taps into subconscious desires, associations, and emotions in ways that are opulent, unpredictable, and always fun.

Champalimaud Design

New York City,
New York, USA

1. The Kent
Private Residence, Drawing Room
New York City, New York, USA
2018

2. Troutbeck
Hotel, Guest Lodge Sitting Room
Amenia, New York, USA
2018

3. Tiffin Room, Raffles Singapore
Hotel, Restaurant
Singapore
2019

1

New York-based designer Alexandra Champalimaud is globally recognized for transforming iconic yet inert properties into renewed destinations. Her work is influenced by a childhood in Portugal and an education in Switzerland and England that has cultivated her international perspective, followed by her training at Lisbon's Fundação Ricardo do Espirito Santo Silva in design and European arts and crafts. Champalimaud's appreciation for historic preservation typifies her fifty-person design firm, which specializes in restorative and luxurious hospitality design. Alongside commercial commissions, the firm also designs fabrics, furniture, and lighting for high-end manufacturers.

The Hotel Bel-Air in Los Angeles and Raffles Singapore are two projects of historical importance that emphasize the firm's passionate approach to bygone eras. In the former, gilded furnishings offer a restrained nod to the 1950s in the Grace Kelly Suite, while an engraved vaulted ceiling from the 1920s frames southern Californian and Art Deco furnishings in the Herb Garden Suite. Preserving the archetype of colonial grandeur at Raffles, the Writer's Bar is enveloped in gold, and tiffin carriers adorn the Tiffin Room—in true revivification of the stalwart's bones.

Champalimaud also brought Art Deco-inspired luxury to a multifamily condo known as the Kent in New York City; a communal drawing room boasts a marble-top bar and an exquisite gold-leafed ceiling, with shellac surfaces inviting multifaceted vantage points. An alternative take on the family theme continues at the historic Troutbeck hotel in Amenia, New York. Here, original exposed beams, wood paneling, and flagstone floors are brought to life with Champalimaud's ability to renew traditional elegance with modern design.

Inducted into the Interior Design Hall of Fame, Alexandra Champalimaud's reputation as a history whisperer in the field of interior design speaks for itself.

2

3

4. Raffles Singapore
Hotel, Lobby
Singapore
2019

5. Hotel Bel-Air
Hotel, Guest Suite
Los Angeles,
California, USA
2011

5

CHZON

Paris, France

Parisian hospitality designer Dorothée Meilichzon designs exceptionally chic cocktail bars, hotels, and restaurants. Since establishing her design agency, CHZON, in 2009, the prolific young designer has completed more than fifty projects in desirable locations, including Ibiza, Venice, and Monaco. Her sharp, contemporary interiors, most notably for the French collective Experimental Group, are warm and inviting, infusing colorful, eclectic spaces with narrative and energy.

Guests arriving at Spain's Menorca Experimental hotel, for example, immediately experience Meilichzon's immersive, storied approach. Her design imagines the hotel as an artist's summer residence, inspired by Joan Miró's retreat in Majorca and Picasso's on the French Riviera. The beguiling result is classic Menorcan style meets artistic bohemia with whitewashed stone, wooden beams, terra-cotta, and handmade glazed tiles providing the backdrop for unique drawings and interior details. Meilichzon and her team commissioned local artisans to produce unusual features, such as curved concrete bed-heads and vanities, using materials recycled from local farms.

Respect for context is also clear at Il Palazzo Experimental, a boutique hotel in a palazzo on Venice's Giudecca Canal. Carefully preserved wooden doors, gloriously high ceilings, and elaborate Gothic windows reflect the magic of Venice's classical past, while Meilichzon's luxurious contemporary details bring the space up to date. In the restaurant, custom marble sofas with scalloped edges and blood-red velvet upholstery sit beneath vintage glass lamps by Venetian designer Luciano Vistosi, paying homage to the Memphis Milano Italian design movement. The smart, tailored bedrooms feature statement postmodern headboards, arched to reflect the city's traditional buildings and upholstered in classic Venetian stripes.

Utterly focused on the consumer's experience, Meilichzon is a dynamic designer who treats the challenges facing the hospitality industry as opportunities to innovate. This fresh, fearless approach has been recognized; she was named Designer of the Year at Maison&Objet 2015 and was included in *Architectural Digest France's* prestigious AD100 list in 2019.

1. Menorca Experimental
Hotel, Guest Bathroom
Menorca, Spain
2019

2. Menorca Experimental
Hotel, Guest Room
Menorca, Spain
2019

3. Menorca Experimental
Hotel, Lobby
Menorca, Spain
2019

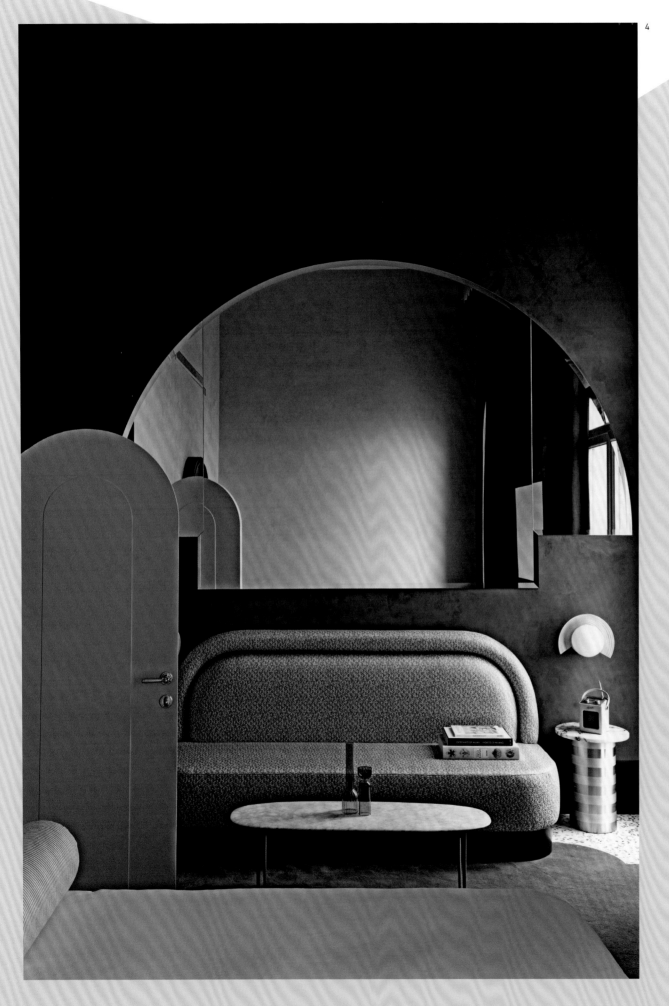

4. Il Palazzo Experimental
Hotel, Guest Suite
Venice, Italy
2019

5. Ristorante Adriatica,
Il Palazzo Experimental
Hotel, Restaurant
Venice, Italy
2019

Commune Design

Los Angeles, California, USA

1. Los Feliz Spanish Colonial
Private Residence, Living Room
Los Angeles, California, USA
2015

2. National Park Cabin
Private Residence, Living Room
Angeles National Forest,
California, USA
2019

3. Santa Monica Apartment
Private Residence, Living Room
Santa Monica, California, USA
2018

Commune Design is a studio predicated on the idea that good design is the work of many minds. The award-winning studio's principals, Roman Alonso and Steven Johanknecht, often collaborate with local artisans and builders, as well as with other designers, architects, and graphic artists. Founded in 2004 in Los Angeles, Commune brings together diverse talents and skill sets, and it ultimately designs projects—residential, commercial, and hospitality spaces, as well as graphics and home and lifestyle products—that have an air of substance and quality. With Commune, there's a sense that you're in good hands.

The studio's touch of unobtrusive luxury is displayed in many of the residential spaces it has designed in California. In an apartment in a 1960s Santa Monica building, for example, the ocean views are echoed by a few perfectly harmonized pieces: a capri-blue credenza, a turquoise daybed. For a historic Spanish Colonial in Los Angeles, Commune selected art to complement the original, intricately hand-painted ceiling. And for a family home in the Berkeley Hills, built in 1915 and previously renovated by the New York-based Studio Geiger Architecture, Commune brought together seating, lamps, and tables from as far afield as Austria and Brazil, now fitting perfectly alongside custom-made American furniture, all touched by the natural light spilling in through tall windows.

Alonso, who grew up in Venezuela, and Johanknecht, who hails from upstate New York, met while working for Barneys New York during the luxury department store's heyday in the late 1980s. The apparent effortlessness of their designs belies decades of collaboration and dedicated effort. They have a Commune ethos that is sometimes perfectly embodied in a project, such as in an off-the-beaten-track California cabin that's reachable only on foot—or by donkey. The cushions by the living room fireplace, which transform an ordinary corner into a cozy spot for a tête-à-tête, are a reward for those who make the trek.

Vincenzo De Cotiis

Milan, Italy

1. Home of Vincenzo and
Claudia Rose De Cotiis
Private Residence, Living Room
Milan, Italy
2017

2. Home of Vincenzo and
Claudia Rose De Cotiis
Private Residence, Living Room
Milan, Italy
2017

3. Home of Vincenzo and
Claudia Rose De Cotiis
Private Residence, Living Room
Milan, Italy
2017

Whether it involves an architectural project, furniture or interior design, or sculpture, Vicenzo De Cotiis's work embraces abstraction, and a continuous conversation between the present and past. The Milan-based architect and artist has a longstanding commitment to Italian craftsmanship that has led to comparisons with Carlo Scarpa and Gio Ponti. His collectible design pieces includes bladelike tables made from slivers of marble and brass, sumptuous hand-dyed velvet sofas, and sinuous silver-plated light fittings, all taking highly poetic forms that go beyond mere comfort or functionality. He frequently combines these precious materials with salvaged wood, metal, or recycled fiberglass. De Cotiis's international projects include private residences, boutiques, and hotels.

He and his wife Claudia Rose live in an enormous eighteenth-century, one-bedroom apartment in Magenta, Milan's historic center. De Cotiis spent considerable time removing layers of paint and wallpaper on the walls and was amazed by what was left behind: evocative, crumbling plaster in muted tones from buff to pink to blue, bleached by years of sunlight into a state, he says, of "marvelous imperfection"—the perfect backdrop against which to display his futuristic creations.

Rooted in the past, the apartment's decor combines dignity and grandeur with a sharp contemporary edge, and a few carefully chosen sculptural pieces that give it a sense uncluttered calm. The light that floods in through the large windows is reflected upward by a deep protruding brass baseboard that skirts the room. De Cotiis often uses concrete in his architectural projects and the apartment's walls have a Brutalist-meets-classicism feel. But the human hand is always discernible: in the layers of plaster, in the painstaking handcrafting of his jewel-like pieces that glint in the light. In common with all of his work, the apartment is neither austere nor perfect; it echoes of the past but is infused with a pathos and an unusually emotive beauty.

Design Research Studio

London, UK

Tom Dixon may have fallen into design by chance, but his empire shows a monumental talent. Today, the self-taught designer's products are found in more than ninety countries, his iconic S Chair sits within the permanent collections of New York's Museum of Modern Art and London's Victoria and Albert Museum, and he was awarded an OBE (a British honor) for his services to design.

Born in Tunisia, Dixon relocated to London as a child and graduated high school with only a qualification in pottery. A six-month stint at Chelsea School of Art was followed by moderate success in the funk-disco band Funkapolitan. In the 1980s, Dixon began experimenting with welding. Within a decade, he'd become a household name, first for Jack, a multifunctional plastic object that resembled a molecule, and then later as Habitat's creative director.

In 2002 Dixon established his eponymous brand, offering a vast array of home products. Five years later he launched Design Research Studio, an interior and architectural firm with high-profile clients, including Sea Containers London, a luxury hotel set along the banks of the Thames. Originally owned by a shipping company, the building's nautical history was referenced with an imposing interior inspired by a 1920s transatlantic cruise liner. In the lobby, the hull of a boat is mirrored in the sweeping curves of a copper-clad wall, while public restrooms feature porthole-shaped mirrors.

The Coal Office—a multidisciplinary London headquarters for Dixon—also drew design cues from its industrial nineteenth-century quarters. Powerful and modern, the space features brick walls crisscrossed with exposed steel pipes that contrast with Dixon's eye-catching sculptural lighting.

After scooping 2019's London Design Medal, Dixon mused, "I'm never really happy with what I did before. I'm only interested in what I'm doing next." Such resistance to complacency has seen this maverick transform not only his own fortunes but also the landscape of British design.

2

3

1. Sea Containers London
Hotel, Lobby Bar
London, UK
2014

2. The Coal Office
Multipurpose Venue,
Restaurant
London, UK
2018

3. The Coal Office
Multipurpose Venue,
Studio and Office
London, UK
2018

4. Sea Containers London
Hotel, Rooftop Bar
London, UK
2014
[overleaf]

Dimorestudio

Milan, Italy

In Italian *dimore* means "dwelling," but in a charming, old-world sense like the French *demeure* or English "abode." Britt Moran established the company in 2003 with Emiliano Salci, and since then the pair has made Dimorestudio into a global architectural and design brand spanning retail, residences, and hospitality. Their gold-plated client list includes Fendi, Dior, Lanvin, and the Arts Club. Hallmarks of the partners' work include ultramodern structural elements, such as bookcases and lighting, printed textiles, custom-made furniture, carefully sourced art, and rich tones. "We take a historical approach to a project to give it some roots, and then we inject it with more of a contemporary feel," explains Moran.

In 2015 Dimorestudio transformed the second floor of a seventeenth-century palazzo in Rome into a VIP apartment to serve as an entertainment space for top Fendi customers. Walls are painted a specially blended blue-gray sage, a nostalgic fin de siècle tone. In the lounge, decorative stucco is juxtaposed with modernist geometric wallpaper, and the firm's elegant cuboid, emerald velvet daybed is available for lounging. Just visible in the room beyond is a design classic: Meret Oppenheim's 1939 claw-footed *Traccia* table. Together, these elements create an opulent, sensuous atmosphere.

More suburban, but no less beguiling, is a 2018 remodel of a 1960s Florentine house. Instead of the predictable austere Minimalism that might be expected in such a setting, Dimorestudio embraced an orderly, refined eclecticism. In the sunken lounge, teal silk wallpaper adorns the upper walls, whilst the lower walls are lined with Calacatta marble, and adjacent to the staircase stands a signature structural element—an amber, green, and pink glass and brass screen, inspired by the staircase in mid-century designer Osvaldo Borsani's home.

Artfully layering past and present, Moran and Salci have invented an alternative idiom for luxury that is distinctive, desirable, and emotionally engaging.

1. Palazzo Privé Fendi VIP Apartment
Store, VIP Lounge
Rome, Italy
2015

2. Dior Dubai
Store, VIP Room
Dubai, United Arab Emirates
2019

3. Fendi Sloane Street
Store, Made-to-Order Bag Room
London, UK
2017

4. Villa in Florence
Private Residence, Living Room
Florence, Italy
2018
[overleaf]

Joseph Dirand

Paris, France

1. Girafe
Restaurant
Paris, France
2018

2. J. M. Weston
Store
Paris, France
2018

3. Four Seasons, The Surf Club
Hotel, Lobby
Miami, Florida, USA
2017

Esteemed architect Joseph Dirand is responsible for some of the design world's most beloved spaces. His beautifully conceived and meticulously executed interiors include the famed Parisian restaurant Loulou and the Four Seasons hotel at Miami's iconic Surf Club.

As the son of legendary photographer Jacques Dirand, the French designer grew up surrounded by images of extraordinary homes and people, giving him a deep appreciation for narrative—and the confidence to establish his own studio in 1999 at only twenty-five years old. Clients such as Balmain and Givenchy come to Dirand for his "ornamental Minimalism" style, with clean, refined designs enriched by lavish, organic materials. Veined marble, polished plaster, and smooth limestone are treated as works of art, laying the foundations for valued antiques and custom furniture.

Capturing the energy of its colorful past, his transformation of the Surf Club, Miami, is a master class in tailored elegance. Dirand and his team reinvigorated the foyer's dramatic arches and ceiling moldings, and added splashes of brass and fluted plaster-cast walls to the serene, all-white bedrooms. For Girafe, a restaurant inside Paris's Palais de Chaillot, Dirand took inspiration from the theatrical splendor of the city's grand cafés of the 1930s. Caramel tones and brass lighting create a restful, luxurious backdrop for his material-focused design. Walls and ceilings are enriched with oak paneling, and sumptuous, velvet-upholstered mid-century chairs by Warren Platner provide seating. The pièce de résistance is the curved statement bar, carved from a single piece of marble.

Dirand has an exceptional understanding of the rhythms of design, using subtle differences in tone and texture that draw the eye and calm the mind. His award-winning interiors—the subject of several monographs—offer visual magic without compromising on comfort or function.

dix design+architecture

Hong Kong;
Milan, Italy

1. Associazione Chianti
Restaurant and Butchers
Hong Kong
2019

2. Renkon
Restaurant
Ho Chi Minh City, Vietnam
2019

3. Renkon
Restaurant
Ho Chi Minh City, Vietnam
2019

4. Yardbird
Restaurant
Hong Kong
2018

1

American architect and interior designer Sean Dix prefers his work to take a back seat, believing the "best design is quiet and subservient." In the twenty years since he launched his firm, dix design+architecture, this principle has informed every aspect of his business—from the hospitality and retail projects across Europe, Asia, and the United States to the Dix furniture collection sold worldwide.

Born in Kansas City, Missouri, Dix's itinerant childhood saw him live in Fiji, the Philippines, and the Pacific island of Saipan. After graduating from the School of the Art Institute of Chicago, he went to the Gerrit Rietveld Academie in Amsterdam and Domus Academy in Milan. Dix first established his firm in Italy's design capital. The lure of Asia, however, eventually convinced him to relocate to Hong Kong in 2008, where he has easy access to the vast Asia-Pacific market.

In 2019 a project in Ho Chi Minh City allowed Dix to bring his creativity to Vietnam's financial hub. Dix applied his usual restraint to the interior of Renkon—a modern *izakaya* restaurant and bar—with stacked breeze blocks for the walls, carefully arranged to allow light in from above; a curving staircase designed by Dix himself; and custom-made wooden stools, named Chopsticks after the X shape of their legs, which contrast against the polished gray walls.

For another *izakaya* restaurant, Yardbird, Dix was inspired by the cafeterias of German workers during the Bauhaus era. Favoring natural materials that age well, such as steel, cast aluminum, and hardwoods, he created an industrial-style space for the popular Hong Kong eatery. To help bring in an element of Yardbird's character, he incorporated subtle design features, such as a row of illuminated pickled ingredients showcased on a shelf. In typical Dix fashion, it's an interior that is functional, understated, and humbly intended to serve a supporting role rather than steal the spotlight.

1. St. Kilda Residence
Private Residence, Kitchen
Melbourne, Victoria, Australia
2018

2. Malvern Residence
Private Residence, Living Room
Melbourne, Victoria, Australia
2019

3. Malvern Residence
Private Residence, Living Room
Melbourne, Victoria, Australia
2019

Doherty Design Studio

Melbourne, Victoria,
Australia

1

Mardi Doherty is known for the colorful, contemporary interiors that she fashions throughout her native Australia. With a résumé that features stints at renowned design firms, including Conran Design Group and David Collins Studio in London, Doherty embarked on a solo career in 2014, armed with an arsenal of experience. Her diverse array of projects span private residences, retail environments, and a function space set within an historic estate. Such industriousness attracted attention; in 2018, Doherty Design Studio was awarded the IDEA Editors Medal.

Doherty's signature obsession with natural sunlight and open spaces can be seen in a recent renovation of a house built by architect Peter McIntyre. The resort-style 1980s architecture, which evokes Palm Springs glamour, boasts unconventional details, from the entry hall's double-height glass atrium to a spaceshiplike exterior. For Doherty, the project required a careful balancing act: she needed to show respect for the building's architectural heritage while overhauling its interior. The result is a sleek reimagining of an era that saw curved glass shelving and rounded bathroom mirrors contrasting against the house's hard edges. The monochromatic interior was replaced by bold color: in the living room the teal and tangerine walls showcase a contemporary artwork in similar tones.

A different tack was taken at the flagship store of baby brand Marquise; the sophisticated, champagne-hued space is minimally decorated, with displays organized around a central tiled island. True to form, Doherty included subtle historic references; a colorful acrylic ceiling feature, inspired by 1960s children's toy PlayPlax, was used to invoke a sense of nostalgia.

Much of Doherty's work feels reflective of her homeland: bright, warm, and modern. It's an approach that extends to her business relationships, as she joked in an interview with *Est Living* magazine, "We encourage our clients to relax and enjoy the journey, and let us do the worrying!"

Sophie Dries Architect

Paris, France;
Milan, Italy

2

3

Parisian polymath Sophie Dries is an architect, interior designer, and artisan with a stellar list of projects and collaborations under her belt. Since establishing her Paris- and Milan-based studio in 2014, at the young age of twenty-eight, Dries has already worked with some of interior design's biggest names, including French designers Pierre Yovanovitch and Christian Liaigre.

Her interiors and custom designs—Dries launched a collection of ceramics in 2017—benefit from her multidisciplinary background; she holds degrees in architecture and furniture design, studied contemporary art history at École du Louvre, and has designed exhibitions for the world-famous Musée d'Orsay in Paris.

Gallery styling and historical references are key to the poetic theme she created for floral artist Arturo Arita's Paris showroom. Embracing the artist's love of Art Deco and inspired by the elaborate Mannerist caves of the late Italian Renaissance, Dries used an enchanting mix of mirrors, glass, geometric shapes, and textured surfaces to transform the showroom into a cavelike wonderland. Whitewashed plaster walls look like stone grottoes, giving a sense of subterranean minerality; their rocky cavities create niches to exhibit Arita's fresh, botanic compositions.

Equally tranquil is the Paris home she renovated for a pair of art collectors. Described by Dries as a contemplative space on account of its classically Parisian architectural style and calm, Minimalist aesthetic, the apartment has a simple elegance with a neutral palette—except for muted aqua tones used as focal points throughout the space. Natural light and art are the starting points for the interior plan; Dries designed the rooms according to specific axes and sightlines, creating unique perspectives from which to view covetable artworks.

A solid understanding of art and curating, with her ability to use lines, lighting, and detail, has given Dries a particular talent for delivering interiors that showcase artworks effectively within the context of spaces, yet they remain serene and unpretentious.

1. Art Collector Pied-à-Terre
Private Residence, Living Room
Paris, France
2019

2. Art Collector Pied-à-Terre
Private Residence, Kitchen
Paris, France
2019

3. Arturo Arita
Store
Paris, France
2019

4. Contemplative
Haussmanian Space
Private Residence,
Living Room
Paris, France
2019

5. Street Art Collector
Family Apartment
Private Residence,
Kitchen
Paris, France
2018

Bernard Dubois Architects

Brussels, Belgium;
Paris, France

Belgian architect Bernard Dubois is a rising star, winning praise for his quiet, meticulously planned spaces and modern, materially driven furniture. His expanding portfolio includes retail boutiques for luxury brands, such as Isaac Reina and Valextra, as well as art galleries and private homes. In 2014, Dubois also represented Belgium at the 14th International Architecture Exhibition of the Venice Biennale, marking an important step at the beginning of his career.

Raised in a family of engineers and physicians, Dubois studied chemistry before turning to architecture. The influence of science is clear in his meticulous three-dimensional rendering of spaces and rigorous project planning, but his sleek Minimalist interiors are artistic and conceptual with a strong narrative arc.

At the Brussels store he designed for Australian skincare brand Aesop, the interior walls and floors are lined with distinctive blond briquettes, once frequently used in 1930s Belgian exteriors but less commonly seen today. For Dubois, they evoke nostalgia—rainy childhood vacations on the Belgian coast—while the vertical pattern adds a warm Mediterranean feel. Against this reference to early twentieth-century architecture, Dubois added oiled-oak joinery and Modern and postmodern touches, such as curvilinear forms, chamfered corners, and repeating arches.

The interplay between past and present is also key to Dubois' design for the Paris home of art collector Thierry Gillier, the founder of Zadig & Voltaire. He used the building's existing architectural features, exposing wooden beams and restoring the grand stone staircase, then chose materials for their tactility and character, from ceppo di gré—a bluish stone from northern Italy—to rough gnarled oak. Crucially, Dubois stuck to an all-white, utilitarian design, with smartly placed walls, to allow for the gallery-type styling of Gillier's collection, which includes artworks by Picasso and Jean-Michel Basquiat and furniture by mid-century masters Charlotte Perriand and Pierre Jeanneret.

Using an exacting and scholarly approach, Dubois—who has also codirected the Architectural Association's Visiting School Brussels since 2016—is able to unite disparate themes and styles into a coherent, original whole.

1. Galilée Apartment
Private Residence, Living Room
Paris, France
2018

2. Aesop
Store
Brussels, Belgium
2018

3. ICICLE
Store
Paris, France
2019

André Fu Studio

Hong Kong

André Fu, founder of the eponymous Hong Kong-based studio, is responsible for some of Europe and Asia's most design-conscious hotels and restaurants. With a portfolio that includes Hong Kong's the Upper House hotel and Villa La Coste, in Provence, France, the architectural designer has spent nearly twenty years creating award-winning spaces for major brands worldwide.

Educated in England, Fu studied architecture at Cambridge University before establishing his studio in 2000, straight after graduating. Since returning to his native Hong Kong, the studious designer has revolutionized modern Asian design with his highly creative, analytical approach. Deeply sensitive to form and proportion, Fu's designs are mesmeric in their treatment of light and scale, creating grand spaces that feel profoundly calming.

Intimate, refined sophistication is displayed at the twenty-seven-story St. Regis Hong Kong, which opened in 2019. Described as a "curated mansion," Fu's inspiration was twofold: the iconic St. Regis New York and the architectural heritage of Hong Kong. His exquisite interiors, with Art Deco details, gas streetlights, and colonial columns, conjure up 1920s America with all the romantic nostalgia of 1960s Hong Kong immortalized in Wong Kar-wai's cinematic masterpiece *In the Mood for Love*.

Also reflecting the 1920s splendor of its American counterpart is Bangkok's iconic Waldorf Astoria. Fu's design for the hotel pays homage to this history, but cleverly and subtly reinterprets Art Deco details to reflect Thai culture. One example is the Peacock Alley bar's spectacular bronze clock—a modern take on the Manhattan Waldorf's famous timepiece—which boasts intricate twists in the metal as a tribute to the hand movements unique to Thai dancing.

Clients come to Fu for understated elegance and his relaxed brand of luxury, delivered by a studio that listens deeply. Fu's atmospheric interiors, which blend European and Asian design, are based upon a deep appreciation for both cultures and genuine love for the indulgence of hospitality.

1. Peacock Alley,
Waldorf Astoria Bangkok
Hotel, Tea Room
Bangkok, Thailand
2018

2. St. Regis Hong Kong
Hotel, Second Floor Lobby
Hong Kong
2019

3. Louise Hong Kong
Restaurant
Hong Kong
2019

Ken Fulk

New York City, New York, and
San Francisco, California, USA

Virginia-born, San Francisco- and New York-based Ken Fulk happily inhabits the role of a modern-day impresario, designing interiors as well as events—he is known for the elaborate parties he organizes as well as the dashing, custom-tailored suits he wears. Fulk's design studio handles everything from branding and graphics to flowers for residential, restaurant, and hospitality spaces. The mix of showmanship and easy glamour that is typical of his designs keeps elegant and elaborate rooms from feeling overproduced or overstuffed. Fulk is refreshingly forthright about his focus on what he calls the "human scale." On a practical level, this means hanging art at eye level; overall, it means personal idiosyncrasies are encouraged rather than sacrificed to abstract principles of design.

At Birch Castle, a five-story mansion in San Francisco's Billionaire's Row, personal history is the guiding concept. One half of the client couple is British, and Fulk integrated British history into an updated, edgy design theme, which includes a mosaic of the British flag, a grand double staircase, and a portrait gallery, where eighteenth-century artworks are hung with a photograph of Kate Moss. In 2015, at the Las Vegas outpost of the beloved New York restaurant Carbone, Fulk addressed a different cultural heritage, channeling Sin City's mid-century Rat Pack allure. The result—inspired by Milan's La Scala opera house—is breathtakingly operatic. In the restaurant's red room, a cascading chandelier that once hung in a Ferrari dealership descends toward tall leather booths, which servers approach for tableside service, a throwback to a more performative era of dining and entertainment.

Fulk never trained formally as a designer, but an early love for hosting, combined with a tireless work ethic, has brought him to a professional pinnacle. If his work seems inimitable, it's because he sets the stage for unique experiences—moments that can't be repeated.

1. Carbone
Restaurant
Las Vegas, Nevada, USA
2015

2. Birch Castle
Private Residence, Staircase
San Francisco, California, USA
2008

3. The Lake House
Private Residence,
The Great Hall
Glen Ellen, California, USA
2015

Fawn Galli

New York City,
New York, USA

Known for her experimental sensibility, Fawn Galli says her "subtle playfulness" lies in the esoteric. Although untrained, Galli's sharp eye first landed her at Christie's furniture department in Paris. In New York, Galli gained industry experience working for architect Robert A. M. Stern and later Peter Marino, an architect of luxury fashion stores, before launching her own interior design and construction management firm in 2005.

Galli's signature interiors have been featured in *Architectural Digest, Elle Decor, House Beautiful*, and the *New York Times*, and a devoted roster of clients entrust her expert use of color and forte for combining old-world elegance with modern sophistication. In a classic 1920s Washington Square Park apartment in New York City's Greenwich Village, for example, Galli helped envision the renovation of an abundant family home. Silk ombre curtains and a custom sofa upholstered in blue velvet by Rose Cumming reflect the joyful indulgence of Galli's clients, a couture designer and composer. An effortless blending of eras is captured by a 1970s Italian floor lamp and 1950s Mathieu Matégot side table set against grass-cloth walls by Roger Arlington. For a classic prewar Central Park West apartment in Manhattan that recalls Villa Necchi Campiglio in Milan, mirror-paneled walls surround a statement stone fireplace to help project light into the peacefully gray living room.

Galli's iconoclastic approach came into play for a client's residence in Short Hills, New Jersey. Acid yellow pops under an Art Deco chandelier in the monochrome living room and another set of Galli's ombre curtains bursts out against a chinoiserie lounge, which features Arts and Crafts wallpaper and an aureate settee.

The designer says the five elements she employs, "nature, clashing, surrealism, bohemian, sparkle," reflect her love of 1970s disco. While eccentric and visually off beat, these elements shift into focus with Galli's ability to create liveable spaces of beauty and wonder.

1. Short Hills
Private Residence, Bar/Lounge
Short Hills, New Jersey, USA
2017

2. Short Hills
Private Residence, Lounge
Short Hills, New Jersey, USA
2017

3. Central Park West
Private Residence, Living Room
New York City, New York, USA
2017

4. Central Park West
Private Residence, Bedroom
New York City, New York, USA
2017

5. Washington Square Park
Private Residence, Living Room
New York City, New York, USA
2015

GOLDEN

Melbourne, Victoria,
Australia

Alicia McKimm and Kylie Dorotic—the founders behind GOLDEN—settled on the name following a rebranding exercise. Their Melbourne-based studio, formerly known as We Are Huntly, had built such a reputation for their work across residential, commercial, and hospitality projects that it scooped an award for Emerging Interior Design Practice at the Australian Interior Design Awards in 2016. But as they evolved as a business, the duo wanted a name that better conveyed their sunny approach to design, one that always strives to evoke feelings of warmth in their interiors.

Judging from the acclaim they have since garnered, the pair certainly seems to have a golden touch. Using a holistic approach when designing an interior, which sees them consider everything from the emotive qualities of a space to the nitty-gritty practicalities, they have reinvented wellness studios, upscale boutiques, and fashionable restaurants. Alongside a number of private commissions, property developers have also utilized their design skills, attracted by their breezy take on contemporary living.

This knack for injecting joy can be seen at Wattle House, a nineteenth-century property in Melbourne featured in design magazines from *Elle Decor* to *Architectural Digest*. Determined to combine the functionalities needed for a young family with a playful eclecticism, McKimm and Dorotic created a texture-heavy home that includes a blush-pink velvet sofa, a hallway mirror fringed with natural grass, and brass accents that contrast against coolly painted walls.

Another private home in the city, the Brighton Residence, has been given a coolly contemporary makeover. The newly built bayside property features slabs of cement that act as room dividers, black wooden wall paneling, and an abundance of glass. Even when the aesthetic differs, GOLDEN's core values shine through: to create expressive, sensory, and harmonious environments, which, above all, capture the client's personality.

1. Laurent Kew
Café
Melbourne, Victoria, Australia
2019

2. Brighton Residence
Private Residence, Rumpus Room
Melbourne, Victoria, Australia
2019

3. Brighton Residence
Private Residence, Living Room
Melbourne, Victoria, Australia
2019

4. Wattle House
Private Residence, Living Room
Melbourne, Victoria, Australia
2018

Grisanti & Cussen

Santiago, Chile

2

There's something almost uncanny about the inimitable spaces created by the Santiago, Chile-based boutique design firm Grisanti & Cussen, founded in 2007. The principals, architect Hugo Grisanti and designer Kana Cussen, are thorough researchers, gifted with a sense for color and texture and interested in sustainable materials and techniques. Yet, what stands out about their commercial, residential, and hospitality projects is the feeling that these well-lit, relaxed rooms are the products of an alternate history—just as real, but a touch more beautiful than the stories we know.

Take the living room the duo created for the furniture brand BoConcept in 2017. Imagined as a home for the protagonist of Tom Ford's movie *A Single Man*, a British professor in 1960s Los Angeles, the room is a remarkably graceful setting built up in geometric shapes, from the earth-tone diamonds of the carpet to the gray-stone-look porcelain tiles of one wall. The room comes to life through subtle signs—warm lighting, a plant here and there. Grisanti & Cussen brought another fantasy to life in 2019 for the Swedish housing company Riksbyggen. The model apartment they designed brings together the formal simplicity of Scandinavian furniture with the lively palettes of Latin America, with the living room walls painted in broad stripes of dusty pink and Spanish blue.

For a unique hilltop home by architect Juan Galleguillos, the firm had to work without blueprints to complete a design that honors both the original architecture, such as circular stone and glass walls, and the needs of the client's family. With its wooden ceilings and stone floors, the house is at one with the landscape. And like the landscape, their gorgeous designs, fanciful as they may seem, offer a sturdy foundation for life. Grisanti & Cussen's work reflects an ongoing, quiet revolution, making it one of the most exciting design outfits in the field.

3

1. Casa FOA
Temporary Display, Living Room
Santiago, Chile
2017

2. Riksbyggen
Show Apartment, Living Room
Uppsala, Sweden
2019

3. Casa Arrayan
Private Residence, Living Room
Santiago, Chile
2016

Luca Guadagnino

Milan, Italy

When Luca Guadagnino, director of *Call Me by Your Name* and *I Am Love* announced a move into interior design, it was not too difficult to fathom. Both movies are visually intoxicating, and both feature beautiful houses that play leading roles in the narrative. His first project was to redecorate the home of his friends Federico Marchetti and Kerry Olsen—a nineteenth-century silk mill on Lake Como—using a bold Modernist palette of mint green, blush pink, and baby blue, and a blend of early twentieth- and mid-century furniture. Guadagnino storyboarded it out like he would a movie: "I'm a storyteller. That's my first job."

His next commission was a Rome store for the skincare brand Aesop, which drew inspiration from the Eternal City's history, colors, and material palette. Dennis Paphitis, Aesop's founder, wanted "a sense of monastic order and tranquillity," and Guadagnino delivered impeccably with a beautiful and meditative interior, starting with travertine marble flooring inspired by the nearby San Lorenzo church's floor. Pink and dark green blocks of marble form the central counter, while the ceiling is lined, unusually, with straw bricks inspired by the thatched roofs of early settlements on the Pontine Marshes outside the city. Each carefully chosen detail speaks of history, people, and stories.

It was followed by the design for Redemption's flagship store in New York. Inspired by the Rolling Stones' notorious six months at Villa Nellcôte on the Côte d'Azur while recording their album *Exile on Main St.* in 1972, it fuses mid-nineteenth-century elegance with 1970s decadence. The main room features white boiserie with a floral pattern and reclaimed chevron parquet wooden flooring; in the VIP dressing room, umber-and-orange geometric wallpaper is paired with low-slung pink and beige velvet sofas.

Mastery of narrative, space, color, and history are all strikingly evident in Guadagnino's interiors—just as they are in his movies.

1. Redemption
Store, VIP Room
New York City, New York, USA
2019

2. Aesop
Store
Rome, Italy
2018

3. Aesop
Store
London, UK
2019

Halden Interiors

Green Brook,
New Jersey, USA

1. San Jose Estate
Private Residence, Living Room
San Jose, California
2015

2. San Jose Estate
Private Residence, Dining Room
San Jose, California
2015

3. Hudson River Pied-à-Terre
Private Residence, Living Room
Weehawken, New Jersey, USA
2020

Kesha Franklin grew up with a library of good design at her fingertips: stacks and stacks of her father's issues of *Architectural Digest* and *GQ*. Although she gained expertise early, by the time Franklin began to think of herself as a designer, she already had a career in corporate event production, which led to further opportunities within the fashion industry. The shift to interior design took time, so it's a good thing that, once committed, Franklin is so dedicated to her vision, working for that culminating moment when a client enters their new home and expresses joy. Franklin is a gifted and sensitive designer, with a knack for bringing together textures and a penchant for introducing carefully selected flourishes to add joie de vivre to any space.

Franklin recently moved her Halden Interiors studio from New York City to New Jersey, and her projects stand on both shores of the Hudson River. For a Harlem duplex in New York, she used geometric shapes for cohesion as well as finishes that bring out the warm glow of the wood surfaces and floors, creating a peaceful island in the city's busy stream.

In a residence on the Jersey side of the river, Franklin's design takes advantage of the bountiful light and space, employing festive bright strokes within an overall relaxed, natural palette—for example, a brass lamp in the living room and a sunflower-yellow ceiling over the dining room table. Franklin's instincts serve her well farther afield, too, as in the case of a private residence she designed in San Jose, California, in 2015. With custom cowhide carpets, Holly Hunt's Stilt Coupe lounge chairs, and bronze and gold touches, along with an altered layout to suit the young bachelor occupant, Franklin did her usual and created an outstanding home: fit for a devotee of *GQ* or the cover of *Architectural Digest*.

Hare + Klein

Sydney, New South Wales,
Australia

1. Cliff Top House
Private Residence, Living Room
Sydney, New South Wales,
Australia
2015

2. Cliff Top House
Private Residence, Living Room
Sydney, New South Wales,
Australia
2015

3. Old Furniture Factory
Private Residence, Dining Room
Sydney, New South Wales,
Australia
2019

Industry veteran Meryl Hare's approach to interiors is neatly encapsulated in the title of her 2014 book, *Texture Colour Comfort*. Providing insight into the three ingredients that sit as the bedrock of her decorating ethos, it's a winning formula that has seen Hare occupy the forefront of Australia's design scene for thirty years.

South African-born Hare lived in Zambia and Swaziland before relocating to Sydney in 1988, where she established Hare + Klein, her acclaimed interiors firm, the following year. However, as a newly arrived immigrant, Hare was initially devoid of clients or the much-needed connections with local suppliers. It was a disadvantage that her determination bulldozed aside: by 2011, Hare had been inducted into the Design Institute of Australia's Hall of Fame.

Hare shies away from pigeonholing her style, preferring instead to remain guided by each client's individual needs. Such an attitude has won her commissions that range from a converted warehouse home in Sydney to thatched villas at an exclusive five-star hotel resort in Fiji. But despite this diversity, a common thread links her projects: gracefully layered textures, a warm color palette, and generously proportioned spaces that promote a sense of ease.

At Cliff Top House—a private property that boasts a spectacular location overlooking Sydney's Bondi Beach—Hare's tactile approach can be seen in the raw, natural materials used throughout. The white-washed dining room features light installations draped in a material akin to a fishing net, which hang above a rustic wooden table; a cozy, taupe lounge is furnished with jute carpeting and relaxed, low-level seating in leather and wicker.

Elegant yet comfortable, it's a home that invites its residents to relax. For Hare, that's her foremost consideration. "We place a lot of emphasis on comfort," she confided in a conversation with a local furniture company. "It's the great luxury in a home."

4. Old Furniture Factory
Private Residence, Bathroom
Sydney, New South Wales,
Australia
2019

5. Woollahra Valley
Private Residence, Living Room
Sydney, New South Wales,
Australia
2019

Hecker Guthrie

Melbourne, Victoria,
Australia

1. Darlinghurst Apartment
Private Residence, Living Room
Sydney, New South Wales,
Australia
2019

2. East Melbourne Residence
Private Residence, Kitchen
Melbourne, Victoria, Australia
2018

3. Carlton North Residence
Private Residence, Living Room
Melbourne, Victoria, Australia
2019

4. Piccolina Collingwood
Gelato Shop
Melbourne, Victoria, Australia
2017
[overleaf]

2

3

Paul Hecker and Hamish Guthrie—who had worked in the same architecture firm in the 1990s—established the Melbourne-based interior design firm Hecker Guthrie in 2001. In the two decades since, the duo has scooped some of Australia's most desirable commissions. Ranging from sleek boutique hotel revamps and 1950s-inspired Italian gelato shops to sophisticated family homes, each project reflects the studio's belief that design should be rooted in storytelling.

This talent for delivering a contemporary retelling of any interior is obvious at the Carlton North Residence, a home with heritage features located in a fashionable Melbourne suburb. Exposed brick walls and traditional fireplaces remain intact, but black metal detailing was added to frame the property's expansive windows. This accent is repeated in various iterations throughout, from doors in the same material to an external wooden wall painted in a matching inky shade. Materials also play a central role: floor-to-ceiling linen drapes, glossy oyster-colored tiling, and wooden flooring bring textural warmth to the space.

Another private property in Sydney channels the owner's love of Japanese and Scandinavian styles. The neutral color palette, paired with an abundance of pale wood, ensures a restful environment, and prominently displayed objets d'art add a sense of individuality.

Despite its multi-sector roster of clients, Hecker Guthrie approaches each project with the same principles. With their small team, the studio creates refined interiors that emphasize natural materials, craft, and thoughtfully curated furnishings. It's an award-winning formula: in 2017 the South Australian Design Institute of Australia recognized Hecker as a Design Icon in his field.

GRANITA↓	PRICES		
MON	1 SCOOP	5.8
RAWBERRY	2 SCOOP	6.8
MELON MINT	3 SCOOP	8.8
D LIME	KIDS	4.8
	0.5L	15.9
TELLA ↓	1.0L	24.9
PPING 1	1.5L	30.9
	GRANITA	5
% NATURAL MILKSHAKE		7

Shawn Henderson

New York City,
New York, USA

Shawn Henderson's cool palettes, spatial acuity, and classical restraint mark him as a master of neo-Minimalist style. In a way, he's been training his entire life: as a child, Henderson looked through design magazines in doctors' waiting rooms. As an adult who's often featured in those magazines, Henderson designs residential spaces that embody and promote a peaceful stillness, achieved through the harmonious balance of textures and forms. Unique in an era of bold eclecticism, his serene designs are modest and confident enough to announce themselves as settings—spaces for life and contemplation.

It's not surprising that many of Henderson's projects are vacation homes—dwellings where people go to rest and recalibrate. For a client in Aspen, Colorado, Henderson designed a tranquil living room with a round cocktail table by Philip and Kelvin LaVerne, positioned below a rectangular wall piece by the artist Theaster Gates. The French blue of a suede couch is echoed, in a minor key, by the soft celadon of an acorn-shaped Japanese vase. In the lounge of a ski chalet in Montana, up in the Rocky Mountains and awash with natural light, Henderson lets the views speak for themselves with the addition of a circular coral-hue couch: an embrace, a touch of warmth in winter, and a perch from which to contemplate the slopes.

One of the most appealing aspects of this sophisticated, understated aesthetic is its ingenious organization. In Henderson's spaces, utility is a prime value. For the designer's own nineteenth-century colonial farmhouse in Hillsdale, New York, he sought to update a core Scandinavian style with contemporary pieces. In the dining room, blue bench seating does double duty, bringing a burst of color to the toned-down space. A portrait of the transcendentalist Henry David Thoreau serves as kind of metonym for Henderson: an American talent influenced by the best minds in the world.

1. Aspen Home
Private Residence, Dining Room
Aspen, Colorado, USA
2015

2. Aspen Home
Private Residence, Living Room
Aspen, Colorado, USA
2015

3. Hillsdale Home
Private Residence, Dining Room
Hillsdale, New York, USA
2018

4. Montana Ski House
Private Residence, Family Room
Big Sky, Montana, USA
2015
[overleaf]

Beata Heuman

London, UK

1. Farm Girl Chelsea
Restaurant
London, UK
2018

2. Paddington Pied-à-Terre
Private Residence,
Kitchen/Living Room
London, UK
2017

3. Sussex Cottage
Private Residence, Living Room
Sussex, UK
2018

4. West London Townhouse
Private Residence, Drawing Room
London, UK
2016

2

3

4

London-based designer Beata Heuman often presents her clients with watercolor sketches of her ideas. This isn't a singular quirk, but a fitting embodiment of the melding of classical design and imaginative charm that has seen her emerge as a breakout star. In 2018 the hype around her was cemented when *House & Garden* magazine crowned Heuman their "Designer of the Year," and more accolades swiftly followed.

For nearly a decade, Heuman cut her teeth working with esteemed decorator Nicky Haslam—an experience that can be seen in her considered use of soft furnishings and unexpected color. Since the establishment of her own studio in 2013, Heuman has become a popular choice among private clients. One of her residential projects—a pied-à-terre in central London—involved remodeling tight living quarters into a brightly hued interior that matches its owner's creative profession. The entrance hall has been reinvented as a snug sunroom, with olive green leather banquettes nestled underneath the windows. In the living room, a raspberry-colored carpet contrasts joyfully against polished black floorboards and grass-cloth wallpaper, and the sky-blue bedroom is enlivened with a bed upholstered in playful red stripes. To avoid veering into the kitsch, Heuman lent gravitas with carefully selected antiques.

At Farm Girl Cafe in London's Chelsea neighborhood, Heuman's originality was given free rein. Drawing inspiration from *The Grand Budapest Hotel*, Wes Anderson's pastel-hued 2014 movie, Heuman transformed the eatery into an equally whimsical space. In the dining room, jewel-toned seating was accentuated by salmon-pink wall arches and illuminated with Hollywood-style gold bulbs, and the restroom boasted starry tiles and brass fittings.

It's little surprise that Heuman has expanded into a line of textiles, lighting, and custom-made furniture. Each piece promises a little slice of her world: creative, colorful, and filled with fun.

5. West London Townhouse
Private Residence, Study
London, UK
2016

6. West London Townhouse
Private Residence,
Living Room
London, UK
2016

Fran Hickman

London, UK

1. Chess Club
Private Members' Club,
Ground Floor Restaurant
London, UK
2017

2. Chess Club
Private Members' Club,
First Floor Bar/Lounge
London, UK
2017

3. Emilia Wickstead
Store
London, UK
2016

With an impressive list of celebrity clients, society favorite Fran Hickman is one of the brightest young names in British design. Since establishing her studio in 2014, the designer has won numerous prestigious commissions, largely concentrated in London, from her career-launching transformation of Moda Operandi's flagship store to the first European pop-up of Gwyneth Paltrow's brand Goop.

Hickman's twelve-strong team includes interior designers and architects, reflecting a holistic approach to design. There is no signature aesthetic, but the studio's portfolio reveals elegant, highly tailored interiors punctuated with playful and dramatic touches. Think unexpected colors and unique architectural features, such as the Barbara Hepworth-inspired sculptural stone staircase designed for a movie director's Notting Hill residence.

Hickman sees interior design as a language where every object, artwork, or piece of furniture is part of the client's story. This ambition is best articulated in her reimagining of commercial spaces, which demonstrate a sound appreciation of architectural history and an ability to infuse a space with narrative. Stone columns, cotton-candy pinks, and sweeping cuts of terrazzo, for example, welcome visitors to fashion designer Emilia Wickstead's dreamlike show-room in trendy Knightsbridge. With a minimal use of color and sinuous curves, there are echoes of Villa Savoye, the Modernist icon designed by Swiss–French architect Le Corbusier, while upholstered wall panels and floral furnishings add warmth and sophistication.

For the studio's first hospitality project, a London members' club, the fledgling team transformed a derelict early nineteenth-century townhouse into a luxurious bolt-hole for a design-conscious crowd. The building's architectural idiosyncrasies were complemented with mirrors, murals, mid-century lighting, and metalwork inspired by French decorator Jean Royère. In a characteristically poetic touch, Hickman adorned the walls with 257 framed butter-flies in homage to Italian architect Carlo Mollino (whose mysterious apartment in Turin, Italy, featured hundreds of butterflies), as a reminder to enjoy beauty in the everyday.

Laura Hodges Studio

Baltimore, Maryland,
and Washington, D.C., USA

2

1. Rosewood
Private Residence, Music Room
Catonsville, Maryland, USA
2019

2. Rosewood
Private Residence, Dining Room
Catonsville, Maryland, USA
2019

3. Chesapeake
Private Residence, Sitting Room
Baltimore, Maryland, USA
2018

The Baltimore-based designer Laura Hodges had a peripatetic childhood, traveling frequently with her family from their home in northern England. Now, she wields a unique awareness of the ways travel and design can intersect. For designers, "travel" is often a synonym for eclecticism, a passion for variety and abundance, inspired by thrilling, unfamiliar vistas. Hodges is a master at harnessing the desires travel can spark, but she's also attuned to the practical aspects of relocation: the sourcing and shipment of materials required for furniture; the implications of certain manufacturing processes; and the ways the environment is affected by the creation of "environments" within homes. LEED- and green-accredited, Hodges is knowledgeable about sustainability and strives for designs that are both elegant and salubrious. This disposition toward harmony can be felt in Hodges's spaces, even if one doesn't know that the objects were sourced from renewable resources, or that the previous furnishings were donated or recycled.

Interiors designed by Laura Hodges Studio tend to have a lighter palette, but carefully selected darker accents provide grounding for each room. For her roster of residential clients, Hodges has accomplished such subtle feats as turning a conventional living room into a music room by introducing an antique piano and reupholstering heirloom chairs. She's turned a penthouse overlooking Baltimore's skyline into a series of aeries, creating subdivisions with light fixtures, including a Bocci chandelier. And for a client in the Maryland countryside, Hodges's choice of a lovely dusty pink bookshelf backing creates a sense of florals in the study—a space that blooms year-round.

Although often still priced like a luxury good, sustainability is increasingly understood to be simply necessary. Fortunately, Hodges, who also runs the Domain design boutique, is at the forefront of designers thinking about the future.

3

4. Chesapeake
Private Residence, Living Room
Baltimore, Maryland, USA
2018

5. Green Branch
Private Residence, Dining Room
Phoenix, Maryland, USA
2019

Laura Hodges Studio

1. A Sophisticated Townhouse
Private Residence, Living Room
London, UK
2013

2. AllBright Mayfair
Private Members' Club,
Beauty and Wellness Salon
London, UK
2019

3. AllBright Mayfair
Private Members' Club,
Coworking and Events Space
London, UK
2019

Suzy Hoodless

London, UK

1

2

3

Dubbed Great Britain's brightest "tastemaker" by *Harper's Bazaar*, stylist-turned-designer Suzy Hoodless has been creating joyful interiors for more than twenty years. A founding member of *Wallpaper** magazine, where she enjoyed a successful career as the interiors editor, Hoodless swapped styling for designing in the late 1990s and established her studio in 2000. In the decades since, she has applied a stylist's eye and curatorial talent to houses, hotels, and restaurants around the world.

Best known for her eclectic, layered designs, Hoodless's rooms and retail spaces—including her own photogenic home with its arresting canary-yellow door frame—are glossy magazine regulars and much-referenced sources of inspiration. A Hoodless interior is a menagerie of styles, curated and collected, combining mid-century furniture with vintage textiles, modern art, and "mood-lifting" colors.

In Hoodless's vision for AllBright, a female-only London members' club that opened in 2019, color and texture are key. Asked to create interiors that felt feminine but not girly, Hoodless delivered an intimate, glamorous design featuring emerald velvets, geometric prints, and walls emblazoned with the bold florals of French artist Raoul Dufy. In a nod to nearby Savile Row's tradition of custom tailoring, she also added fine wools and houndstooth checks.

Equally special are the darkly atmospheric interiors she designed for a family townhouse in London's Notting Hill. Sensitive to the nineteenth-century building's period features and an impressive modern renovation, Hoodless's design complements both elements. In the living room, walls are kept neutral and clean, and the original window shutters are offset against a striking marble fireplace.

Hoodless's commercial spaces celebrate tailoring and glamour, yet her residential projects can be described as a celebration of organic, slow design—artfully curated homes that evolve naturally over time.

4. Suzy's Own Home
Private Residence, View from
Living Room to Library
London, UK
2018

5. Suzy's Own Home
Private Residence, Kitchen
London, UK
2018

Young Huh Interior Design

New York City,
New York, USA

1. Hamptons Residence
Private Residence,
Drawing Room
The Hamptons, New York, USA
2015

2. Mantoloking Residence
Private Residence, Living Room
Mantoloking, New Jersey, USA
2016

3. Mantoloking Residence
Private Residence, Living Room
Mantoloking, New Jersey, USA
2016

1

New York-based designer Young Huh is the creative behind Young Huh Interior Design, a full-service firm that's been turning heads in the design world ever since the 2019 Kips Bay Decorator Show House. For the event, Huh designed a room that "broke the internet," creating an amazingly vibrant attic space fit for an artist's atelier. However, the designer has been working hard on residential and commercial projects since 2007, when she founded her firm after deciding to turn away from a budding law career. Huh's decision was based on the idea that there's no substitute for enjoyment. In working life as in interiors, one's aim should simply be delight.

Thankfully, Huh's artful compositions, marked by sophisticated palettes and a love of faux architectural details (as well as a penchant for silk Fromental wallpaper), are anything but simple. In a client's Hamptons, New York, home, for example, a symphony of patterns builds throughout the living room: a refined, diagonal-stripe sofa is lit by a stout, attractive lamp with a pink graduated base and animated by fur-covered pillows. For another client's home in Mantoloking, New Jersey, Huh brings together crisp whites and apple greens, grounding the room with a Chinese silk rug and topping it off with cloud-motif wallpaper on the ceiling. One corner houses a chess table, another a grand piano; but thanks to the verdant palette and Huh's calculated pairing of prints, the space feels most like a pleasure garden, a curated extension of the outside world. It's elevated and purposeful, but also suited for play.

Distant as it may be from the law court, the design office is a place with its own codes and customs, and Huh has been an outspoken and supportive member of the design community, which is fortunate to count her as a member. Huh's pursuit of happiness is the pursuit of happiness for all.

Humbert & Poyet

Monaco

1. Villa Odaya
Private Residence, Living Room
Cannes, France
2019

2. Villa Odaya
Private Residence, Living Room
Cannes, France
2019

3. 26 Carré Or
Private Residence, Bathroom
Monaco
2020

4. Beefbar Paris
Restaurant, Dining Room
Paris, France
2018
[overleaf]

1

In an interior designed by Emil Humbert and Christophe Poyet, all is luxury, order, and restraint. Their work shows a profound knowledge of design history, drawing especially on early Modernism and the Jazz Age. Yet across the gamut of their projects, which include retail spaces, luxury residential developments, private clients, and top restaurants, they never resort to mere pastiche.

Humbert, an architect, graduated from the École Nationale Supérieure d'Architecture Paris-Belleville, while Poyet, an interior architect, is a graduate of Académie Charpentier, the prestigious Parisian school of interior design. They met in 2007 and set up their studio in Monaco a year later, swiftly building up a worldwide portfolio of projects.

Humbert & Poyet interiors combine a classical Modernism with a sharp, contemporary edge that appeals to clients who are visually and culturally aware. Villa Odaya, for example, in Cannes, references its Côte d'Azur artistic heritage throughout. On the magnificent staircase, the designers have used the geometric forms and color palettes of Matisse and Picasso, which perfectly complement the Mediterranean landscape. In the lounge, totemic sculptures by Bertrand Créac'h and 1950s chairs by Pierre Jeanneret are perfectly matched with the soft, bulbous forms of the Thédore living room furniture they designed themselves.

Not far down the coast in Monaco, the studio revved up the opulence at the exclusive residential development 26 Carré Or. Reflective surfaces shimmer throughout: gold-streaked marble in bathrooms, gilt faucets, and intricately detailed brass screening and wall paneling; monochrome geometric floor tiles are another breathtaking focal point. The interiors are luminous, flooded with light. In different hands the project could have easily spilled over into flamboyance or flashiness. But despite the ubiquitous luster, extravagant materials, and smart Art Deco detailing, a rigorous Minimalism and classical balance keeps everything elegantly under control.

2

3

Tamsin Johnson

Sydney, New South Wales,
Australia

After more than a decade in the business, sought-after Australian designer Tamsin Johnson is a master in the art of effortless sophistication. Meticulously curated, her eclectic interiors have a playful, laid-back energy that belies the rigorous precision behind their execution.

Antiques, mid-century and contemporary furniture, collected objects, and modern art are grouped together in bright, white spaces with such harmony that it is evident Johnson has a deep understanding of design and provenance. She credits her father—an antiques dealer with whom she scoured European flea markets as a child—for her discerning eye and innate appreciation of craft. A fashion career, a design degree in London, and four years at the Sydney-based studio Meacham Nockles McQualter laid the foundations for her solo success. Johnson established her studio in 2011 and, after five years of delivering acclaimed interiors, added a retail showroom to her portfolio.

Overlooking Sydney's Tamarama Beach, Johnson's bungalow-style home—which she shares with tailor husband Patrick Johnson, whose ateliers she has also designed—is adorned with covetable furniture and artifacts. Audoux-Minet rope chairs and a Philip Arctander Clam chair sit comfortably with linens, a custom marble dining table, and a beautiful wooden chair handmade by Johnson herself.

The same uncontrived elegance is on show at Rae's on Wategos, a whitewashed Mediterranean-style boutique hotel in Australia's picturesque Byron Bay, which Johnson designed top to bottom in 2017. To its fresh, pared-back palette, she has added clamshell sconces, rattan furniture, and accents of wood and travertine. Artworks, sculptures, and fabrics by local artists add further personality and character.

Johnson's rapidly expanding portfolio of interiors benefits from her dual design heritage, combining European twentieth-century design with contemporary craft and an understated, coastal charm that feels quintessentially Australian. It's no wonder the design world has fallen for her brand of Antipodean chic: luxurious, unpretentious yet impeccably tailored, and reassuringly relaxed.

1. Raes on Wategos
Hotel, Penthouse Suite
Byron Bay, New South Wales,
Australia
2016

2. Tamarama Residence
Private Residence, Living Room
Sydney, New South Wales,
Australia
2016

3. Tamarama Residence
Private Residence, Living Room
Sydney, New South Wales,
Australia
2016

4. Tamarama Residence
Private Residence,
Living Room
Sydney, New South Wales,
Australia
2016

5. Palm Beach Residence
Private Residence,
Outside Sauna/Bar
Sydney, New South Wales,
Australia
2020

Kit Kemp

London, UK

2

1. The Whitby Hotel
Hotel, Events Lobby
New York City, New York, USA
2017

2. The Whitby Bar, The Whitby Hotel
Hotel, Bar
New York City, New York, USA
2017

3. Hyde Park Gate
Private Residence, Drawing Room
London, UK
2020

In her three decades as an interior designer, Kit Kemp has scooped multiple awards, cofounded an internationally acclaimed hotel chain, and received an MBE from Queen Elizabeth II. Kemp shows no sign of slowing down: her book *Design Thread* was published in 2019 and in 2020 she became the first guest editor of *Homes & Gardens* in its century-old history.

Since she and husband Tim launched the debut Firmdale Hotel in 1985, the brand has become synonymous with a highly individualistic aesthetic that makes their quirky properties feel like home. Resolutely British in her tastes, Kemp's designs focus on an abundance of color, characterful (and often clashing) textiles, and eye-catching collections of contemporary art. This Maximalist approach is apparent at the reinvented Charlotte Street Hotel, London, which draws upon the area's rich history to inform its interior. Paying tribute to the Bloomsbury Group—a collective of creatives that included Virginia Woolf—Kemp enlivened traditional British style with her trademark experimentalism. In the drawing room, floral armchairs are clustered cozily in front of a fireplace and framed by custom wallpaper; the library's wooden paneling and collection of paintings are modernized by adding antique chairs upholstered in vibrant prints.

Across the Atlantic, the Whitby Hotel is the duo's second venture in Manhattan. Lavishly decorated with fabric-lined walls and eccentric objets d'art, the eighty-six-room hotel was announced the winner of *Tatler* magazine's New York Knockout award after its opening in 2017. A series of towering alabaster sculptures by the artist Stephen Cox stand in the lobby, and fifty-seven wicker baskets hang in a riotous overhead display at the bar.

Throughout her career, Kemp has never lost the sense of playfulness that distinguishes her designs from the solemn formality of other hotels. As she declared to *Condé Nast Traveler* magazine in 2019: "I think color does make you happy—it's as simple as that."

3

4. Hyde Park Gate
Private Residence, Hall
London, UK
2020

5. Charlotte Street Hotel
Hotel, Guest Suite
London, UK
2017

Rita Konig

London, UK

1. North Farm
Private Residence,
Drawing Room
Teesdale, UK
2018

2. North Farm
Private Residence,
Kitchen/Dining Room
Teesdale, UK
2018

3. North Farm
Private Residence, Library
Teesdale, UK
2018

During her two decades as an interior designer, Rita Konig's charmingly English aesthetic has amassed a dedicated following on both sides of the Atlantic. Focusing on residential projects, Konig's love of lush, layered fabrics and textures, eye-catching gallery walls, and artfully mismatched furnishings has cemented her standing as an arbiter of style.

Konig's early years provided an education in interiors. Her mother, esteemed designer Nina Campbell, decorated stately homes across Great Britain, including the Duke and Duchess of York's official residence. As a child of design royalty, Konig grew up attending trade shows in Paris and later worked in her mother's shop. At twenty-six years old, her first client approached her for a private project; later, after moving to New York and becoming editor of *Domino* magazine, Konig continued her interiors work with commissions that include a sprawling brownstone. She has also dispensed advice as a columnist for *House & Garden* magazine and in 2019 partnered with the Create Academy to offer an online course teaching others about her design process.

Konig's columns document the decision-making behind the renovation of North Farm, a nineteenth-century farmhouse that she and her husband own in rural northeast England. While she was determined not to do anything "overly elaborate or too decorated," as she revealed to *Elle Decor* magazine in 2019, Konig's signature style remains obvious. In one of the three living rooms, patterned wallpaper is complemented by heavy twill curtains and luxuriant seating upholstered in corduroy. Walls painted Lilac Pink in the kitchen's dining area, and another living room in a bold shade of green, accentuated by pops of pink and purple from the soft furnishings, add a sense of eclecticism to the more traditional antiques.

"So much of what makes a room is the stuff in it," Konig confided in a 2020 interview with the *Glossary* magazine. As a self-confessed lover of pretty objects, she's harnessed her magpie tendencies to forge a celebrated career.

Kråkvik & D'Orazio

Oslo, Norway

1. Fogia 2019
Catalogue Shoot,
Temporary Display
Stockholm, Sweden
2019

2. Jotun Lady
Catalogue Shoot,
Temporary Display
Copenhagen, Denmark
2020

3. Jotun Lady
Catalogue Shoot,
Temporary Display
Copenhagen, Denmark
2020

2

3

When Alessandro D'Orazio, an Italian art and architecture graduate, first moved to Oslo, he established a design store selling items from his native Italy. After segueing into interiors, he encountered Jannicke Kråkvik, a local stylist, and their romantic relationship expanded to a professional one when they founded their creative studio in 2003. A decade later, the pair expanded their enterprise with the opening of Kollekted By, an interior design store based in Oslo.

Specializing in interior styling and design, Kråkvik & D'Orazio is known for its striking Minimalist aesthetic that defies cliché. The studio's skillful use of color—which has resulted in a decade-long collaboration with Norwegian paint company Jotun—often sees interiors bathed in restful, earthy shades that complement the cool Nordic light. At Milan Design Week in 2016, Kråkvik & D'Orazio championed Norwegian design on an international stage; for its *Structure* exhibition, a selection of furniture, ceramic, lighting, and textiles was curated to such success that it landed on *Dezeen*'s list of unmissable shows.

Many years of collaboration has seen the studio's founders perfect a communication-heavy working style that incorporates their differing cultural backgrounds and styles. "I tend to overfill a setting, to begin with, so we can then both remove things piece by piece until it almost hurts," explained Kråkvik in an interview with arts-based consultancy Zetteler. "That's when the magic happens."

Such enchantment was on display at a shoot for Swedish design brand Fogia. Interested in the unique role that light plays in a notoriously sun-deprived region, Kråkvik & D'Orazio styled an interior in which concrete walls and floor-to-ceiling windows are lent warmth by the tactility of natural materials, such as leather and bamboo. Throughout, a gentle light dapples the space.

For this creative couple, it's easy to find inspiration: they simply look outside. Marrying an aesthetic grounded in colors and materials drawn from Norway's subliminal landscape with a razor-sharp attention to proportions and space, their style is sparse, uncompromising, and uniquely Nordic.

Joanna Laajisto

Helsinki, Finland

Helsinki-based Finnish architect Joanna Laajisto designs elegant, quietly contemporary commercial interiors. Working across the retail, hospitality, and business sectors, as well as in product design, Laajisto's eponymous studio, founded in 2010, places function and quality front and center.

Laajisto has traveled widely and spent ten years in Los Angeles training at the Interior Design Institute and working for Gensler Architects before returning to Finland with an ambition to help rebrand the country's international reputation. It bothered her that lazy stereotypes about Finnish culture persisted when the country she knew was inclusive and technologically sophisticated. In the decade since, Laajisto—who in 2018 was awarded Interior Architect of the year by the Finnish Association of Interior Architects—has played a central role in the development and reputation of contemporary Finnish design.

The studio's clean, sleek designs embody the spirit of Nordic functionalism but use luxurious materials and soft, intimate lighting to add touches of warmth. Illustrating this approach is Coutume, a double-height café Laajisto designed at Paris's Institut Finlandais. Caramel tones, low-level lighting, and gently curved ash benches, the latter designed by Laajisto herself, complement the abundance of natural light. Adding an element of drama, she hung a large, deeply textured gold-bronze rug on the otherwise unadorned walls. The piece makes an artlike statement, suspended high enough to catch and reflect the Parisian sun.

Closer to home, Laajisto is part of a dynamic team renovating Helsinki's iconic Hotel Torni. Her design is characteristically clean and modern; a restful backdrop of neutrals highlights elegant, curved furniture, custom architectural touches, and colorful abstract art.

Laajisto's acclaimed interiors are designed with such clear intent and executed with such precision that the results are seamless: spaces that blur the line between commerce and comfort, making shopping, dining, or working an altogether easier more congenial experience.

1. Hotel Torni Helsinki
Hotel, Guest Suite
Helsinki, Finland
2021

2. Coutume, Institut
Finlandais Paris
Multipurpose Venue,
Store and Café
Paris, France
2018

3. Coutume, Institut
Finlandais Paris
Multipurpose Venue,
Store and Café
Paris, France
2018

LH.Designs

**Los Angeles,
California, USA**

1. 28th Street
Private Residence, Bedroom
Hermosa Beach, California, USA
2018

2. Palo Verde
Private Residence, Staircase
Long Beach, California, USA
2018

3. 25th Street
Private Residence, Bathroom
Hermosa Beach, California, USA
2019

Linda Hayslett became a designer after deciding that she wanted a kind of permanence her previous career in fashion couldn't provide. Runway trends change every season, but Hayslett's interiors eschew ephemerality in favor of a sleek, friendly, sturdy style, providing clients with an environment that's invariably thoughtful and lively, uncluttered and dynamic. Hayslett lived for a long time in New York, and although her studio, LH.Designs, is based in California, there's a compact East Coast energy to her residential and commercial spaces, distinguishing them from classic, laid-back Californian interiors.

After retraining for a career in interior design, Hayslett entered the industry by integrating design with construction, armed with a sense for scale and a contagious enthusiasm for the work—and she has since acquired a roster of equally excited clients. She worked her magic for one couple, first-time homeowners who were at odds with each other— one was drawn to mid-century Modern, while the other was set on farmhouse chic. In an effort to make both of their fantasies come true without turning their Long Beach townhouse into a battlefield, Hayslett pulled off a design feat, combining the wood floors of a farmhouse aesthetic with the playful ergonomics of mid-century design classics, and threading it all together with contemporary touches, such as asymmetrical light fixtures and striking black accents.

In the seaside community of Hermosa Beach, where Hayslett has designed several homes, she has risen to a different kind of challenge, finding a way to enliven the Minimalism of the architecture without contradicting it. Floor cushions adorn the floor of a bedroom in one home, while a gray quartz countertop in another grounds the bathroom and amplifies the sunlight. Hayslett can bring warmth to such cool, monochrome palettes—grays, blacks, and whites— with a well-placed luxe finish. She still has an eye for fashion, after all.

1. John Anthony
Restaurant
Hong Kong
2018

2. Tingtai Teahouse
Teahouse, Tearooms
Shanghai, China
2018

3. Tingtai Teahouse
Teahouse, Tearooms
Shanghai, China
2018

Linehouse

Shanghai, China;
Hong Kong

Shanghai- and Hong Kong-based architecture and design studio Linehouse is the brainchild of Chinese–Swedish architect Alex Mok and New Zealand interior designer Briar Hickling. The young design duo, who both have extensive experience designing commercial interiors in Asia and beyond, met in Shanghai while working for the Chinese architectural practice Neri&Hu. After working on hospitality projects for clients worldwide, the enterprising pair established Linehouse in 2013.

Artistic vision and narrative flair are central to Linehouse's design for Hong Kong's John Anthony, a chic dim sum restaurant named after the first Chinese man to be naturalized as a British citizen. Inspired by Anthony's journey from East to West, the eco-friendly design blends modern glamour and Eastern detailing with British colonial decor. Terracotta tiles reclaimed from abandoned houses in China are used alongside sustainable rattan screens, a timber bar, wicker furniture, and floral upholstery, while tall glass tubes of gin infused with botanicals hang above the bar. The result is a beguiling hybrid of both cultures: a British tea hall with the retro charm of a Chinese canteen.

Also blending Old World with New World is the Tingtai Teahouse, a former factory space in Shanghai's art district, which conjures up the spirit of a Chinese teahouse while retaining a Minimalist, Scandinavian aesthetic. The double-height first floor, with its clerestory windows, original brick walls, and exposed concrete foundations, is lined with a series of elevated stainless steel teahouses. Paneled in smoked oak and framed with full height glass, they connect guests to the open space yet provide an intimate retreat in which to enjoy the ritual of tea.

Named Emerging Interior Designer of the Year in 2019 by design bible *Dezeen*, the pair are building a solid reputation as one of the most exciting studios in Asia, winning praise for their storied, contemporary interiors and bold, spatial vision.

Isabel López-Quesada

Madrid, Spain

1. Paris Apartment
Private Residence, Drawing Room
Paris, France
2018

2. Paris Apartment
Private Residence, Drawing Room
Paris, France
2018

3. Madrid House
Private Residence, Drawing Room
Madrid, Spain
2019

"A home for me is everything, it's like the center of our universe," says Isabel López-Quesada in a film for client Zara Home. At the age of thirteen, she realized she had a vocation to make interior spaces more beautiful—and only seven years later she opened her own design studio in Madrid. Now, López-Quesada works mainly with private clients across Europe and North America, but she has also designed the headquarters for several Spanish corporations, including Iberia Airlines and Acciona, and decorated Spanish embassies in Doha, Qatar; Dakar, Senegal; and Tokyo. Her approach bears an eclecticism stemming from her wide travels; it combines tradition and modernity, and it always brings nature indoors.

In a Paris apartment, for example, she effortlessly mixes mid-century furniture with nineteenth-century features: Chandigarh chairs by Pierre Jeanneret sit beautifully amid wood paneling, ornate coving, and an original fireplace. Carefully curated modern art graces the walls, and a striking metallic pendant light makes a bold statement. Splashes of bright color come from turquoise armchairs on a gold carpet, a multicolored bedspread, and printed cushions. Little clutter disrupts the order, but selected books are artfully dotted around the apartment. Pink hydrangeas, a branch of blossom, and a sculptural cactus add the finishing touches. "I think it's incredibly important to add nature inside," she says; López-Quesada collaborates regularly with Spanish florist Inés Urquijo.

In a Madrid residence, the feel is more of a family home but equally eclectic and cultured. A serene monochrome color palette lets the art on the walls take center stage. Symmetry creates pleasing harmony, with couches and identical tables facing one another and a pair of matching mirrors framing the fireplace; plants provide a softening, sculptural counterbalance to the order. Every room she creates is an individual world, a sanctuary formed of different elements that combine to create a soothing, uplifting, and authentic space—a place to really, truly feel oneself.

1. South Yarra House
Private Residence, Living Room
Melbourne, Victoria, Australia
2017

2. South Yarra House
Private Residence,
Dining Room
Melbourne, Victoria, Australia
2017

3. Fitzroy House
Private Residence, Library
Melbourne, Victoria, Australia
2016

Fiona Lynch

Melbourne, Victoria, Australia

1

A leading name in Australian design, Fiona Lynch creates artful, impeccably considered interiors with a brooding, evocative edge. Her Melbourne-based studio, which covers residential and commercial commissions, has designed some of the city's most tailored homes, stores, and museums, and Lynch regularly collaborates with artisans and makers for Work Shop, the studio's curatorial series.

Lynch's projects, such as a former boot factory in Fitzroy and a nineteenth-century row house in South Yarra (both fashionable districts in Melbourne), are exceptionally refined and materially driven. Neutral walls are deliberately unadorned to give way to rich cuts of heavily veined marble, hand-carved furniture, and custom architectural details, such as sculpted Brutalist fireplaces and monolithic stone tables.

In her award-winning Fitzroy project, Lynch ensured her bold design respects the architectural bones of the factory, which was converted into a living space in the 1980s by architect Ivan Rijavec. The building's industrial style and steel-framed windows inspired Lynch's dark-stained joinery, which blends seamlessly into the space. Dark floor-to-ceiling shelving displays the client's art and books, and cabinets curve beautifully around corridors. Black marble and ebonized wood create drama in the kitchen, but they are softened with fluted glass and brass fittings.

Custom joinery is a key feature in one of Lynch's other residences in South Yarra where the team used carefully chosen materials to delineate the spaces and create architectural interest. The open shelving in the living area was crafted in oak, then painted and lined in bronze; in the dining room a painted white oak cabinet perched on a marble plinth features bi-fold doors and an unusual tubular handle.

Favored by design-conscious clients, Lynch is a confident and considered designer whose talent for spatial planning and sensitivity to materials is speedily gaining international attention.

4. Fitzroy House
Private Residence,
Entryway
Melbourne, Victoria,
Australia
2016

5. Ottawa House
Private Residence,
Bathroom
Melbourne, Victoria,
Australia
2020

Maison Vincent Darré

Paris, France

Unafraid of color, criticism, or "bad taste," flamboyant French designer Vincent Darré creates extravagant, fearless interiors that are as sophisticated as they are surreal. In the mid-2000s, after a glittering two decades in fashion—Darré was head of Moschino and has worked with Yves Saint Laurent, Prada, and Karl Lagerfeld—the ebullient Frenchman turned to interior design and, with limitless creative energy, began designing dreamlike, operatic interiors for fashion's elite to live out their fantasies.

Nearly twenty years on, and with a stellar client list and sumptuous monograph, Maison Vincent Darré's interior projects continue to provide fertile ground for its chief designer's experimental, outlandish imagination. A Darré interior, which always begins with a watercolor drawing, is a joyful explosion of rainbow color and decorative excess, where mirrors shaped like futuristic unicorns hang above giant gilded lobsters and furniture inspired by mythical creatures.

His eponymous Paris gallery is an office, showroom, and entertaining space where everything is for sale. Each room of the eighteenth-century mansion is decorated with Darré's creations and artworks by friends and collaborators. Corridors painted with Roman ruins take guests to a drawing room with antique paneling and an orange ceiling and onwards to a sky-blue bedroom where Darré's Chimera sofa, in mohair velvet, is illuminated by a twisted bronze pendant by French sculptor Marc Bankowsky.

His commercial projects and installations, if slightly less elaborate, are no less magical. His 2018 design for the museum store at Villa Noailles—a Modernist Côte d'Azur retreat built by architect Robert Mallet-Stevens in the 1920s—has a whitewashed, plaster-wall interior, where stucco moldings shaped like androids display wares by emerging furniture and product makers.

Inspired by the Baroque, Renaissance, and Dada movements, Darré's wonderfully avant-garde interiors are a true celebration of the decorative arts. Executed with great panache, they have cemented his reputation as a preeminent tastemaker and an industry favorite.

1. La Boutique, Villa Noailles
Store
Hyères, France
2018

2. Maison Vincent Darré
Offices and Showroom,
Dining Room
Paris, France
2020

3. Maison Vincent Darré
Offices and Showroom,
Living Room
Paris, France
2020

Mlinaric, Henry and Zervudachi

London, UK; Paris, France;
New York City, New York, USA

1. Chalet in Rougemont
Private Residence,
Living/Dining Room
Rougemont, Switzerland
2011

2. House in Tokyo
Private Residence,
Main Living Room
Tokyo, Japan
2010

3. House in Rio
Private Residence,
Living Room
Rio de Janeiro, Brazil
2016

Esteemed London-, New York-, and Paris-based firm Mlinaric, Henry and Zervudachi (MHZ), has been designing beautifully chic, understated homes and high-profile public spaces for more than forty years. With Mick Jagger and Lord Rothschild among the names on its client list and a portfolio that includes London's Royal Opera House, MHZ has an impressive pedigree that matches its global influence and incredible wealth of experience.

Established in 1964 by the now-retired British interior designer David Mlinaric, and headed by principal Tino Zervudachi, MHZ is currently organized into three distinct companies: Mlinaric, Henry and Zervudachi in London; Tino Zervudachi & Associés in Paris; and Tino Zervudachi LLC in New York. Although each office operates independently, the work is underpinned by a shared philosophy; MHZ produces designs that are modern and innovative, a true symbiosis of classic and contemporary design.

The extraordinary chalet it designed in the Swiss Alps is a case in point. Striking contemporary art, modern luxuries, and cutting-edge technology mingle seamlessly with mid-century furniture, such as Ours Polaire sofas by French designer Jean Royère and an Eye coffee table by French architect Pierre Chapo. A committed decorative palette of neutral walls, warm woods, and rich grass-green upholstery ties the open-plan spaces together and connects the interior with the snow-capped landscape beyond.

The private Tokyo residence MHZ designed in collaboration with architect Kengo Kuma is a spectacular temple to Japanese design heritage, with knockout modern features, such as finely paneled bathrooms with freestanding wooden bathtubs reminiscent of traditional Japanese bathhouses. The treatment of light and scale is masterful, creating a vast space in the heart of a buzzing city that feels quiet, discreet, and profoundly restful.

By virtue of its skill, global reach, and experience, MHZ's exceptional portfolio is unusually varied. What is clear, however, is the unifying characteristic of the firm's projects: laid-back, natural-looking rooms that, whether traditional and decorative or contemporary and restrained, are impeccably considered and enduringly elegant.

Greg Natale

Sydney, New South Wales,
Australia

One of Australia's premier interior designers, with global influence and two books to his name, Greg Natale has been creating flamboyant, rich interiors for nearly twenty-five years. The ebullient designer established his highly successful Sydney-based studio in 2001. Inspired by fashion styling and movie set design, he creates vibrant, tailored spaces world-wide, and in 2020 he opened a concept store in Sydney selling curated finds and his own custom products. Like his interiors, they are loud and proud expressions of his own personal taste for audacious colors, metallic, and mirrors—perhaps not for those of a Minimalist persuasion.

With its blood-red glazed walls, adorned with vintage treasures and contemporary art by the likes of American Pop artist Keith Haring, Natale's own apartment is a seductive bedecked space. Now on its third interior redesign, the sumptuous apartment in Sydney's iconic Horizon building has a dramatic yet intimate feel, which reflects Natale's interior design identity and the alluring worlds he likes to recreate. The rich maroon walls are matched by rich carpets of the same shade and accented by gold lighting, conjuring up a sense of old-fashioned, star-studded Hollywood movie premieres.

Equally captivating is the grand country estate he designed for an Australian family. The five-bedroom residence is packed with pop colors and lavish finishes cocooned in a moody shell of black-stained wood. Natale lined the walls and floors in blackened American oak, using a parquetry pattern on the floors and vertical paneling on the walls. He punctuated the black-on-black design with brass details, patterned rugs, and contemporary art by icons such as Andy Warhol.

Daring and dynamic, with total confidence in his bold, cinematic style, Natale is a fearless and cele-brated designer. His ambitions for every project are clear: homes, restaurants, and retail spaces will be infinitely more alive and glamorous as a result of his Midas touch.

1. Barwon River House
Private Residence, Sports Bar
Geelong, Victoria, Australia
2017

2. Darlinghurst Apartment III
Private Residence, Family Room
Sydney, New South Wales,
Australia
2019

3. Barwon River House
Private Residence, Entryway
Geelong, Victoria, Australia
2017

4. Inner West House
Private Residence, Family Room
Sydney, New South Wales,
Australia
2018
[overleaf]

Paola Navone / Studio OTTO

Milan, Italy

1. Candlenut, COMO Dempsey
Retail and Restaurant Complex,
Restaurant
Singapore
2017

2. Ippoh Tempura Bar,
COMO Dempsey
Retail and Restaurant Complex,
Restaurant
Singapore
2017

3. Ippoh Tempura Bar,
COMO Dempsey
Retail and Restaurant Complex,
Restaurant, Bar
Singapore
2017

4. Dempsey Cookhouse and Bar,
COMO Dempsey
Retail and Restaurant Complex,
Restaurant
Singapore
2017
[overleaf]

1

1. Candlenut, COMO Dempsey
Retail and Restaurant Complex,
Restaurant
Singapore
2017

Unconventional and free-spirited, architect and designer Paola Navone says she finds inspiration in everything. She puts her original approach down to working for postmodern avant-garde furniture design collectives Studio Alchimia and the Memphis Group in the 1980s, and over the last few decades has been a pioneer in the field of male-dominated Italian design. Studio OTTO, her multidisciplinary company in Milan, has an international client base that includes Virgin Hotels, COMO Hotels and Resorts, a range of private clients, and retailers—such as Armani/Casa, Crate and Barrel, and Poltrona Frau. Hallmarks of her work include blending the artisanal and the industrial: imperfection, elements of the exotic, organic shapes, and bright, sometimes clashing colors. She often brings in a do-it-yourself aesthetic, recycling and repurposing materials, and in her furniture design she is known to deconstruct familiar forms.

Between 2016 and 2019 Navone completed an ambitious, wide-ranging interior design project for COMO Dempsey's gourmet food retail and restaurant complex in Singapore, including the food hall Culina and several high-end eateries. For Candlenut, the world's first Michelin-star Peranakan restaurant, she used aspects of Eastern interior design to create a laid-back, eclectic space, mixing up straw lamp-shades, louvered wall paneling, wicker and metal chairs, ceramics, and shades of luscious jade green. Multitudes of baskets feature in Ippoh Tempura Bar, piled high, along with more ceramics plus chairs in her signature cobalt blue.

She took a more formal approach at the Dempsey Cookhouse and Bar, which takes its cues from the brilliant white interiors of the hotel Raffles Singapore. Botanical and genteel, it features ornate white furniture, monochromatic floor tiles, abundant indoor plants, and oversize Chinese lantern-style lighting. Whatever the space Navone designs, it will be sophisticated, exuberant, and spark curiosity, but she says her approach is to simply make people feel at home: "I always enjoy creating relaxing, delicate, and never aggressive atmospheres that make every-one feel at ease."

Neri&Hu

Shanghai, China

1. Tsingpu Yangzhou Retreat
Hotel, Tea Room
Yangzhou, Jiangsu Province, China
2017

2. Suzhou Chapel
Chapel
Suzhou, Jiangsu Province, China
2016

3. Sulwhasoo Flagship
Store
Seoul, South Korea
2016

1

1. Tsingpu Yangzhou Retreat
Hotel, Tea Room
Yangzhou, Jiangsu Province, China
2017

2. Suzhou Chapel
Chapel
Suzhou, Jiangsu Province, China
2016

3. Sulwhasoo Flagship
Store
Seoul, South Korea
2016

Shanghai-based Neri&Hu is a dynamic architectural design studio with an interdisciplinary approach, designing buildings, interiors, furniture, and products worldwide. Established in 2004 by partners Lyndon Neri and Rossana Hu, both architects, the award-winning studio has an international team with a clear emphasis on architectural research and academic debate—in 2018 Neri and Hu held the prestigious position of Norman R. Foster Visiting Professor of Architecture at Yale University in Connecticut. Using research as a design tool, Neri&Hu respond to global architectural challenges, such as overcrowding in cities, with innovative, sustainable solutions.

The studio's monolithic Suzhou Chapel, near the eastern Chinese city of Suzhou, is a vision of architectural excellence: a white plaster cube perched on a foundation of reclaimed bricks, wrapped in perforated and pleated metal. An important site within the Sangha well-being resort, the building takes inspiration from local architecture, but through cutting-edge design presents as an almost floating, translucent structure. Inside, the main hall is lined with wooden batten strips stretching upward to a vaulted ceiling, from which hangs a grid of bronze pendants that cast a warm glow across an otherwise sober, monastic space.

In the Chinese city of Yangzhou, Tsingpu Yangzhou Retreat, a twenty-room hotel near a scenic lake and national park, is also rooted in its local architectural context. Asked to adapt and reconfigure existing buildings, the studio took inspiration from the area's traditional homes based around courtyards. The team used this feature and a series of pathways to connect the structures, allowing each richly textured interior to flow seamlessly into the outdoor space.

With a rigorously researched approach that considers experience, material, form, and light equally, Neri&Hu is a leader in modern sustainable design. The diverse team continues to win praise and awards for creating architectural and design landmarks in unexpected, often rural, locations.

David Netto Design

Los Angeles,
California, USA

A gifted writer and talented designer, David Netto enjoys articulating his design philosophy both in theory and in practice. Since withdrawing from Harvard's graduate program in architecture and opening his own studio in 2000, Netto has focused on residential projects, outfitting homes in his particular brand of Modernism, a style to which he seeks to restore the liberating eclecticism of its early pre-war period.

Netto's extensive knowledge of art and design history, and his openness to the serendipities of daily life, join to create textured, full, unfussy spaces that feel at once familiar and exciting. A firm advocate of prioritizing the personal, Netto believes interiors should accommodate the people who live in them, not the other way around. In 2017, for example, Netto furnished a house in Amagansett, New York, with simple white rugs, blond wooden chairs and benches, and white shelving—all contrasting beautifully with the deep electric blues of the flower-patterned wallpaper. A Connecticut residence he designed in 2018 has a classic Greek meander pattern running along the top of the great room's walls, and cozy wicker bubble chairs resting beside a restored, partly exposed, brick fireplace. For a residential project completed in 2019 in London, Netto uses two large mirrors to amplify the light in the room—and provide a tantalizing peek into the client's library.

At home—he lives with his family in a Richard Neutra-designed glass house in Los Angeles—Netto stays loyal to his design principles. Works by Cy Twombly and Al Held hang alongside drawings by his children; there's a Jean Arp sculpture inside and a trampoline out back. This peaceful coexistence of art and the quotidian is a crucible for Netto's acclaimed designs. Finding inspiration in influences as wide ranging as Wes Anderson, François Truffaut, and Bong Joon-ho movies, as well as ocean liners and old photographs, Netto is always working.

1. London Residence with Garden
Private Residence, Living Room
London, UK
2019

2. Connecticut House
Private Residence, Living Room
Greenwich, Connecticut, USA
2018

3. Amagansett House
Private Residence, Music Room
Amagansett, New York, USA
2017

Norm Architects

Copenhagen, Denmark

1. The Audo
Multipurpose Venue, Guest Suite
Copenhagen, Denmark
2019

2. The Audo
Multipurpose Venue, Café
Copenhagen, Denmark
2019

3. Sticks'n'Sushi
Restaurant
London, UK
2018

Since its founding in 2008 by Jonas Bjerre-Poulsen and Kasper Rønn Von Lotzbeck, the Copenhagen-based architecture and design firm Norm Architects has quickly established itself as a leader in the Scandinavian design tradition. Taking on a multi-disciplinary approach, the studio's eclectic output ranges from beautifully Minimalist residential homes in Sri Lanka and Japan to earthy black ceramics and stone-top coffee tables.

Such versatility proved invaluable when Norm Architects was selected to design the Audo in 2019. Located in a Neo-Baroque building along Copenhagen's waterfront, the concept space needed to act as a hotel, coworking and events venue, café, library, and headquarters to Danish design brand Menu. In short, it had to reflect the hybrid nature of modern life in which work and play increasingly intersect. Faced with a 26,900-square-foot (2,500-square-meter) space, the firm created subtle aesthetic demarcations between different zones to reflect their functions. The downstairs lobby takes an industrial tone, with concrete flooring and a black metal ceiling from which pendant lights hang. On the top floor, however, each of the ten guest suites boasts earth-colored plaster walls, oak flooring, and contemporary furnishings in warm, organic tones.

In Sticks'n'Sushi, a Japanese restaurant in London's upscale Chelsea neighborhood, Norm Architects took a similarly experiential approach, merging elements of Danish and Japanese design. Inside the three-story building, diners travel up toward light: the lower ground floor—a dark space with textured walls that encourages intimacy—leads to the restaurant's central zone, in which a blackened steel bar and cement flooring are softened with iconic pieces of Danish furniture. By the top floor, the neutral palette and oak furnishings creates a bright, expansive space.

For founders Bjerre-Poulsen and Rønn Von Lotzbeck, their diverse portfolio remains underpinned by a singular desire: to create timeless work. In all their projects, a raw Scandinavian simplicity, coupled with a focus on craft, shines through.

Note Design Studio

Stockholm, Sweden

1

1. Summit House
Coworking Space, Reception
London, UK
2019

2. Summit House
Coworking Space,
Kitchen/Working Area
London, UK
2019

3. Hidden Tints
Private Residence, Kitchen
Stockholm, Sweden
2017

2

3

Note Design Studio—a multidisciplinary collective that specializes in architecture, interiors, products, and graphic design—made its intentions clear when the company was founded in 2008: it wanted to get noted. And in the decade since, the studio has done exactly that through projects that sensitively pay homage to historic features but at the same time incorporate contemporary design elements.

Summit House, a workspace in central London, showcases this interplay between modernity and antiquity across a 42,200-square-foot (3,920-square-meter) space. Drawing inspiration from the Swedish Grace design period of the early twentieth century, the elegant interiors complement the building's original Art Deco features. Such respect for the past, however, didn't hamper Note Design Studio's creativity: the rust-colored lobby features a bird's-eye maple reception desk set beneath a tiered structure that recedes behind it. Coupled with geometric terrazzo flooring, the result feels almost like an optical illusion. Throughout the property, a warm, autumnal palette is heightened by the use of tactile materials, such as armchairs upholstered in bouclé and felt.

Color also takes center stage at Hidden Tints, a period property in Stockholm that served as a fashion brand's headquarters before being transformed into a family home. Stripping away the office accoutrements, the studio discovered mustard-colored paint dating back to the nineteenth century. The paint, along with three tiled ovens, served as the basis of their palette, eventually evolving into an eight-tone range that sees mossy green cabinets in the kitchen and salmon-pink and sunny-yellow tiled cabinets hanging beneath the property's ornate cornices.

Many tenets of Scandinavian design are placed at the heart of Note's design philosophy. Yet its approach to Minimalism is never cold, nor is it dull. Instead, it celebrates heritage, translated into a contemporary context.

4. Hidden Tints
Private Residence, View from
Living Room to Children's Room
Stockholm, Sweden
2017

5. Norobata, Grow Hotel
Hotel, Restaurant
Stockholm, Sweden
2019

Marie-Anne Oudejans

Jaipur, India

2

1. Bar and Caffé Palladio
Bar, Café, and Store, Entryway
Jaipur, India
2013

2. Bar and Caffé Palladio
Bar, Café, and Store, Bar
Jaipur, India
2013

3. Bar and Caffé Palladio
Bar, Café, and Store, Retail Space
Jaipur, India
2013

From her adopted home in the Indian city of Jaipur, Dutch fashion designer turned interior decorator Marie-Anne Oudejans designs unforgettable jewel-like spaces.

Her route into interior design could be described as a modern-day fairy tale. In 2010, while working for her own fashion label, Tocca, and traveling by plane, a chance conversation with a fellow passenger led to a serendipitous decision: Oudejans would move to India, a country she'd always adored from afar. A year later, she was settled in the Pink City—so named after Jaipur was painted the peachy hue for a royal visit in 1876—and living in an apartment within the romantic Hotel Narain Niwas Palace. The epicenter of traditional Indian craft, including stone carving, woodworking, and textiles, Jaipur sharpened Oudejans' eye for color, pattern, and craftsmanship. It remains an endless source of inspiration for the convivial designer.

When Oudejans was asked to redesign some of the hotel's public spaces, she relished the opportunity. The outstanding Bar Palladio, owned by hotelier and friend of Oudejans, Barbara Miolini, is the finest example of the designer's creative flair: a vision of azure and royal blues, classic stripes, block-printed textiles, and playful details, inspired by the spirit of travel and the extravagant lifestyles of India's maharajas in the early 1900s. Oudejans designed every feature, with all details beautifully executed by local artisans, from the vibrant piping on every cushion to the custom murals of exotic birds on the bar's walls. In a playful touch, reminiscent of her childhood and "obsession" with tents, Oudejans hung canopies with orange scalloped edging on the ceilings. It conjures the magical feeling of warm desert nights.

With a truly adventurous nature and a talent for combining joyful colors with exquisite, highly imaginative details, it's no wonder that Oudejans has now opened her own design agency and is capturing the attention of design lovers and travelers worldwide.

3

1. Paris 9th District
Private Residence, Living Room
Paris, France
2017

2. Offices Paris Champs-Élysées
Offices, Reception Area
Paris, France
2020

3. Mauritius Villa
Private Residence, Living Room
Bel Ombre, Mauritius
2017

Stéphane Parmentier

Paris, France

1

Esteemed interior architect Stéphane Parmentier turned to design after nearly twenty years in fashion working for Givenchy, Lanvin, and Karl Lagerfeld before launching his own fashion label. Following a prestigious opportunity to redesign the interiors of Singapore Airlines' first and business class cabins, the French designer embarked upon the well-trodden path from haute couture to interior design, establishing his eponymous atelier in 2003. In the decades since, Parmentier has cemented his place in the upper echelons of interior design, winning awards for his elegantly modern aesthetic and luxurious simplicity. This is expressed in residential and commercial interiors; custom-designed objects and furniture; creative direction; and collaborations with leading brands such as Hermès.

Parmentier's inspirations—from Classical Greek and Roman architecture to Japanese Minimalism—are evident in the spectacular monochromatic apartment he designed for a Paris-based collector. An all-white palette extends to the walls, floors, curtains, and modular sofas in the grand Haussmanian-style drawing room, providing a neutral backdrop for highly collectible art and furniture, such as a pair of iconic mid-century Easy chairs by Swiss-French architect Pierre Jeanneret. Ornate decorative moldings, a gilded over-mantel mirror, and a huge marble fireplace contrast beautifully with the angular lines of the apartment's modern and contemporary features.

A monochrome design and rich natural woods look equally majestic in the beach house he designed in Mauritius. While muted in color, the interior is anything but subdued, with giant oversize sofas, table lamps, and sculptures lending drama and gravitas to the sober tropical sanctuary.

Parmentier's innate appreciation of texture, form, and proportion is evident throughout his portfolio, as is the often-symbiotic link between high fashion and interior design. In both lives, Parmentier's exceptionally refined eye and stylistic flair have been central to his success.

2

3

Ben Pentreath

London, UK

1. Chelsea Apartment
Private Residence, Living Room
London, UK
2014

2. Chelsea Apartment
Private Residence, Living Room
London, UK
2014

3. Welsh House
Private Residence, Bedroom
Coed Darcy, Wales, UK
2012

A classically English designer whose clients include the Duchess of Cambridge, Ben Pentreath designs elegant interiors that blend heritage colors and period details with modern art and fine antiques. Since establishing his practice in 2004, the London-based architectural designer, who is also a successful author, blogger, and retailer—his store, Pentreath & Hall, is a collaboration with British designer Bridie Hall—has amassed an impressive residential portfolio.

The designer encourages his clients to begin collecting as soon as their project starts. This is because beloved art, objects, and furniture are integral to his layered, curated aesthetic, which takes inspiration from historical architecture but remains refreshingly modern. In London's Chelsea, Pentreath and his team transformed a bland, uninspiring pied-à-terre into a sophisticated, textured haven, painting the entrance hall a deep plum tone and adding architectural interest with eighteenth-century engravings. The walls elsewhere are neutral but adorned with colorful abstract art, and antique and mid-century furniture is balanced with bright patterned lampshades and pastel upholstery. The result is impeccably tailored, yet playful.

For a large-scale regeneration project in Wales, the team was asked to design a collection of simple vernacular houses. The practice infused these new, empty spaces with warmth and character, adding wooden tongue-and-groove paneling painted in traditional British rural colors of taupes, creams, and greens, as well as antique Welsh dressers, paisley prints, and Pentreath-designed wooden furniture. The buildings were transformed into handsome, yet modest, homes with nostalgic charm.

A masterful designer with a commitment to preserving historical architecture and aesthetic traditions, Pentreath has a unique ability to make period details and more classic interiors feel relevant and up-to-date. His residential designs, whether in the town or country, are often a fusion of periods and patterns—from historic William Morris prints to graphic Middle Eastern ikats—but the common denominators are always quality and just the right amount of restraint.

Perspective Studio

Stockholm, Sweden

2

3

Robin Klang's path into interiors has been a circuitous one. After establishing his name as Sweden's first male fashion blogger, he transitioned into work as a stylist for *Café*, a monthly men's magazine, before being headhunted as a buyer for clothing retailer H&M. It was in that role, traveling globally, that Klang began to consider interiors.

The result is Perspective Studio, a Stockholm-based interiors firm founded in 2016. In parallel, Klang opened a boutique in the city that acted as a bricks-and-mortar showcase for his brand of craft-focused Minimalism. While Klang's Scandinavian heritage is clear in his appreciation for natural materials and pared-back spaces, he also draws inspiration from the Japanese philosophy of *wabi-sabi*, an outlook that sees beauty in imperfection, which translates in aesthetic terms to a rustic simplicity. His store—which has since shuttered and migrated online—sells a curated selection of one-of-a-kind antiques, artworks, and smaller household objects that reflect this distinctive vision.

In a residential Stockholm project, titled Torsgatan, Klang transformed his own apartment into a show-room for the exquisite collection of pieces that fills it, and opened the space for the public to view by appointment only. A stiff-backed wooden chair is positioned opposite an assembly of ceramic pots in varying sizes, while moody abstract artworks in charcoal textures hang from the stormy-colored walls. In another area of the home, shelves are arranged with a gallery-worthy display of vases and weighty coffee table tomes. The effect is spartan, elegant, and yet underlain with a subtle sense of the homespun.

At another private Stockholm home, Kaptensgatan I, Klang embraced a softer palette with blush tones that soften the more austere dark wood furnishings and dramatic black doors. Again, objects take center stage, such as in the living room, where a striking bust sits atop a wooden plinth. A deep splinter runs lengthwise down it—a perfectly imperfect piece, just as Klang intended.

1. Kaptensgatan II
Private Residence, Living Room
Stockholm, Sweden
2020

2. Kaptensgatan I
Private Residence, Living Room
Stockholm, Sweden
2019

3. Torsgatan
Private Residence/Showroom,
Living Room
Stockholm, Sweden
2019

Emmanuel Picault

Mexico City, Mexico

French-born designer Emmanuel Picault is a self-taught talent who, for the last twenty years, has made Mexico the creative epicenter of his life and award-winning work. Responsible for some of Mexico City's most fashionable venues, including nightclub M. N. Roy (named after the former resident, who founded the Mexican communist party), Picault has played a central role in helping to regenerate parts of the city and establish it as a preeminent destination for art and design. In 2001 he founded his cult gallery and studio, Chic by Accident, which showcases creative collaborations and his sizable collection of mid-century furniture, Mexican masks, and curiosities.

Nestled within Mexico's tree-clad Tepozteco mountain range in the village of Santa Catarina sits an extraordinary stone and concrete house, which Picault bought and designed in 2015. Taking inspiration from Modernist master architects, such as Le Corbusier and Frank Lloyd Wright, as well as from the historic ruins at Petra and Mexico's Aztec temples, the interiors equally embody Picault's distinctive style. Raw clay and rough concrete surfaces are softened by luxurious metals, oversize lighting, and an array of eclectic objects. With only one door that can be locked, the house is almost completely open to the elements.

In Xucú, in the Mexican province of Yucatán, Picault transformed a once-neglected nineteenth-century hacienda into a beautifully rustic space that respects the passing of time and its impact on architecture. Embracing the historic structure's crumbling appearance, he used the ruins' appeal to glorious effect, weaving his interiors throughout the craggy stone space.

Strongly influenced by the "emotional architecture" pioneered by architect Luis Barragán and sculptor-painter Mathias Goéritz in the 1950s, Picault's work, as both a designer and gallerist, is driven by his desire to create avant-garde spaces with warmth, humor, and soul.

1. Xucú Hacienda
Private Residence, Living Room
Xucú, Yucatán, Mexico
2015

2. Santa Catarina House
Private Residence, Living Room
Near Tepoztlán, Morelos, Mexico
2015

3. Xucú Hacienda
Private Residence, Lobby to
Main Bedroom
Xucú, Yucatán, Mexico
2015

Reath Design

Los Angeles, California, USA

1. Little Holmby
Private Residence, Living Room
Los Angeles, California, USA
2018

2. Little Holmby
Private Residence, Playroom
Los Angeles, California, USA
2018

3. Altadena
Private Residence, Pool Room
Los Angeles, California, USA
2019

4. Franklin Hills
Private Residence, Entryway
Los Angeles, California, USA
2019

Frances Merrill's profoundly charming Los Angeles studio Reath Design turns residential and commercial interiors into little charms, too. She chooses saturated colors and wild patterns that seem to have no business being in the same room, but somehow they work together splendidly. Merrill takes risks, and they usually pay off. It doesn't hurt that this designer—who collaborates with her clients to create interiors to help their everyday living—has an eye for textiles and a welcoming attitude for experimenting with the unusual. If a better life is the goal, risky juxtapositions are warranted.

Merrill has left a bright trail across Los Angeles. For a 1926 Spanish Colonial in the Little Holmby neighborhood, Merrill and her Modernist architect client devised an enormous, custom-made sectional couch upholstered in a velvet palm-tree print. Through her selection of runners, she carefully modulated the tone in a Monterey Colonial in Franklin Hills, raising the temperature with a red patterned rug on the first floor, then lowering it with a deep teal one on the stairs leading to the second story. And for a gorgeous mid-century home in Altadena, Merrill worked with the client to create a lively tension between the house's austere, steel-and-glass architecture and its rainbow-hued decor, echoing the house's clean lines while introducing vibrant colors via a custom, Mulberry-striped banquette.

Being fond of dusty pinks and washed blues and greens, Merrill can seem like a Californian native; however, she grew up in New York and studied literature before moving to the West Coast and into design. But unforeseen turns are this designer's forte, making her one of the most intriguing designers working today. Individual lives are Merrill's real stock-in-trade, and all of her prodigious skill is put to work making spaces that people find invigorating—making their lives a little better every day, which adds up to a lasting difference.

Redd Kaihoi

New York City,
New York, USA

Miles Redd and David Kaihoi have worked together for more than a decade, but in 2019 they made it official—they became business partners, and the eponymous design studio Miles Redd, LLC, (established in 1998) changed its name to Redd Kaihoi. What has thus far remained consistent is the duo's unselfconscious love of resplendent residential interiors: walls painted or wallpapered in dramatic yellows, greens, blues, and reds; bold accent pieces; ubiquitous florals and animal prints; chinoiserie; and choice antiques and select contemporary furnishings.

Redd had spent a decade as the creative director of Oscar de la Renta Home, and Kaihoi switched to design while working as an art installer. During the last few years, they have honed their trademark style to produce a number of awe-inspiring residential spaces. In 2017, for example, they completed a San Francisco Bay Area family home in which they decorated the living room walls in light turquoise satin and upholstered the seating in silk velour and floral linen. Animal statuettes, fresh flowers, and paintings hanging from the front of recessed bookshelves add to the charm of the space. For a Texas farmhouse, Redd Kaihoi put a playful spin on the living room display, which features a sculpted buck's head instead of the usual mounted hunting trophy. Another of the studio's glowing achievements in recent years is the transformation of an attic in a Houston mansion. For this new "guest house within a house," as Kaihoi calls it, the pair created a breathtakingly imaginative, eighteenth-century-inspired hideaway, complete with a "conservatory" (sunroom), bar, and screening room. Theater prop busts that emulate Roman sculpture take pride of place in the opulent, celebratory interior.

Redd credits Kaihoi with a strong editorial sensibility, a talent for keeping only what's necessary. It will be exciting to see whether the designers' official partnership brings about any shifts in their joyous "more-is-more" approach.

1. Bay Area Home
Private Residence, Living Room
San Francisco, California, USA
2017

2. Bay Area Home
Private Residence, Living Room
San Francisco, California, USA
2017

3. Bay Area Home
Private Residence, Main Bedroom
San Francisco, California, USA
2017

4. Texas Farmhouse
Private Residence, Living Room
Bellville, Texas, USA
2018
[overleaf]

5. Texas Farmhouse
Private Residence, View from
Dining Room to Breakfast Room
Bellville, Texas, USA
2018
[overleaf]

Redd Kaihoi

Retrouvius

London, UK

Maria Speake—a reclamation expert who has always found herself drawn to pieces rejected by others—and her husband, Adam Hills, met while studying architecture at Glasgow School of Art. In 1993 they launched their pioneering business Retrouvius, which sought to salvage architectural pieces from sites prior to demolition; soon afterward, they received their first interior design commission and relocated to London. Their award-winning design studio and architectural salvage business has garnered a devoted following for Speake's ability to transform reclaimed building materials, furniture, and textiles into distinctive interiors. Their diverse projects span both urban and rural settings, and include a 1970s superyacht, four interiors for fashion designer Bella Freud, a hotel refurbishment on England's south coast, and a privately owned sixteenth-century priory.

Retrouvius's warehouse—a treasure trove of salvaged stock—has an enthusiastic clientele, some of whom turn to the studio when it comes to designing their own homes. Sam Roddick, the founder of Coco de Mer, was one such client; in 2009 she asked Speake to redesign her sprawling nineteenth-century residence. The breakthrough project—which landed on the cover of the *World of Interiors* magazine—showcases Speake's emphasis on craftsmanship with its abundance of reclaimed fireplaces, vintage furniture, and rough stone flooring.

More recent undertakings include a home in West London owned by a family with small children. Careful to remain considerate of their needs, Speake opened up the interior by removing a wall and creating durable, multipurpose spaces. However, practicalities didn't come at the cost of elegance: from the contrast struck between the dining room's mustard-colored walls and wooden furnishings to the dusky jewel tones found in the hallway, the property is imbued with retro glamour.

Retrouvius prioritized provenance, reuse, and natural materials long before it was fashionable. This reverence for sourcing and sustainability means their interiors aren't just timeless—they also have a story to tell.

1. Bella's Home
Private Residence, View from
Living Room to Bedroom
London, UK
2019

2. Bella's Home
Private Residence, Living Room
London, UK
2019

3. Martha's Home
Private Residence, Living Room
London, UK
2018

4. Martha's Home
Private Residence, Kitchen
London, UK
2018
[overleaf]

5. Sam's Home
Private Residence, Living Room
London, UK
2009
[overleaf]

Richards Stanisich

Sydney, New South Wales,
Australia

1. Hotel Rose Bay
Pub
Sydney, New South Wales,
Australia
2017

2. Darlinghurst Residence
Private Residence, Kitchen
Sydney, New South Wales,
Australia
2017

3. Beach House
Private Residence, Bathroom
Sydney, New South Wales,
Australia
2017

2

3

When Jonathan Richards and Kirsten Stanisich founded Richards Stanisich, their interior architecture practice, in 2018, it signaled a natural evolution for the long-term collaborators, who had spent many years together at a Sydney design studio. In the short time since, they have received a number of high-profile commissions that—coupled with the debut of their first piece of furniture—confirm their status as an unstoppable creative duo.

The partners are enthusiastic advocates of Australia's burgeoning pool of talent. In a video for *Vogue*, architect-trained Stanisich extolls the unique virtues of the national aesthetic, which sees glamour married with trademark Australian ease. "I think we've got this really great way of mixing a luxurious side to our interiors with a really relaxed and accessible energy," she explained.

This style is displayed at Beach House, a coolly contemporary private residence overlooking Sydney's world-famous Bondi Beach. Seeking to evoke a seaside spirit, Richards Stanisich has created a home rich in sensory experiences. Natural light plays a fundamental role, with Japanese-inspired sliding panels installed on the west-facing windows to gently diffuse the sunshine that washes through the open-plan interior. A textural element was granted with natural materials, such as the grayish-blue tiles that lead down a curved corridor and the wooden architraves that subtly demarcate each doorway. Accompanying the beachside vibe are pops of pure glamour, such as a retro bathroom lined floor to ceiling in blush-pink mosaic tiles.

Richards Stanisich's comfortable Minimalism was introduced to the Darlinghurst Residence, a heritage home in a chic Sydney suburb. In one corner, a rich color palette features a burnt-orange leather banquette and midnight blue walls that channels mid-century design; yet a concrete-wall bathroom is unmistakably modern. It's an interior that encapsulates Richards Stanisich's vision of Australian design: elegant and sophisticated, yet always imbued with ease.

Right Meets Left Interior Design

New York City,
New York, USA

2

1. Private Brooklyn Brownstone
Private Residence, Parlor
Brooklyn, New York, USA
2016

2. Junior League of Detroit
Show House
Private Residence, Ladies' Lounge
Detroit, Michigan, USA
2018

3. Sands Point Family Home
Private Residence,
Hall and Staircase
Sands Point, New York, USA
2017

3

New York designer Courtney McLeod, the founder of Right Meets Left Interior Design, is known for her brio: bold, bright upholstery and wallpapers are characteristic of her work. Such vivacious colors may feel like risks for others, but for McLeod, who worked fifteen years in finance, a vivid palette is a sure thing. Yet, thanks to a calibration of delicate accents, layered textures, and choice patterns, her spaces are playful and serene, not an assault on the senses.

With a home in Harlem and an office in the Flatiron District, McLeod is an echt New Yorker, but influences from her hometown of New Orleans frequently find their way into her designs. This was reflected in the Junior League's Designers' Show House—a design event in Detroit that raises funds for community projects—where McLeod transformed a tiny room with no ceiling into a showstopper: a charming lounge wallpapered in an Art Nouveau-style floral pattern by Aux Abris, reminiscent of the Big Easy's iconic architecture. And if McLeod gets to infuse her rooms with personal references, her clients do, too. For a family's traditional brownstone in Brooklyn's Cobble Hill neighborhood in New York, McLeod used an heirloom armoire and a beloved abstract painting as the keystones in a lively update of the home's parlor floor. With three distinct areas for socializing and relaxation (the latter holds an enviable tweed, Tuscan-yellow daybed), the space became less formal and more hospitable. Elsewhere, for a family home on Long Island, McLeod used Japanese tea paper wallpaper by Porter Teleo to elegantly enliven a century-old house.

Although relatively new to the design world, McLeod is aware of the business side of her work. "Right Meets Left" refers to the two hemispheres of the brain—the analytical left and creative right. The name is a good reminder that the two parts work in unison—in McLeod's work, nothing is overlooked.

Rockwell Group

New York City, New York, and Los Angeles,
California, USA; Madrid, Spain

1. Nobu Downtown
Restaurant, Bar
New York City, New York, USA
2017

2. 15 Hudson Yards
Private Residence,
Skytop Lounge
New York City, New York, USA
2019

3. Clockwork, Fairmont Royal York
Hotel, Lobby Lounge
Toronto, Ontario, Canada
2019

4. Nobu Downtown
Restaurant
New York City, New York, USA
2017
[overleaf]

When David Rockwell's mother first introduced him to the theater, it was a profound experience that showed him the emotional impact of set and interior design. Inspired, he trained as an architect and in 1984 founded the cross-disciplinary Rockwell Group in New York City. Known for its award-winning architectural projects and stage sets, the firm also comprises an extremely successful interior design practice, covering a vast range of international settings, from bars and restaurants to offices, hotels, residential, and cultural institutions. Versatility is Rockwell Group's signature, but whatever the project, storytelling always plays a leading role.

As in scenography, the firm constructs a narrative around an interior space so that no design decision is arbitrary. For the lobby refurbishment of Toronto's 1920s Fairmont Royal York hotel, which connects to Union Station, Rockwell Group paid homage to the aesthetics of the golden age of rail travel. The lobby atrium, with its double-height clock tower, has a nocturnal palette of copper and deep navy blue, suggesting the setting sun in an inky evening sky, blended with Art Deco-style furniture and lighting and the hotel's original wood-paneled ceiling. The space resonates with romance and adventure: a place for journeys to begin, if only in the imagination.

In the restaurants of celebrated hospitality group Nobu, Japanese cuisine is blended with Peruvian ingredients, and this cultural fusion of Asia-meets-South America extends to Rockwell Group's treatment of the downtown New York branch. A gigantic, twisting, black ash scuplture by John Houshmand hanging above the bar is inspired by Japanese brush calligraphy; an undulating wooden ceiling canopy takes its cues from *kirigami*, a type of origami that uses cuts as well as folds; and seating upholstery is in a rich Peruvian red. The monumental architecture, with its neoclassical columns, completes the breathtaking staging. Ultimately, it is a respect for history, culture, and above all drama that permeates Rockwell Group's work.

Roman and Williams

**New York City,
New York, USA**

2

1. Verōnika
Restaurant
New York City, New York, USA
2019

2. Verōnika
Restaurant, Bar
New York City, New York, USA
2019

3. Roman and Williams Guild
Store and Café
New York City, New York, USA
2017

Walking into a space designed by Roman and Williams is like entering a story that unfolds in thrilling, unexpected ways. The New York-based duo behind the design studio, Robin Standefer and Stephen Alesch, began working together in set design in Los Angeles, and their thoughtful, eclectic aesthetic endows spaces with the immersive magic of a Hollywood movie. The couple founded Roman and Williams in 2002, and over nearly two decades of collaboration, they've brought the unique combination of Standefer's fine arts background and Alesch's architectural experience to bear on a wide range of projects worldwide, from residential to retail to nightclubs. February 2020 also saw the opening of their first museum project, a spectacular renovation of the Metropolitan Museum's British Galleries in New York.

Continuity is foundational to a Roman and Williams design. To preserve and highlight a space's most interesting cultural and architectural features, the pair draws on an extensive design vocabulary. In 2019 Roman and Williams turned their sights on Verōnika, a restaurant inside Fotografiska, New York's newest museum of photography. Located in a historical, nineteenth-century Beaux-Arts building, Verōnika is a paean to the early history of photography, with its soft color palette and warm lighting, but it's also eminently contemporary in its fluency of reference. A bohemian wall mural, arches, and curvy mohair banquettes come together seamlessly in a space that also contains panels from an original stained-glass window, now incorporated into the restaurant's wall. The light design plays up the contrast between the glass and the black St. Laurent marble bar, an exemplar of the natural materials Roman and Williams prefers.

In 2017 the couple opened Roman and Williams Guild, a flagship store in Manhattan that carries furniture, lighting, and accessories designed by Standefer and Alesch, as well as artisan-made objects collected on their travels. The store also holds a flower shop and café. It's a complete and enchanting sensory experience, a Roman and Williams story that can be the start of new stories in many homes.

3

Roman and Williams

Romanek Design Studio

Los Angeles,
California, USA

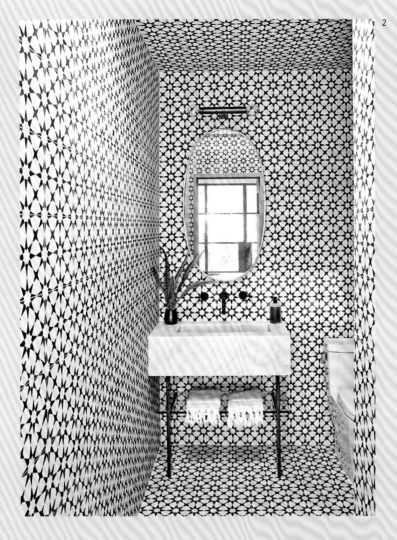

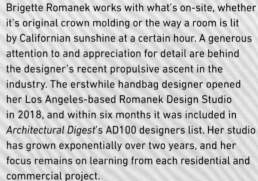

1. The Bu
Private Residence, Den
Malibu, California, USA
2019

2. The Bu
Private Residence, Bathroom
Malibu, California, USA
2019

3. Brigette's Home
Private Residence, Living Room
Los Angeles, California, USA
2017

Brigette Romanek works with what's on-site, whether it's original crown molding or the way a room is lit by Californian sunshine at a certain hour. A generous attention to and appreciation for detail are behind the designer's recent propulsive ascent in the industry. The erstwhile handbag designer opened her Los Angeles-based Romanek Design Studio in 2018, and within six months it was included in *Architectural Digest*'s AD100 designers list. Her studio has grown exponentially over two years, and her focus remains on learning from each residential and commercial project.

Romanek's generosity and gift for observation make her highly attuned to her clients' needs. For a family home in Malibu, she realized a design grounded in sturdiness and elegance. A blackened wood staircase inspired by the Japanese *shou sugi ban* technique (in which wood is charred to waterproof it) links the house's open-plan first story with a second story in which black-framed glass partitions separate the rooms. The designer's own home in the Laurel Canyon neighborhood of Los Angeles is a former recording studio that once hosted the Beatles and Jimi Hendrix—a historic structure rich in musical lore that Romanek ingeniously adapted for her family's use. New arched windows in the living room suffuse with light a space keyed for classic comfort, furnished with buttery lounge chairs and a Hans Wegner chaise longue that provides a whimsical stroke. The house's library lives up to the name, stuffed with art and design books to be perused on a brown velvet couch.

Romanek has a knack for using tiles and a gift for incorporating her clients' art collections, but what tracks across all of her projects is a love of greenery. It's not uncommon to see flowers, potted trees, or just a well-placed, green-leafed branch in her designs. It will be thrilling to watch this designer's growth in the upcoming years.

4. Brigette's Home
Private Residence, Library
Los Angeles, California, USA
2017

5. Brigette's Home
Private Residence, Den
Los Angeles, California, USA
2017

5

Romanek Design Studio 215

Daniel Romualdez

New York City,
New York, USA

1. Roush
Private Residence, Library
New York City, New York, USA
2003

2. Romualdez Residence
Private Residence, Living Room
Los Angeles, California, USA
2005

3. Romualdez Residence
Private Residence, Bedroom
Los Angeles, California, USA
2005

"What I like to do," says architect and interior designer Daniel Romualdez, "is to abstract an idea—a house in the country, a beach house—and whittle it down so it's not the obvious, literal thing." This is a design approach that has netted him a constellation of high-profile clients, including Daphne Guinness, Tory Burch, Cornelia Guest, Aerin Lauder, and Mark Rockefeller. Born and raised in Manila, Philippines, it was assumed Romualdez would follow his parents into a career in diplomacy. But he persisted with his dream to work on interiors, initially in the offices of Thierry Despont, before opening his own firm in New York City in 1993. Although it is hard to pin down a signature style for Romualdez, a passion for context and strong narrative runs through each of his projects. He effortlessly mixes vintage pieces with his own furniture designs and draws frequently on luxurious textiles, such as leather, silk, parchment, and fur.

The distillation of one idea and avoidance of the obvious is evident in Romualdez's own Gilcrest house in Los Angeles—in this case a winter retreat. It would have been predictable to design this glass-walled white cube in stark, mid-century Modern style. While is it certainly Minimalist, with pale walls and light-flooded rooms, the emphasis is emphatically placed on simple luxury and comfort, which carries throughout.

In the living room, a Romualdez-designed couch and daybed, both in raw silk, are complemented by a painting by conceptual artist Sean Landers. A geological specimen placed atop a coffee table made of logs creates an earthy, natural connection. In the bedroom, a replica of the gilded four-poster bed he created for his Manhattan apartment forms a stunning centerpiece, its headboard covered in tactile Cavallini cowhide by Edelman Leather. Neutral, calming tones dominate. The sum of parts is glamorous, polished, yet cozy—qualities that his clients value.

RP Miller

New York City, New York, and Aspen,
Colorado, USA; Mexico City, Mexico

1. Kentucky Farmhouse Retreat
Private Residence, Study
Louisville, Kentucky, USA
2018

2. Kentucky Farmhouse Retreat
Private Residence, View from
Study to Living Room
Louisville, Kentucky, USA
2018

3. Kentucky Farmhouse Retreat
Private Residence, The Barn
Louisville, Kentucky, USA
2018

4. Mexico City Residence
Private Residence, Living Room
Mexico City, Mexico
2019
[overleaf]

Fifth-generation Californian Rodman Primack grew up globally, traveling between California's Laguna Beach, Idaho's Sun Valley, Mexico, Japan, and Portugal. His design and textiles firm, RP Miller, recently went global, too, straddling North America with offices in New York and Mexico City. Primack's early passion for collecting art, textiles, and pottery has also followed him into adulthood. Until recently, he combined his design career with work as an auction house executive and art fair creative director. Well-connected and forever curious about who's making what, Primack also collaborates with talented specialists through RP Miller. Now, contemporary art and traditional crafts from around the world find their way into Primack's residential projects—however, he is judicious about his more-is-more aesthetic, knowing when a well-painted wall can provide just as much pleasure as piles of objets d'art.

For a family's weekend getaway in Louisville, Kentucky, which RP Miller designed in 2018, playful patterns and bright prints were used to create a welcoming haven. Local artist Monica C. Mahoney lent her talents to the project by painting the pool table, now a unique geometric centerpiece that complements the prepossessing Memphis Group boxing-ring beds in the property's guesthouse. Primack's brio is on full display in the study, which is wallpapered in wax prints—traditional Central and West African fabrics.

His ability to modulate serves Primack well. In the Mexico City apartment he shares with his partner, Rudy Weissenberg, the designer's signature tones rise to a sustained, joyous crescendo. In the living room, a custom rug from Agnes Studio lies below a 2018 painting by Donna Huanca, which presides over a space filled with plants and overstuffed Afra and Tobia Scarpa leather lounges. The lounges are a family heirloom that look, in their present context, astonishingly contemporary. Juxtaposed in Primack's designs, old and new things become classics.

Achille Salvagni

Rome, Italy; London, UK;
New York City, New York, USA

In a short film by Freddie Leyden, Achille Salvagni declares, "Rome is in my soul, in my bones; it's part of my architecture, my body." Without doubt, Salvagni's interiors and furniture are infused with the classicism of the ancient city, but he holds any Roman excess firmly in check. The designer attributes this to a year's study in Stockholm during his mid-twenties, after which he traveled across Sweden, Finland, and Norway to track down every building that bore the mark of Finnish architect Alvar Aalto. For him, Scandinavian design was the ultimate counterpoint to all things Italian, and the experience was profound: "It was like breathing modernity," he says.

Salvagni masterminds entire spaces, working out the flow of rooms and designing everything right down to the door hinges. Since setting up in 2002, he has built a worldwide reputation and glittering clientele, and his commissions include superyachts, city apartments, and mansions. Gold, onyx, walnut, marble, and Murano glass are staples of his material palette, and he collaborates with Italian craftspeople whose techniques have not changed for centuries— who, in his words, "transform very boring elements into jewels." In 2013 he established his own atelier for limited-edition furniture and lighting.

The Apollo display in his London showroom sums up this fusion of modernity and traditional hand-crafting. Here, a space capsule, inspired by the movie *2001: A Space Odyssey*, provides the Minimalist backdrop for several Salvagni pieces in rounded, primal forms, such as Roma, his walnut and twenty-four-carat gold cabinet with ovoid legs, and the interplanetary globules of the Bubbles wall sconce in onyx and gilt bronze. Here and elsewhere, Salvagni's interiors are never coldly intellectual: he uses eruptions of color—hot pink, fuchsia, bright red, and gold, always gold—to shock the retina and rouse the emotions. His spaces vibrate with tradition, but they also become something strange, beautiful, and new.

1. Kyoto, Achille Salvagni Atelier
Gallery and Showroom,
Temporary Display
London, UK
2017

2. Cocktail Hour,
Achille Salvagni Atelier
Gallery and Showroom,
Temporary Display
London, UK
2016

3. Apollo,
Achille Salvagni Atelier
Gallery and Showroom,
Temporary Display
London, UK
2018

Tom Scheerer

New York City,
New York, USA

2   Tom Scheerer is a scion of the American East Coast, yet his allegiance isn't to tradition but to comfort and elegance. Scheerer's favorite piece of furniture is an Eero Saarinen Tulip table, a design he admires for its efficiency and grace. These same qualities are ones that the highly respected designer, who formed his company in 1995, strives for in his spaces. Scheerer creates designs that are never intimidating but are always striking and serene.

In a Scheerer-designed room, an occasional Modernist piece, such as the Saarinen table, might be placed alongside antique bentwood chairs, rattan furniture, and printed wallpapers. These rooms often come with a view of the city or the sea—his projects over the past five years have taken him from Dallas, Texas, to Antigua, the Bahamas, New York City, and the Hamptons on Long Island. Scheerer is accustomed to travel and keeps residences in Paris and New York, which is ideal for his constant browsing for objects to incorporate into later designs. In a Georgian-inspired Dallas apartment, these might be a pair of candlesticks on a fireplace mantle or horse figurines on a bookshelf.

Unfussy but exacting, Scheerer is a master of subtle, effective gestures. For the neutral palette interiors of an East Hampton house he designed in 2017, the enlivening accent is a color instead of decorative objects—a blue-and-white striped rug in one room, an eggshell-blue sofa in another. Scheerer also believes a little green can work in any room. At an outdoor dining patio of a house in Antigua, his beloved gathering of straw hats on a wall doubles as a group of wall-hung plants. At a house in the Bahamas, woven bags and a circular, sunlike decorative centerpiece join the hats. Perhaps the straw hat is a perfect representation of Scheerer's approach to design: an object that's beautiful, necessary, but not precious.

3

1. East Hampton Beach House
Private Residence, Living Room
East Hampton, New York, USA
2017

2. Zanzibar
Private Residence, Living Room
The Abacos, Bahamas
2016

3. Zanzibar
Private Residence, Dining Room
The Abacos, Bahamas
2016

Glenn Sestig Architects

Ghent, Belgium

1. Hieronymus
Store
Zurich, Switzerland
2014

2. Hieronymus
Store
Zurich, Switzerland
2014

3. Penthouse Mulier
Private Residence, Kitchen
Antwerp, Belgium
2016

4. Penthouse Mulier
Private Residence, Library
Antwerp, Belgium
2016

2

3

Muted luxury and refined utilitarian design are the specialities of urbane interior architect Glenn Sestig. Based in Belgium, Sestig—who established his studio in 1999—favors the timeless appeal of natural stone, which he has used with admirable effect in homes, stores, nightclubs, and galleries.

His monolithic contemporary spaces have a Minimalist sensibility and a precise architectural approach; these include notable collaborations made with other Belgian creatives, such as the fashion designer Raf Simons and interiors brand Obumex. For Sestig, interior design and architecture are inseparable, one informing the other, so he prefers projects where he is in control of both.

If the space is an architectural icon, however, Sestig relishes the opportunity to blend the old and new. In 2016 he restored Antwerp's Riverside Tower, a Brutalist penthouse designed in 1972 by Belgian Modernists Léon Stynen and Paul De Meyer. Both architect and client shared the same intent: to restore the concrete masterpiece to its former glory and accentuate its natural beauty with new features. Sestig added a spectacular sculptural kitchen, all carved in titanium travertine, and reexposed concrete walls and floors, softening them with warm, integrated lighting.

Scale, proportion, and natural stone are also paramount in Sestig's commercial spaces. At the Zurich flagship store of luxury paper and leather goods brand Hieronymus, he conjured a unique retail experience with a contemporary stone environment. The concept store is divided into distinct zones using bronze mirrors, vast metal shelves, and subtle shifts in material and tone.

Although restrained, even austere, Sestig's designs retain a sense of warmth and tactility. The continuous, gridlike lines of his award-winning designs appear tranquil, creating elegant urban spaces that feel ordered and soulful.

4

SevilPeach

London, UK

SevilPeach has redefined the way people live and work for more than twenty-five years. Founded in 1994 by architects Sevil Peach Gence and Gary Turnbull, with an ambition to stay small while thinking big, the award-winning London-based practice offers a full architecture and interior design service. Praised for its highly creative, ergonomic approach, SevilPeach has designed stylish workplaces and sleek retail spaces for companies worldwide, including Vitra, Microsoft, and Swiss Re.

When the Finnish furniture brand Artek asked for a gallery-style space in which to present furniture by its founder, the architect Alvar Aalto, as well as its parent company, Vitra, SevilPeach transformed its Helsinki headquarters from a muddled maze of corridors and offices into an airy, modern space. Inspired by Aalto's functionalist principles and use of natural materials, the team reimagined the interior using locally sourced birch plywood, clutter-concealing curtains, and vibrant pops of color.

The headquarters of Danish textile company Kvadrat, completed in 2018, tells a similar story. Always attentive to light and space, SevilPeach has opened up the two-story building to create communal workspaces, social areas, and meeting rooms, as well as a studio, product library, and showroom for customers to browse in a familial, relaxed environment. Key areas are clearly defined by sweeping curtains in company fabrics and are linked by a central streetlike passageway. Floor-to-ceiling windows and accents of green upholstery connect visitors to the surrounding coastal landscape.

Residential projects are treated with the same sense of care. An artist's home, for example, was sculpted with natural light to create a bright, lofty space with a touch of magic—a freestanding teak bathtub that overlooks the garden.

Regardless of type or scale, SevilPeach's projects benefit from its trademark combination of creativity and restraint. Fuss-free decorating lets architectural features shine, while spaces are imaginatively designed with the utmost consideration for the people who will use them.

1. Artek HQ
Offices and Showroom,
Corridor
Helsinki, Finland
2017

2. Kvadrat HQ
Offices and Showroom,
View through Meeting Room to
Showroom
Ebeltoft, Denmark
2018

3. Kvadrat HQ
Offices and Showroom,
Meeting Room
Ebeltoft, Denmark
2018

4. Kvadrat HQ
Offices and Showroom,
Library/Dining Room
Ebeltoft, Denmark
2018

5. Steeles Road
Private Residence, Bathroom
London, UK
2008

SheltonMindel

New York City,
New York, USA

American architect Lee F. Mindel brings a synergy to his architectural and interior design practice that, combined with his knowledge of furniture design and contemporary art, reveals the shrewd aestheticism behind his craft. Having founded SheltonMindel in 1978, architecture graduates Peter L. Shelton and Mindel first landed a gig designing cult movie director Brian De Palma's apartment. Since then, Mindel has said that the authenticity running through his late collaborator's work remains his benchmark.

As inductees into the Interior Design Hall of Fame and recipients of the 2011 Cooper Hewitt National Design Award, presented by the Obamas, SheltonMindel's influence looms large. Projects include commissions for Ralph Lauren, Fila, and Soros Capital Management, private Gulfstream jets, and multiple residences for Sting and Trudie Styler and the Lauder family. Mindel's 2015 collaboration with James Turrell is a lucid response to the installation artist's giant three-dimensional light-filled egg chamber resting at the center of the client's rectilinear office building. Mindel says he took cues from the logic of artist Dan Flavin when configuring his "almost chandelier" electrical fixtures and in applying his own visual theory to the office floors, which were demarcated by a series of monochromatic color palettes.

The Manhattan Triplex, for which SheltonMindel won a 2020 NYC×DESIGN Best Apartment Award, gestures toward a home's authority to both contain and expand domestic experience. A two-story penthouse was combined into a single-family triplex, in which the structural logic of a tree connects the three floors—warm larch wood, a blue lacquered wall, graphic furnishings, and geometric patterns all play on this kinetic metaphor. Furthering the nature theme, a three-story screen of perforated wooden blocks allows dappled light to pour into the living room, where a dainty wire giraffe by sculptor Benedetta Mori Ubaldini adds a touch of playfulness.

For SheltonMindel, the unified and clean-lined approach of classic Modernism paired with the opulence of neoclassical aesthetics purifies contemporary interior design into artistry—something Mindel does so skillfully.

1. 56 Leonard, Indoor/Outdoor
Sculpture Garden
Private Residence, Bedroom
New York City, New York, USA
2019

2. LFM Loft
Private Residence,
Stairway to Rooftop Garden
New York City, New York, USA
2019

3. London Townhouse
Private Residence, Cinema
London, UK
2017

4. Manhattan Triplex
Private Residence,
Living Room
New York City,
New York, USA
2018

5. Manhattan Triplex
Private Residence,
Living Room
New York City,
New York, USA
2018

Space Copenhagen

Copenhagen, Denmark

1. Allegra, The Stratford
Hotel, Restaurant and Bar
London, UK
2019

2. Mezzanine Cocktail Bar,
The Stratford
Hotel, Bar
London, UK
2019

3. The Lounge, The Stratford
Hotel, Bar
London, UK
2019

2

Describing their approach as "Poetic Modernism," Danish architectural studio Space Copenhagen has been designing sharp contemporary interiors and heirloom-quality furniture for more than fifteen years. Established by friends Signe Bindslev Henriksen and Peter Bundgaard Rützou, both architecture graduates from the Royal Danish Academy of Fine Arts, the studio takes a dichotomous approach to design, combining contrasting styles—from classic and modern to sculptural and minimal—to deliver intriguing original spaces and products. Their extensive portfolio includes destination restaurants, such as Noma in Copenhagen, and collaborations with major design brands, including GUBI and &Tradition, as well as private homes.

In 2019 the studio designed the interiors, including furniture and accessories, for the Stratford, a hotly anticipated 145-room hotel in London. Taking inspiration from 1950s New York, when such luxury hideaways welcomed long-term residents, their design celebrates classic, old-school glamour but with a futuristic twist. To a calm and consistent palette of muted neutrals and organic materials, the team added its own custom furniture featuring free-form shapes, rich woods, and metallics. The impact is streamlined and sophisticated, with the eye drawn to the hotel's standout features, such as its long, sweeping stone bar and the lobby's triple-height triangular ceiling.

The studio's distinctive brand of modern Nordic chic is also evident at Restaurant 108 in Copenhagen, an extraordinary brick and concrete space where hard Brutalist edges meet soft classic details, such as walls paneled in restful sea green shades, sweeping linen curtains, and blown-glass pendants. This artful mix of the organic and industrial illustrates the studio's approach to balancing opposites in their designs, and it gives the restaurant's interiors a unique depth and character.

With a fresh, intuitive approach, the duo behind Space Copenhagen have the ability to anticipate human behavior and make an impact on it through their much-admired designs, creating environments that encourage a more mindful, poetic style of living.

3

4. 11 Howard
Hotel, Lounge
New York City, New York, USA
2016

5. Restaurant 108
Restaurant
Copenhagen, Denmark
2017

The Stella Collective

Melbourne, Victoria,
Australia

1. Zoobibi
Store and Café
Melbourne, Victoria, Australia
2018

2. Zoobibi
Store and Café
Melbourne, Victoria, Australia
2018

3. Artedomus Sydney
Showroom
Sydney, New South Wales,
Australia
2017

Hana Hakim brings a rebellious element to the spaces she masterminds. As founder of the Stella Collective, a Melbourne-based design studio with a global reach, Hakim describes her approach as focused around finding each client's "white tiger." This determination to identify a singular quality in each project is what sets Hakim's interiors apart—and distinguishes her as a rising star.

Born in London and educated at London's Chelsea College of Art and Design, Hakim relocated to Australia two decades ago. In 2015 she established her own practice, selecting a former department store as her office and painting its ornate cornice moldings gold. Projects have since ranged from coffee shops to a collection of light-filled town-houses intended to evoke the breezy romance of an Ibizan villa.

Hakim's heritage often finds its way into her work. Her father is Syrian, and she spent childhoods visiting the ancient city of Aleppo, which has since been destroyed by the civil war. When concept store Zoobibi commissioned her to design a retail space for their collection of home wares, she drew upon these memories of her father's familial home. Recreating the beauty of Syrian architecture, from the central water fountain to the arched doorways and Arabesque-inspired geometric tiles, was a deeply personal undertaking for the designer.

In the case of Artedomus's showroom, the "white tiger" was the products themselves. Channeling the glamour of Old Hollywood sets, Hakim created an aspirational series of spaces to exhibit the brand's exclusive stoneware in an environment more akin to a luxury apartment than a retail space. It proved to be a winning formula—Hakim's ability to construct such an immersive experience resulted in a People's Choice Award from media brand Frame in 2018. It was an apt tribute to a designer whose flair for story-telling produces mesmerizing results.

Robert Stilin

**New York City,
New York, USA**

Based in New York City and the Hamptons, Robert Stilin has decorated the homes of the affluent for more than twenty-five years. In the late 1980s, while running a Palm Beach, Florida, lifestyle store, a client came in, bought nearly everything, and invited him to decorate their residence—and Stilin has never looked back. His designs incorporate furniture with crisp, clean lines, along with luxurious textiles, such as cashmere, neutral palettes with pops of color, and natural wood on floors or ceilings. An avid art collector, he also integrates contemporary works into his interiors.

For a couple's Upper East Side apartment in New York, Stilin created an urban, contemporary feel that never becomes cold or austere. The couple are avid skiers, and Stilin acknowledged this by including fur-covered dining chairs and mohair rugs for Alpine coziness, as well as vintage lounge chairs upholstered in brown alpaca wool. The carefully selected art hanging on the walls provides a seamless theme throughout the space. Splashes of color zing against muted earthy tones, and chestnut-colored glass pendant lights in the dining room provide a retro focal point. In the living room, a linen-covered sofa designed by Stilin and a 1970s leather-and-stainless steel cocktail table complete the look.

For a Tribeca loft apartment dating to 1866— a former American Express coaching house—the designer used a mixture of vintage, antique, and contemporary pieces. The clients, a couple with two children, dreamed of having a home bar to enjoy a drink, so Stilin helped to design one in zinc, walnut, and brass that suited a domestic setting. This is a smart, relaxed grown-up sanctuary, with plentiful top-quality upholstered seating, rustic and industrial pieces, and artworks adorning the walls. Whatever the context, Stilin's interiors are urbane, yet practical and intimate.

2

3

1. Upper East Side Residence
Private Residence, Living Room
New York City, New York, USA
2015

2. Upper East Side Residence
Private Residence, Dining Room
New York City, New York, USA
2015

3. Tribeca Residence
Private Residence, Living Room
New York City, New York, USA
2015

Studio Ashby

London, UK

2

1. Floral Court
Private Residence, Living Room
London, UK
2019

2. The Robertson Small Hotel
Hotel, Reception
Western Cape, South Africa
2017

3. Holland Park Villas
Private Residence, Living Room
London, UK
2019

4. TVC Apartment
Private Residence, Living Room
London, UK
2016
[overleaf]

Sophie Ashby often credits her preternatural success to her nomadic childhood. Born to an English father and a South African mother, she grew up between the two countries and lived in fourteen family homes by the time she was eighteen. In 2014, after being asked to take on a lucrative commerical project, she founded her London-based design practice, Studio Ashby. The designer has a sharp eye for combining antiques and modern furniture with striking photography and contemporary "world art" to fashion dream interiors for others.

In 2017 Ashby was commissioned to makeover the Robertson Small Hotel, a ten-bedroom luxury bolt-hole on South Africa's Western Cape. Ashby—an enthusiastic aesthete with a particular fascination for contemporary African art—brought her expertise to the period property, adorning its walls with a custom collection of works by local artists. This emphasis on regional character continues throughout as Ashby mirrored elements of the breathtaking terrain with an earthy palette and organic textures that transitions guests from indoors to out.

A favorite among developers, Ashby has conceived the interiors for Holland Park Villas, a contemporary apartment building in West London. The elegant neighborhood served as inspiration during the design process: Ashby envisioned a cultured resident who enjoyed browsing the boutiques of nearby trendy Portobello Road. The result is a series of residences whose vibrant pops of color are offset by carefully selected antiques. Another residential commission led to the penthouse at London's upscale Floral Court development being transformed into a boldly captivating space, with unique pieces that included a burr-elm coffee table and a dining table with dried flowers arranged beneath its glass surface.

In the apartment she shares with her husband, fashion designer Charlie Casely-Hayford, Ashby's signature aesthetic is on full display. Unsurprisingly, artworks cover the walls, including an enormous print by beloved Nigerian photographer Lakin Ogunbanwo.

3

Studio Daminato

Singapore

2

Interior architect Albano Daminato, the founder of the Singapore-based design practice Studio Daminato, is a master of Minimalism and elegant restraint. After more than ten years in the industry, Australian-born Daminato established his studio in 2001. In the decades since it has designed jaw-droppingly swanky contemporary spaces around the world, from Bali to Lake Como, and is rapidly gaining global attention. In 2020 Daminato made his debut into *Architectural Digest* magazine's prestigious AD100 list.

Studio Daminato's interiors combine the best of Scandinavian Modern, Japanese Minimalism, and contemporary ergonomic design, and Daminato's experience in architecture shows throughout. The studio designs from the ground up, planning and commissioning every detail, from door handles to smart architectural solutions, such as hidden doors, banquette seating, and integrated storage.

Villa Peduzzi, overlooking Italy's Lake Como, is one of the studio's most admired projects. The grand mansion, built in 1909 for Italian engineer Rocco Peduzzi, has been so beautifully reimagined and skillfully executed that the effect is mesmeric. The restful creamy-toned bedrooms and living areas are furnished with discreet oak joinery and twentieth-century Scandinavian design, and the walls are fitted with handwoven linen panels. Natural textiles and tactile surfaces, such as handcrafted glazed tiles, Italian stone worktops, and fluted oak, are resplendent throughout, illuminated by light wells, wraparound windows, and meticulously designed lighting.

The studio's custom furniture is among the standout features at Arnalaya Beach House, a holiday retreat in Bali where the team managed the entire interior project, from design planning to styling. Bamboo paneling, beautiful bentwood chairs, and dark teakwood furniture with accents of rattan reflect Indonesia's cultural heritage, while every modern comfort and detail has been considered, including freestanding bathtubs and smooth terrazzo floors.

Eschewing trends and overly decorative flourishes, Daminato favors simple materials in a neutral palette, which he layers to create interiors that have immense depth, soul, and tactility.

3

1. MJ Residence
Private Residence, Main Bedroom
Undisclosed Location
2010

2. Lake Como Villa
Private Residence, Piano Salon
Como, Italy
2019

3. Arnalaya Bali
Private Residence, Dining Room
Bali, Indonesia
2014

Studio Jacques Garcia

Paris, France

1. La Réserve Paris Hotel and Spa
Hotel, Library
Paris, France
2015

2. Hôtel Barrière
Le Fouquet's Paris
Hotel, Guest Suite
Paris, France
2019

3. Hôtel Barrière
Le Fouquet's Paris
Hotel, Guest Suite
Paris, France
2019

Legendary decorator Jacques Garcia is a global talent, famed for designing some of the world's most extraordinary iconic hotels, from Hotel Costes in Paris to La Mamounia in Marrakech.

The Frenchman spent his childhood visiting flea markets and chateaus with his father, a Spanish immigrant with great artistic and intellectual curiosity. Together, the pair marveled at France's grand castles and imagined the lives within. It could be argued that Garcia's career has been spent trying to recreate the same sense of wonder and history for hotel guests.

Take two recent projects, La Réserve Paris Hotel and Spa, an Haussmanian mansion near the Champs-Élysées, and Hôtel Barrière Le Fouquet's, providing luxurious accommodation attached to the famous Paris restaurant Le Fouquet's. The former is unmistakably Garcia, a traditionally opulent space with all the romance of Belle-Époque Paris: rich dark woods, engraved marble fireplaces, and gilded chairs.

The latter—owned by hoteliers Dominique Desseigne and the late Diane Barrière-Desseigne (who gave Garcia his first opportunity to decorate a hotel in 1992)—is a more contemporary space but still reflects Garcia's love of classical French style with its fine antique furniture; it also has Haussmanian-style detailing. His most treasured commodities—space, volume, and light—are abundant and emphasized with a warm off-white palette that graces the walls, curtains, and upholstery. The result is pure elegance: a grand Parisian space that feels as comfortable and intimate as a private home.

At the age of ten, Garcia and his father were refused entry to the Ritz, leading to uncomfortable questions about class and status. The experience drove Garcia's fierce ambition to make his spaces accessible to anyone with a passion for art and beauty. This intent, executed with great panache, revolutionized the French hotel industry. Although undeniably lavish, Garcia's spaces are never pompous. Their success relies not on exclusivity but on the magic and mastery of his design.

1. Apartment Jean Goujon
Private Residence, Living Room
Paris, France
2014

2. Flamingo Estate
Private Residence, Study
Los Angeles, California, USA
2018

3. Flamingo Estate
Private Residence, Living Room
Los Angeles, California, USA
2018

Studio KO

Paris, France;
Marrakech, Morocco

1

The cutting-edge architectural practice Studio KO is the brainchild of partners Olivier Marty and Karl Fournier. The French architects founded their studio in 2000 and, from offices in Paris and Marrakech, Morocco, they have since designed some of the world's most talked-about stylish spaces, from London's Chiltern Firehouse to Marrakech's Yves Saint Laurent Museum.

The studio's earthy, elemental buildings and clean, linear interiors share neutral tones with vibrant accents, abundant natural light, and walls of concrete, terrazzo, and terra-cotta. Authentic material choices root their work in nature, resulting in humble, graceful designs and monolithic buildings that settle unobtrusively into their surroundings. This striking yet grounded approach has led to multiple awards and a successful monograph, published in 2017.

Each work is distinct: the duo eschews a signature aesthetic, instead preferring to seek inspiration from the context of their projects. However, the magnificent Flamingo Estate, which sits in the hills above Los Angeles, bears all the hallmarks of their architectural philosophy and creative vision. The 1940s flamingo-pink house (a former adult-film studio) was meticulously renovated, along with its stunningly landscaped gardens created by Arnaud Casaus, to produce a playful yet sophisticated mansion. The team added custom features and stylistic statements, such as a wooden frieze featuring the owners' dogs, which wraps around the living room, and striped green-and-white wall panels and ceiling rafters. They sourced, or approved, every item in the house, from tableware to art, such as David Hockney's exuberant *Caribbean Tea Time* folding screen from 1987. The three-year process took the team from LA to Morocco, via desert souks and Parisian flea markets—a creative journey the owners described as "life changing."

With major projects afoot, the French architects are indisputably at the top of their game. Yet, despite their success, they remain as refreshingly modest and effortlessly debonair as their portfolio.

2

3

Studio Mumbai

Mumbai, India;
Milan, Italy

1. Ganga Maki Textile Studio
Weaving and Dyeing Complex,
Weaving Studio
Dehradun, Uttarakhand, India
2017

2. Ganga Maki Textile Studio
Weaving and Dyeing Complex,
Residential Living Room
Dehradun, Uttarakhand, India
2017

3. Copper House II
Private Residence, Living Room
Chondi, Maharashtra, India
2012

The architectural and design philosophy of celebrated Indian architect Bijoy Jain—founder of Studio Mumbai and a visiting professor of architecture at the Accademia di architettura in Mendrisio, Switzerland— is rooted in the most fundamental of human ambitions: to provide shelter, security, and a nurturing space, using materials and an economy of means dictated by the immediate landscape. For Jain and his studio, this begins with a search for three key elements: water, air, and light, which together create an environment that is universal to all geographies and cultures.

Jain worked in Los Angeles and London before establishing his practice in 1995 (becoming Studio Mumbai in 2001). It was in the United States that he discovered land art and artists such as Michael Heizer, Mary Miss, and Robert Smithson; however, it was only on his return to India that he was able to reconnect with the vast and abundant landscape of his homeland, which continues to inform his work today.

The relationship between architecture and the environment is key to Jain's design for the award-winning Copper House II, a contemporary dwelling in Maharashtra, India. The elegant building, with its patinated copper roof and gently stepped levels, blends into the landscape with such sensitivity that it seems like it has always been there. Designed around a stone courtyard, handmade wooden screens and fluted glass offer intimacy and isolation.

The Ganga Maki Textile Studio, at the foothills of the Himalayas in India, shares a similar spirit. Designed for Japanese weaver Chiaki Maki, the stone, brick, and lime weaving complex is centered around a courtyard and includes residential quarters, workshops, indigo farms, and other weaving and dyeing facilities. The gentle yet imposing structures rise and fall in their surroundings.

Whether constructing buildings, interiors, or installations, Jain's highly unique creations share a simplicity, materiality, and empathy for the environment—one made from water, air, and light.

Studio Peregalli

Milan, Italy

"Contemporary" is not a word one would normally use to describe Studio Peregalli's approach, but their work occupies an important place in today's interior design landscape. Roberto Peregalli and Laura Sartori Rimini are famed for their ability to create rooms that appear to be from a previous age. They are not merely reproductions of the past but an artistic homage to an idea, time, or place. "Our interiors aim to give the impression they've always been there," Sartori Rimini explained to *Elle Decor* in 2015. Especially beguiling is how they use their insight and creativity anachronistically, jumping from century to century across rooms, or within a room itself.

This can be seen in a family home they worked on in Hampstead, London, an Arts and Crafts-style mansion built in 1881. The organizing narrative was Great Britain as a seafaring nation, suggesting that the house was filled with the precious objects of travel and exploration. The doors of the husband's dressing room are covered in Spanish tiles from the 1600s and 1800s; in the library different pieces hailing from France, Russia, and England and spanning a period of three hundred years are effortlessly blended.

For socialite Katherine Bryan's apartment in a Paris townhouse, the studio wanted to recreate what Peregalli described as, "our idea of France—something eighteenth century, poetic." There is plenty of gold paint, but it is Italian. French gold leaf, the type used in Versailles, was too harsh and too bright. The exquisite dining room was designed to have a certain Flemish flavor, suggesting the era of a Rubens painting, yet it features contemporary mirrors painted with flowering vines.

Peregalli and Sartori Rimini could be likened to curators or art directors: their interiors are remarkable assemblages of curiosities that create a dreamlike effect. That in itself is a postmodern thing to do, and, in a sense, they are inventing a brand-new reality.

2

3

1. Paris Residence
Private Residence, Living Room
Paris, France
2015

2. Paris Residence
Private Residence, Dining Room
Paris, France
2015

3. London Residence
Private Residence, Living Room
London, UK
2015

Studio Shamshiri

Los Angeles,
California, USA

1. Los Altos
Private Residence, Living Room
San Diego, California, USA
2019

2. Sonia Boyajian Jewelry Studio
Showroom
Los Angeles, California, USA
2019

3. Sonia Boyajian Jewelry Studio
Showroom
Los Angeles, California, USA
2019

Pamela and Ramin Shamshiri, siblings born in Tehran who moved to the United States as children, founded Studio Shamshiri in 2016. The duo were founding partners at Commune Design, another Los Angeles-based design studio, and their years of experience are evident in the confident and thoughtful approach they apply to each of their commercial and residential projects. Working out of a restored 1920s Hollywood building, Studio Shamshiri has charted an ethical course, eschewing synthetic materials in favor of natural ones whenever possible, and acknowledging a responsibility not only to their clients, but also to the commercial and residential spaces they work on, as well as the surrounding communities.

If that sounds altogether too serious, it shouldn't. Studio Shamshiri is versatile and resourceful, developing captivating designs influenced by the siblings' memories of Tehran, their love of Italy (where their mother is from), and little gems of design and architectural history, from early twentieth-century lace to the work of the Austrian–American architect Rudolph Schindler. In 2019, Studio Shamshiri created a showroom for the Los Angeles jeweler Sonia Boyajian deeply influenced by the artist Georgia O'Keeffe's studio in Santa Fe, New Mexico—down to the angles of the hand-carved display niches. Also in 2019, the studio addressed a different challenge: the Maison de la Luz in New Orleans, a new property of the Ace Hotel group. Echoing both a grand French hotel and down-home Southern hospitality, the hotel's authoritative, elaborate interiors are an intricately crafted fantasy, from the flirty fringes on the custom-made armchairs to the moody, retro, acid-etched globe lighting.

Studio Shamshiri considers good design to be integral to a good life, and the past four years have been auspicious for this collaboration. It will be fascinating to watch these talented designers advance on their path to better design and better living.

4. Bar Marilou, Maison de la Luz
Hotel, Bar
New Orleans,
Louisiana, USA
2019

5. Maison de la Luz
Hotel, Living Room
New Orleans,
Louisiana, USA
2019

Studio Sofield

New York City,
New York, USA

1. Palm Beach I
Private Residence, Living Room
Palm Beach, Florida, USA
2015

2. Tom Ford
Store, Men's Salon
Beverly Hills, California, USA
2014

3. Tom Ford
Store, Perfumery
New York City, New York, USA
2017

William Sofield has been described as a Modernist by temperament and a historicist by training. He is adept at blending different periods, objets d'art, and eccentric touches, but he always does so with restraint and classical balance. The result is an exquisite beauty that has a deep impact on the emotions and the imagination. Founding the interdisciplinary Studio Sofield in 1996, his approach has gained him a roster of retail clients, including Tom Ford, Salvatore Ferragamo, Ralph Lauren, Gucci, and Yves Saint Laurent; large-scale residential commissions worldwide; and prestigious environmental and exhibition design projects.

When studying architecture at Princeton University in New Jersey, Sofield focused on art history and European cultural studies, a background that informs his vision. He places an important emphasis on his clients' needs and tastes and tailors a space to the locale. His New York City offices are themselves an exercise in seduction and amazement.

Sensitivity to location is evident in a private Palm Beach, Florida, residence. The double-height living room is flooded with marine light and dominated by an enormous silver travertine fireplace streaked with tones of sand and ocean blue. Social areas are furnished with beautifully upholstered couches and chairs: accents of coral pink, leaf green, and ice blue pick up the natural outdoor hues of the garden and sky. While architecture and furnishings all have sharp Modernist lines, the overall effect is never hard or cold but retains an atmosphere of calm, comfortable luxury. Sofield's design for Tom Ford's Beverly Hills salon reflects Ford's own aesthetic, which is slick, polished, and tactile. Velvet sofas and Newport White marble wall panels create a tempting opulence in the store, and a statement mobile by Alexander Calder—one of Ford's favorite artists—finishes off the space. In these two projects, the characteristic Sofield hallmarks of vast knowledge, refined taste, and deep understanding of a client's preferences prevail.

Studioilse

London, UK

1. Ett Hem Hotel Stockholm
Hotel, Lounge
Stockholm, Sweden
2012

2. Swedish Summer House
Private Residence, Kitchen
Southern Sweden
2019

3. The Savoy Helsinki
Restaurant
Helsinki, Finland
2020

4. Wellbeing Collection,
Nanimarquina
Textile Collection,
Temporary Display
Barcelona, Spain
2019

The award-winning interior design practice Studioilse is the brainchild of British designer Ilse Crawford, an eminent tastemaker with an eye for talent and a timeless, ethical approach. Crawford was the founding editor of *Elle Decoration UK*, where she was instrumental in recognizing and promoting the early promise of some of the world's top interior designers, including Belgian architect Vincent Van Duysen. After nine years in design journalism, she moved into the industry herself, establishing Studioilse in 2001. The London-based studio's exceptional portfolio includes luxury hotels, such as Soho House New York, private homes, and collaborations with major brands, including Aesop, Anya Hindmarch, and IKEA—for which Crawford designed a furniture collection in 2015.

Thanks to Crawford's inimitable touch, the elegant Ett Hem guesthouse, based in an Arts and Crafts building in Stockholm, has become a favorite among the design cognoscenti. Studioilse combined classic Scandinavian details—neutral tones, clean lines, natural woods—with Crawford's custom furniture, an artfully curated mix of mid-century pieces, and vintage lighting. Home comforts, such as walls lined with books and glass cabinets full of ceramics, contribute to the hotel's relaxed intimacy and unpretentious appeal; it's a commercial space that feels like a restful residential home.

Across all projects, Studioilse balances the aesthetic and ergonomic with an emphasis on well-being and sustainability. Its collection of cream and earth-toned rugs, hammocks, and tapestries, designed for Barcelona-based textiles company Nanimarquina, for example, uses only hand-spun local fibers, without bleach or dyes, to reduce the environmental impact of production. The firm also brings accessible design excellence to low-or no-budget projects with social value. For a London community kitchen designed with chef Massimo Bottura, Crawford created an environment that not only appeals to guests but is also a desirable place to hire, which helps to fund its operation. Regardless of the client, scale, or category, Studioilse's ouput demonstrates a truly holistic approach, and a firm commitment to improve the lived, human experience.

5. Wellbeing Collection,
Nanimarquina
Textile Collection,
Temporary Display
Barcelona, Spain
2019

6. Private Home Sweden
Private Residence, Bathroom
Stockholm, Sweden
2017

Takenouchi Webb

Singapore

1. Empress
Restaurant
Singapore
2016

2. Esora
Restaurant
Singapore
2018

3. Whitegrass
Restaurant
Singapore
2018

3

Design duo Marc Webb and Naoko Takenouchi met on a project in the Thai city of Chiang Mai. In 2006 they established Takenouchi Webb and, in a reflection of the way their personal and professional lives have intersected, their firm's debut project—a historic chapel converted into a sleek restaurant—served as their wedding venue. Hospitality has continued as their area of expertise. Drawing upon the strength of their combined backgrounds—British-born Webb is an architect; Takenouchi was a restaurant designer in Tokyo—the pair have scooped numerous awards for the restaurant and bars they've designed in their home of Singapore.

Their designs often draw upon existing prompts from the site. For the Chinese restaurant Empress, built as a modern extension to the Asian Civilizations Museum in Singapore, Takenouchi Webb integrated its classical facade into their plans. The firm created an open-plan dining room showcasing the museum's external wall on one side and views of the Singapore River on the other. Throughout, subtle Chinese features appear, such as the Asian-inspired geometric screens that serve as room dividers. Red—China's much-loved national color—was chosen for the dining chairs' leather upholstery, adding a rich pop to the restaurant's sophisticated palette of gray marble and dark wood.

In contrast, the pint-sized Esora restaurant in Singapore is soft and soothing. Housed in a traditional Asian "shophouse" (a building for both residential and small business use) Takenouchi Webb transformed the Japanese restaurant's interior into a Minimalist sanctuary. A slab of silvery marble encloses the bar, which is complemented by wooden slatted screens and dining sets in the same pale pine. Above the chef's counter, a curved skylight overlaid in honeycomb *washi* paper fills the space with diffused light.

As a married, multinational team, Takenouchi Webb offers a unique fusion of perspectives to redefine Asia's design scene—one swanky spot at a time.

David Thulstrup

Copenhagen, Denmark

1. Noma
Restaurant
Copenhagen, Denmark
2018

2. Peter's House
Private Residence, Living Room
Copenhagen, Denmark
2015

3. Noma
Restaurant
Copenhagen, Denmark
2018

2

3

For acclaimed architect and designer David Thulstrup, the feeling that a space evokes is of fundamental importance. After working for Jean Nouvel and Peter Marino, he founded his studio in Copenhagen in 2009. Since then he has built a reputation for a detail-oriented approach that often sees him creating specially made pieces for his projects.

When Thulstrup was asked to design the new interiors of the world-famous Noma restaurant, he decided to approach it from a residential perspective. The premises—now housed in an eleven-building complex in a hippie enclave of Copenhagen—has been coined "The Village" by chef and co-owner René Redzepi. This sense of homegrown domesticity informs every aspect of Thulstrup's perspective, from the wooden boards that line the restaurant's ceilings and walls to the weighty smoked-oak plank that serves as a dining table. Drawing inspiration from the earthy landscape outside, materiality plays a central role in the design process. The service kitchen's custom-made terrazzo floor is crafted from river stones; a handmade cream brick wall in the lounge references retro Danish design. Much of the furniture is custom made, such as the ARV dining chair that Thulstrup created in collaboration with a local workshop, nodding to Scandinavia's lineage of traditional craftsmanship.

Similar precision was deployed at Chimney House in Copenhagen, a former water pumping station reimagined as a contemporary home for Danish design brand VIPP's concept hotel venture. Thulstrup has added bold architectural interventions, including a steel staircase that slices up the interior. True to form, he considered the smallest details, such as custom metal door handles for the bathroom.

On his website, Thulstrup states, "Everything is carefully selected, curated, or designed and nothing screams more than the other." It's an outlook that has defined his meticulous approach to design, ensuring a brand of Minimalism distinct in its depth.

4. Vester Voldgade
Private Residence, Living Room
Copenhagen, Denmark
2020

5. Chimney House
Hotel, Living Room
Copenhagen, Denmark
2018

5

Faye Toogood

London, UK

British designer Faye Toogood has never felt constrained by a particular discipline. Her creative output—ranging from furniture and other home furnishings to fashion and sculptural works—has been integral to her celebrated interior design practice, which sees coolly contemporary interiors populated with her own unique pieces.

After acquiring a history of art degree, Toogood's career began as decoration editor for the *World of Interiors* magazine. By 2008, she'd founded her eponymous studio, Toogood, whose works have been snapped up by leading art museums around the world. Toogood's roster of clients is diverse. Design-savvy individuals have commissioned her services for private homes in Ibiza, Spain, and Mayfair, London, and her fashion clients include Mulberry and Carhartt. The designer's own home has received her careful attention. When she and her husband bought the former residence of Swiss architect Walter Segal, she embarked upon an ambitious renovation. Paying homage to the building's 1960s origins, she created a pared-back simplicity that utilizes milky-white acoustic board ceilings, pine paneling, and original brick walls in neutral shades.

In 2016 Toogood brought her inimitable aesthetic to the Tapestry, a luxury residential development in King's Cross, London. The owner—a well-known television producer—wanted his penthouse apartment to have a sense of uncompromising Minimalism. Painting the walls a grayish-green shade of "slush," as she coined it, Toogood then polished them into a textured, swirling pattern that contrasts with the traditional parquet flooring. The public spaces remain imposing—a corner of the living area has Toogood's signature Roly-Poly chairs beneath a glass atrium—but Toogood took a different tack in the bedrooms. One of them has a velvet-upholstered bed and heavy drapes complemented by the mermaidlike shades of her artwork.

Unlike many of her contemporaries, Toogood lacks formal design training. But for this polymath, it's proven instrumental in establishing a practice that, like her, refuses to be pigeonholed.

1. North Hill
Private Residence, Living Room
London, UK
2018

2. Tapestry Penthouse
Private Residence, Living Room
London, UK
2017

3. Carhartt WIP Kings Cross
Store
London, UK
2017

4. Mulberry Regent Street
Store
London, UK
2018
[overleaf]

Virginia Tupker
Interiors

Darien, Connecticut, USA

1

A rising star of the interior design world, British-born, U.S.-based decorator Virginia Tupker has won praise for her distinctive designs across the United States. Design bible *Architectural Digest*, which included Tupker in its prestigious AD100 list in 2020, has described her as a "neotraditionalist"—one of a new generation of designers reviving a more traditional, bohemian aesthetic.

Tupker initially worked as interiors editor for *House & Garden* and *Vogue*, before a serendipitous commission to furnish a colleague's home led to a new career. Requests from fashion's elite soon flooded in, from a barn in the Hamptons, New York, for Moda Operandi cofounder Lauren Santo Domingo to a Manhattan apartment for fashion writer Derek Blasberg.

With a focus on rich colors, classic textiles, and fine antiques, Tupker's interiors often have a nostalgic, theatrical feel. A custom tattersall check by Ralph Lauren was used masterfully in Blasberg's bedroom, covering the walls, bed canopy, headboard, and a chaise longue. Tupker was unfazed by his requests for a sunken living room, an intimate "gossip room," and a secret passageway connecting the foyer to his bright blue study. She delivered all three with aplomb, according to Blasberg, sketching ideas and listening intently.

Tupker's more pared-back projects are no less impactful, revealing both her imagination and responsiveness as a designer. For a young family's chic beach house in Bridgehampton, New York, she committed to a largely blue-and-white design, carefully layering shades and patterns of each color to complement, not detract from, the home's colorful art, rattan lampshades, and wooden furniture.

Tupker's largely American portfolio is strongly influenced by her native Europe, from British country house classicism to the work of Italian architect and set designer Lorenzo Mongiardino. The resulting interiors, while hard to define, have a timeless elegance, making her a popular choice for fashionable clients looking for glamour from a bygone era.

1. Upper East Side Apartment
Private Residence, Living Room
New York City, New York, USA
2018

2. Bridgehampton Beach House
Private Residence, Living Room
Bridgehampton, New York, USA
2018

3. Upper East Side Apartment
Private Residence, Bedroom
New York City, New York, USA
2018

2

3

Vincent Van Duysen

Antwerp, Belgium

1. HH Penthouse
Private Residence,
Hall and Staircase
New York City, New York, USA
2015

2. VVD II Residence
Private Residence, Living Room
Antwerp, Belgium
2003

3. VVD II Attic
Private Residence,
Living Room/Studio
Antwerp, Belgium
2015

2

3

Belgian architect Vincent Van Duysen is a world-renowned tastemaker with a seminal portfolio. His timeless, textured interiors, have earned him prestigious awards, A-list clients, and five monographs during his thirty-year career.

Like the best of his trade, Van Duysen is an artisan, designing every small detail from the ground up. Restrained in color and sparsely furnished, his interiors share an intense physicality, born from an intuitive sense of material and form. He credits this, in part, to his early work with Italian architect Aldo Cibic, whose focus on abstraction and elemental shapes is an enduring inspiration.

Van Duysen's own apartment in Antwerp, Belgium—with bone colors, time-weathered woods, and custom modern touches—is a marvelous fusion of the raw and the refined. A decade after renovating the former notary house, Van Duysen peeled back the layers of time once again to create a "hermit's retreat" in the attic. Paying homage to its heritage, he sourced seventeenth-century oak to form a new floor and functional wall. The old conceals the new: a huge bluestone bathtub and gray gloss-lacquered shower.

This lightness of touch and respect for historical context is evident in Van Duysen's first hotel, August, in Antwerp. His team spent four years transforming the nineteenth-century Augustine convent into a sober, monochromatic sanctum. Guests sleep under wooden rafters that conjure the spirit of old Flemish farmhouses, while public spaces, such as the bar inside the former chapel, reflect their neoclassical past with tailor-made fixtures and fittings.

An illustrious ambassador for Belgian design, Van Duysen's influence cannot be overstated. His signature style of earthy beige tones, pale woods, black accents, and off-white linens—which was neither ubiquitous nor popular when he began his career in the 1990s—has been instrumental in defining the much admired, much emulated contemporary Belgian aesthetic.

4. VDC Residence
Private Residence,
Summer Living Room
Kortrijk, Belgium
2010

5. August
Hotel, Bar
Antwerp, Belgium
2019

Vincent Van Duysen

Gert Voorjans

Antwerp, Belgium

1

284

Antwerp, Belgium-born Gert Voorjans is not interested in creating historical rooms, but instead takes a rational approach to assembling art, textiles, and pieces of furniture that, together, create a magically warm, stimulating ambience. There will be bold dashes of color—a chartreuse green or a bright violet—and striking contrasts; he is not afraid to pair a silk damask wallpaper with a Sterling Ruby abstract painting. This approach has attracted clients such as Mick Jagger, fashion journalist Nina Garcia, and a range of residential, corporate, and retail commissions. Whatever the project, he achieves a refined European coziness that is carefully tailored to the client's tastes.

Voorjans was born into a family of furniture traders and carpenters and studied interior architecture in Hasselt, Belgium, when he learned to really "see" the bones of a building and to work with, instead of against, its structure. Something of a dandy himself, his projects have often been intimately linked to fashion. Since 1995 he has designed all the stores for his friend Dries Van Noten. Bucking a trend for Minimalist white cube retail spaces, he creates boutiques of elegance and comfort, using flat planes of color, lampshades, couches, curios, and paintings and customizing the store to its locality. The Tokyo branch, for example, blends concrete Minimalism with a luxurious leather couch, gold carpets, and a pair of 10-feet (3-meter) high, seventeenth-century Gérard de Lairesse mythological paintings.

Under his touch, even Schloss Untersiemau in Bavaria, a drafty medieval castle, is transformed into a comfortable family home. Voorjans brings witty anachronistic grandeur into play with trompe l'oeil ceilings, classical statuary, and pink marble columns, but he also adds characteristically zingy printed textiles, pale wood flooring, and Pop art pieces, which creates a relaxed and modern family space. Eclecticism, craftsmanship, and a joyful exuberance combine to achieve a highly cultured yet never stuffy luxury.

1. Schloss Untersiemau
Private Residence, Music Room
Coburg, Germany
2015

2. Schloss Untersiemau
Private Residence, Garden Room
Coburg, Germany
2015

3. Dries Van Noten Tokyo
Store
Tokyo, Japan
2009

4. Jim Thompson
Showroom/Salon
Antwerp, Belgium
2020

5. AD Intérieurs
Temporary Display,
Artist's Dressing Room
Paris, France
2017

Joyce Wang

Hong Kong;
London, UK

Since Joyce Wang opened her studio in 2011, she has designed lush, cinematic interiors around the world for clients that include the Hollywood Roosevelt hotel in Los Angeles and the Mott 32 restaurant franchise. In 2019 her aptitude for high-octane glamour was showcased in another medium at Art Basel Hong Kong when, in collaboration with Swarovski, Wang created a kaleidoscopic light installation made from hundreds of crystals.

Hawaii-born Wang was educated in the United Kingdom, studied architecture and materials science at the Massachusetts Institute of Technology in Cambridge, then collected degrees in London and the Netherlands. This international upbringing has shaped her style, which delves deep into the intricacies of different cultures to deliver visionary results.

Inspired by the immersive approach of legends such as Carlo Scarpa and Adolf Loos, Wang's designs transport visitors into another world. At the Peruvian restaurant Ichu, Wang pays homage to the country's mountainous terrain with excavated fossils, a stepped timber ceiling, and artworks that mirror the jagged beauty of raw rock formations. It doesn't matter that Ichu is in Hong Kong—each facet of the restaurant, from materials to color palette, evokes a vibrant South American landscape thousands of miles away.

At the Mandarin Oriental Hotel, near London's Hyde Park, the early twentieth-century property's extensive renovation is a nod to its leafy surroundings. Noting the ducks paddling outside, Wang introduced a feather motif pattern on silk-covered wall panels in the hotel's suites; the changing seasons are referenced in abstract rugs that mirror the patterns cast by falling leaves. Hand-etched mirrors, velvet-upholstered chairs, and jeweled detailing on the light fixtures completed her vision: an English fairy tale brought to life.

For Wang, this element of escapism is crucial. "I design spaces that make people feel great," she confides on her website. "I want people to feel confident, to lose themselves, and to have fun."

1. Ichu
Restaurant, Private Dining Room
Hong Kong
2018

2. Mandarin Oriental Hyde Park
Hotel, Penthouse Suite
London, UK
2019

3. Mandarin Oriental Hyde Park
Hotel, Penthouse Suite
London, UK
2019

4. Mott 32 Singapore
Restaurant
Singapore
2019
[overleaf]

Kelly Wearstler

Los Angeles,
California, USA

1. Beverly Hills Residence
Private Residence, Living Room
Beverly Hills, California, USA
2018

2. Beverly Hills Residence
Private Residence,
Powder Room Vestibule
Beverly Hills, California, USA
2018

3. Malibu Residence
Private Residence, Living Room
Malibu, California, USA
2009

Los Angeles-based designer Kelly Wearstler hardly needs an introduction, but as with her stunning designs, the details of her success are hard to resist. Wearstler credits her love of natural materials and processes—gorgeous marble, luxe fur, metal surfaces with a romantic patina—to her childhood in South Carolina spent by the shore. Her early passion, combined with an education and training in Boston and New York, led to Wearstler becoming a worldwide phenomenon by the 2000s, known for her unique Maximalist vision for boutique hotels and her vibrant commercial and residential projects.

Spaces designed by Wearstler draw on a range of influences: 1930s Hollywood glamour, mid-century European design, fashion, the graphic arts. Unlikely combinations of eras and forms are provocative yet thoroughly thought out, buoyed by a postmodern sensibility in which anything goes but everything comes together. At a Hillcrest residence in Beverly Hills, for example, seating upholstered in a delicate geometric pattern is at home alongside a bold metal-and-glass table in a room crowned by the home's original neoclassical moldings. In a renovation of a 1901 townhouse on New York's Madison Avenue, Wearstler uses color and form ingeniously in a bedroom, adding warmth with a playful, orange-and-lilac bed that has a headboard shaped like a pair of demurely smiling lips.

At a 2019 project in the luxury hotel Santa Monica Proper, visitors can rest in arched alcoves in the lobby after passing by a hand-carved, seashell-inspired reception desk—a detail evoking Wearstler's childhood and the hotel's location. The designer's omnivorous interest in contemporary art and talent for spotting estate sale treasures have ensured that her aesthetic constantly evolves, with the best of art and design, past and present, brought together to introduce visitors to new possibilities.

4. Madison Avenue
Private Residence, Bedroom
New York City, New York, USA
2017

5. Santa Monica Proper
Hotel, Lobby
Santa Monica, California, USA
2019

Bunny Williams

New York City,
New York, USA

1. New York City Pied-à-Terre
Private Residence, Living Room
New York City, New York, USA
2014

2. Palm Beach Residence
Private Residence, Living Room
Palm Beach, Florida, USA
2016

3. Palm Beach Residence
Private Residence,
Breakfast Room
Palm Beach, Florida, USA
2016

Nothing less than an interior design legend, Bunny Williams honed her craft during a twenty-two-year tenure at the esteemed design firm Parish-Hadley. She established her own studio in 1988 and is known for her refined aesthetic, decorating homes for those with a love of art, travel, and history. Her work can be seen in country estates, city apartments, and coastal retreats across the United States and beyond.

In 2003, Williams took on Elizabeth Lawrence as an intern, and after only fourteen years the two became business partners. Lawrence is now tasked with co-leading the studio, delivering what it described as "thoughtful design" to the next generation of clients—a harmonious blend of classical, historic and contemporary touches, with careful attention to detail. The result is layered, lived-in interiors that are opulent but never flashy. Surprising color twists are typical; the entrance hall to Williams's own New York residence, for example, is electric blue.

In a New York City apartment designed by the studio, twisted black columns frame the living room, giving it a slightly baroque feel. These are cleverly juxtaposed with Modernist geometric flooring. The seating is neutral, sharply designed, beautifully upholstered, and arranged with symmetry. A chunky glass coffee table injects a sense of metropolitan chic, while books, flowers, and the hallway beyond provide pops of joyous color. The design for a Palm Beach residence in Florida is on a much grander scale, yet the approach avoids stuffy period pastiche. The unexpected cherry-blossom pink breakfast room walls have been teamed with contemporary floral art and a striking patterned rug. In a living room, the atmosphere is congenial, with sociably arranged seating, cozy wood paneling, an eye-catching rug, and more exuberant wall art.

Indisputably, Bunny Williams has been responsible for fashioning a quintessential American style: beautiful, cultured spaces that are both contemporary and timeless—and above all, comfortable, practical, and liveable.

Woodson & Rummerfield's House of Design

Los Angeles, California, USA

1. Hollywood Residence
Private Residence, Living Room
Hollywood, California, USA
2017

2. Los Angeles Residence
Private Residence, Dining Room
Los Angeles, California, USA
2016

3. Los Angeles Residence
Private Residence, Bedroom
Los Angeles, California, USA
2016

4. Palm Springs Residence
Private Residence, Living Room
Palm Springs, California, USA
2015

Los Angeles designers Ron Woodson and Jaime Rummerfield, the eponymous principals behind Woodson & Rummerfield's House of Design, have coined a new word to describe their studio's style: "modage." A portmanteau of "modern" and "vintage," it's an apt description of the aesthetic Woodson and Rummerfield have envisioned for the houses of Los Angeles. The duo not only fill their clients' rooms with curated vintage pieces and custom-made contemporary furniture but also with an unmistakable, irrepressible attitude that invigorates these high-octane interiors with a feeling of festivity. For Woodson and Rummerfied, good design is an occasion for celebration. Their high-drama, high-style sensibility is fed by the glamour of Old Hollywood and the eclecticism of contemporary fashion. (Coincidentally, *High Style* is also the name of the book Woodson and Rummerfield published in 2008, itself a beautiful object to behold.)

Since 2004 the designers have helped develop Los Angeles's now-recognizable, glitzy but tasteful ethos: exuberant strokes of peacock blue and bitter-lemon green, plenty of white, elegant finishes, and textured rugs. For a client with a house in the historic neighborhood of Fremont Place and a prodigious art collection, for example, they orchestrated a wall of Andy Warhol's *Marilyn Monroe* overlooking a staircase with a Diane von Furstenberg emerald-colored runner, which sports a leopard making its way upstairs. Elsewhere in the house, another Warhol shares space comfortably with an antique-style bust, one of the designers' signature ornaments.

In recent years Woodson and Rummerfield have been active in the effort to maintain and preserve historic homes, such as those in Fremont. Their nonprofit SIA Projects works to get landmark status for historic structures, enlists professionals who can help with preservation, and spreads awareness about the value and importance of such architecture. Historically conscious and very much plugged in, these designers are prepared to help the party continue.

5. Hancock Park Residence
Private Residence, Living Room
Los Angeles, California, USA
2017

6. Hancock Park Residence
Private Residence, Entryway
Los Angeles, California, USA
2017

Yabu Pushelberg

New York City, New York, USA;
Toronto, Ontario, Canada

1. London EDITION
Hotel, Lobby Bar
London, UK
2013

2. Katsuya Brickell
Restaurant
Miami, Florida, USA
2018

3. Paradise Club,
Times Square EDITION
Hotel, Nightclub
New York City, New York, USA
2019

4. Berners Tavern,
London EDITION
Hotel, Restaurant
London, UK
2013
[overleaf]

2

3

Over its forty years of experience, the acclaimed Toronto- and New York-based design studio Yabu Pushelberg has left an indelible mark on the profession. Founded in 1980 by George Yabu and Glenn Pushelberg, this two-man partnership began by outfitting a local dry cleaner and the city's then-new Club Monaco locations. It has since gone on to design commercial and hospitality properties around the world, including Bergdorf Goodman's flagship New York store and multiple Park Hyatt and Four Seasons hotels.

Yabu Pushelberg is a master of hotel design. Recognizing a hotel's inherent mutability and understanding the way visitors use its spaces is fundamental to its design process. Travelers staying at the London EDITION hotel, for example, can "people watch" in the lobby from exquisite Donald Judd-inspired green velvet sofas, or have a drink at the blackened-steel bar. For the hotel's restaurant, Berners Tavern, the studio created an atmosphere that is both intimate and festive, with rift-cut oak tables, mohair banquettes, and walls overflowing with curated art. In 2017 the studio achieved a similar effect at Miami's Katsuya Brickell restaurant, using large, playful, headlike installations hanging from the ceiling to contrast with the restaurant's low-level lighting and wooden surfaces. In 2019, at the Times Square EDITION hotel in Manhattan, Yabu Pushelberg delivered another iconic dining space, this time beneath a "green" ceiling of plants, while using a calm, muted palette for the rooms to create a respite from the busy streets.

Today, Yabu Pushelberg is a powerhouse of sleek, conscientious, monumental design. The studio continues to expand, hiring specialized staff to approach design projects holistically, developing everything in-house—from architecture to lighting. This ceaseless professional momentum may be what allows Yabu and Pushelberg's personal lives to remain steady, having also been a couple all this time.

Teo Yang Studio

Seoul, South Korea

1

Teo Yang has a flair for translating the past into the present day. A rising star in Seoul's sought-after creative scene, the interior designer's singular vision plucks distinctive design cues from facets of Korean heritage and places them in a contemporary context. His clientele extends from the illustrious, such as South Korea's first lady, to the ordinary; in 2016 Yang transformed a rest stop into the world's most Instagram-worthy highway bathroom.

Although his namesake design studio specializes in residential and commercial projects, Yang's creativity often extends beyond interiors. For *Wallpaper** Hand-made, the magazine's annual exhibition project, he drew upon the rich symbolism of Korean garden design to craft a trio of sculptural birdbaths. Luxury brands have been quick to court him, too: a collaboration with Fendi produced a regal resin-and-lacquer version of their Peekaboo handbag, and Swiss watchmaker Vacheron Constantin commissioned him to create miniature 3-D-printed pagodas for an exhibition.

In Yang's own home, Gyedong Hanok Residence, this trademark retelling of classical aesthetics is displayed with a dazzling effect. After purchasing the *hanok*—a low-rise, traditional wooden house built around a central courtyard—Yang carefully renovated the space with deference to its historic features. Vaulted wooden beams and intricate geometric patterns on the sliding doors complement Yang's impressive collection of Asian art and artifacts.

In Samseong-dong Residence—a private home owned by an art collector—Yang's nods to Korean design are subtler. The sleek interior, with its pale wooden floors and matching ceilings, is streamlined, with corridors interrupted by only a built-in bench or exhibited artworks. In the enveloping calm of the television room, sliding screen doors at one end create a mood that feels almost spalike.

The ethos behind Yang's creations, regardless of the client, is expressed in his motto, "past in the future," which is apparent in his approach to mixing modern with tradition.

1. Gyedong Hanok Residence
Private Residence, Living Room
Seoul, South Korea
2020

2. Samseong-dong Residence
Private Residence, Living Room
Seoul, South Korea
2020

3. Samseong-dong Residence
Private Residence, Media Room
Seoul, South Korea
2020

4. Wellness K, Kukje Gallery
Restaurant and Wellness Center,
Locker Room and Lounge
Seoul, South Korea
2020

1. Ixelles
Private Residence, Entryway
Brussels, Belgium
2016

2. Ixelles
Private Residence, Living Room
Brussels, Belgium
2016

3. Château de Fabrègues
Private Residence, Dining Room
Aups, France
2012

Pierre Yovanovitch

Paris, France; New York City, New York, USA

A visionary interior architect with an haute couture background, Pierre Yovanovitch is one of the most celebrated and sought-after designers of his generation. With offices in Paris and New York, he boasts an exceptionally refined, distinctive portfolio, which includes some of the world's most design-conscious addresses, from the homes of leading art collectors to the fashionable Hélène Darroze restaurant at London's Connaught Hotel.

After eight years of designing menswear for the legendary fashion designer Pierre Cardin, Yovanovitch began to apply a couturier's eye to interiors, establishing his namesake atelier in 2001. Cardin's elegantly avant-garde aesthetic remains a major influence, but Yovanovitch's style of modern French design is matchless. Classical spaces are transformed into contemporary works of theater, infused with drama and whimsy and filled with unusual colors and curvilinear geometric shapes. Nowhere demonstrates this better than Château de Fabrègues, the designer's home in Provence. The seventeenth-century castle and chapel are the ultimate expression of his taste and creativity: a symbiosis of art and architecture and a veritable museum of twentieth-century design, including mid-century Scandinavian masterpieces. Humble pine furniture by Swedish architect Axel Einar Hjorth sits perfectly with otherworldly lighting by Finnish designer Paavo Tynell and striking contemporary art. It is a playful, idiosyncratic temple of design where artistic freedom reigns supreme.

Hôtel Le Coucou, Yovanovitch's fifty-five-room masterpiece in the French Alps, also transports visitors into an artistic, playfully sophisticated world. Guests enter via a pine-paneled lobby under a spectacular glass-domed ceiling that features an owl-themed fresco by the artist Matthieu Cossé and can relax in a statement spa that, with its repeating arched coves, resembles a painting by Giorgio de Chirico.

With a string of prestigious awards, including *Wallpaper** magazine's Designer of the Year 2019, and a successful monograph under his belt, Yovanovitch is an extraordinary talent, revered for creating exciting, inspirational interiors that are symphonic and wholly unique.

4. Le Coucou
Hotel and Spa, Lobby
Méribel, France
2019

5. Le Coucou
Hotel and Spa,
Guest Suite
Méribel, France
2019

BIOGRAPHIES

A Work of Substance
Maxime Dautresme
Born 1978 in Rio de Janeiro. Based in Hong Kong. Established 2010. **Selected Commissions:** Goodman Westlink, Hong Kong, 2019; Khromis, Hong Kong, 2018; The Fleming, Hong Kong, 2017; Osteria Marzia, Hong Kong, 2017; Origin Grill, Shangri-La Hotel, Singapore, 2017. **Clients include:** Sulwhasoo, Hermès, Rosewood Hotels, Shangri-La Group, and Black Sheep Restaurants. **Awards:** Merit, DFA Design for Asia Award, 2020; winner, Hong Kong's Best New Restaurant, T.Dining Best Restaurants Awards, 2019; finalist, *Interior Design*'s Best of Year Awards, 2018; winner, Restaurant & Bar Design Awards, 2018.
aworkofsubstance.com
@aworkofsubstance

JJ Acuna / Bespoke Studio
James Acuna
Born 1980 in Manila, Philippines. Based in Hong Kong and Manila. Established 2015. **Selected Commissions:** XiaoTing at Four Seasons Hotel Macau, 2021; Hansik Goo, Hong Kong, 2020; The Central Sweets, Yangon, Myanmar, 2018; Tokyo Tokyo Trinoma Flagship, Manila, 2018; Little Bao at 72 Courtyard, Bangkok, Thailand, 2016. **Press and Publications:** *Forbes*, February 2020; *South China Morning Post*, January 2020; *Design Anthology*, July 2020; *Tatler Homes Singapore*, October 2020; *Wallpaper**, April 2017. **Clients include:** ZS Hospitality Group, Nha Trang Catering Service, Hansbury, Sands China, and Analogue Enterprises. **Awards:** Interior Designer of the Year, Design Anthology Awards, 2019; longlist, Emerging Designer of the Year, Frame Awards, 2019; Best Interior Design, T.Dining Best Restaurants Awards, 2018.
jjabespoke.com
@jja.bespoke.studio

Apartment 48
Rayman Boozer
Born 1960 in Anniston, Alabama. Based in New York. Established 1994. **Selected Commissions:** Rent the Runway, New York, 2018; Build Series Production Studio, New York, 2017; Vox Media Creative Lounge, New York, 2017; AOL Flagship Offices, New York, 2014; and numerous private residences. **Press and Publications:** *Better Homes & Gardens*, September 2019; *Elle Decor*, March 2019; *AD*, January 2019. **Clients include:** Verizon Media, Build Series, AOL, Vox Media, and numerous private clients. **Awards and Events:** *Elle Decor* A-List; Design on a Dime, 2019; Hampton Designer Showhouse, 2017; Black Artists + Designers Guild, founding member.
apartment48.com
@apartment48 / @raymanboozer

ASH
Ari Heckman, Jonathan Minkoff, Will Cooper, and Andrew Bowen
Heckman born 1983 in Providence, Rhode Island; Minkoff born 1984 in Washington, D.C.; Cooper born 1987 in Fort Worth, Texas; Bowen born 1990 in Bay Shore, New York. Based in New York and Los Angeles. Established 2009. **Selected Commissions:** Hotel Peter & Paul, New Orleans, 2018; The Siren Hotel, Detroit, Michigan, 2018; Glassworks Bushwick, Brooklyn, 2018; The Dean Hotel, Providence, Rhode Island, 2014. **Press and Publications:**

More Than Just a House: At Home with Collectors and Creators (Rizzoli, 2020); *Vogue Living Australia*, October 2020; *AD*, August 2020; *Forbes*, September 2019; *New York Times*, March 2019. **Awards:** AD100
ashnyc.com
@ash_newyork

Batiik Studio
Rebecca Benichou
Born 1986 in Nice, France. Based in Paris. Established 2014. **Selected Commissions:** numerous private residences; **Press and Publications:** *Elle Decoration France*, October 2020; *Côté Paris*, July 2020; *Milk Decoration*, November 2019; *Architectures ÀVivre*, July 2019; *AD*, September 2019. **Clients include:** Amélie Maison d'Art and numerous private clients.
batiik.fr
@batiikstudio

Kelly Behun
Born in Pittsburgh. Based in New York. Established 2001. **Selected Commissions:** 1228 Madison Avenue, in collaboration with Robert A.M. Stern Architects, 2021; numerous private residences; and exclusive product and furniture lines with The Rug Company, Hudson Valley Lighting, and The Invisible Collection. **Press and Publications:** *Interiors: The Greatest Rooms of the Century* (Phaidon, 2019); *AD*, June 2019; *May I Come In?: Discovering the World in Other People's Houses* (Abrams, 2018); *Elle Decor*, November 2015; *The Complete Kagan: Vladimir Kagan, A Lifetime of Avant-Garde Design* (Pointed Leaf Press, 2004). **Clients include:** numerous private clients. **Awards:** AD100, *Elle Decor* A-List.
kellybehun.com
@kellybehunstudio

BENSLEY
Bill Bensley
Born 1959 in Orange County, California. Based in Bangkok, Thailand, and Bali, Indonesia. Established 1989. **Selected Commissions:** Shinta Mani Wild, BENSLEY Collection, Southern Cardamom National Park, Cambodia, 2019; Capella Ubud, Bali, Indonesia, 2018; Rosewood Luang Prabang, Nauea Village, Laos, 2018; JW Marriott Phu Quoc Emerald Bay Resort & Spa, Bai Khem, Phu Quoc, Vietnam, 2017. **Press and Publications:** "Sensible Sustainable Solutions," white paper for the hotel industry (January 2020); *Designing Paradise with Bill Bensley*, television series, 2019; *Escapism Volume 1* (Kodansha, 2017); *Paradise by Design: Tropical Residences and Resorts by Bensley Design Studios* (Periplus Editions 2008). **Clients include:** Dinglong China, Six Senses Hotels Resorts Spas, Four Seasons Hotels and Resorts, Rosewood Hotels & Resorts, Marriott International, and Capella Hotels & Resorts. **Awards:** AD100; Interior Designer of the Year, IDCS, 2020; Platinum Winner, Muse Design Awards, 2020; TTG Luxury Travel Awards, 2020; Eco-Spa of the Year, Destination Deluxe Awards, 2019.
bensley.com
@billbensley

Sig Bergamin
Born 1953 in São Paulo, Brazil, where the firm is also based. Established 1980s. **Selected Commissions:** Bal Harbour Apartment, Miami, 2019; Iporanga Beach House,

Guarujá, Brazil, 2019; Tropical House, São Paulo, 2019. **Press and Publications:** *AD Middle East*, March 2019; *Maximalism* (Assouline, 2018); *AD*, March 2017. **Clients include:** numerous private clients. **Awards:** AD100; *Elle Decor* A-List.
sigbergamin.com.br
@sigbergamin

Deborah Berke Partners
Deborah Berke
Born in New York, where the firm is also based. Established 1982. **Selected Commissions:** 21c Museums Hotels, multiple locations; 432 Park Avenue, New York; and numerous private residences. **Press and Publications:** *Wallpaper**, July 2020; *New York Times*, April 2020; *Galerie*, October 2019; *Wall Street Journal*, June 2019; *House Rules: An Architect's Guide to Modern Life* (Rizzoli, 2017). **Clients include:** Yale University, Princeton University, Brown University, University of Pennsylvania, and Harvard Law School. **Awards:** AD100; winner, Interior Design, National Design Awards, Cooper Hewitt, Smithsonian Design Museum, 2017.
dberke.com
@deborahberkepartners

Nate Berkus Associates
Nate Berkus and Lauren Buxbaum Gordon
Berkus born 1971 in Orange County, California; Buxbaum Gordon born 1980 in Chicago. Based in New York, Chicago, and Los Angeles. Established 1995. **Selected Commissions:** Celebrity Cruise Sunset Bar, 2021; West Hollywood Residence, 2020; Upper East Side Residence, New York, 2020; andSons Chocolatiers, Beverly Hills, 2019; Chicago Townhouse, Chicago, 2017; Nate Berkus Suite at the Loews Regency, New York, 2015. **Press and Publications:** *Robb Report*, October 2020; *Elle Decor*, October 2020; *Hamptons*, Summer 2020; *Elle Decor*, Summer 2020; *AD*, May 2020; *The Things That Matter* (Spiegel & Grau, 2012) *Home Rules: Transform the Place You Live into a Place You'll Love* (Hyperion, 2004). **Clients include:** Charlize Theron, Ricky Martin, Karlie Kloss, Katie Lee, and Oprah Winfrey. **Awards:** AD100; *Elle Decor* A-List; honorary Doctorate of Fine Arts in Interior Design (Berkus), New York School of Interior Design, 2019.
nateberkus.com
@NateBerkus / @LaurenBuxbaumGordon

Linda Boronkay
Born 1982 in Budapest, Hungary. Based in London. Established 2008. **Selected Commissions:** Four Seasons Fort Lauderdale, Florida, due for completion in 2022; Soho House Hong Kong and Soho House Mumbai, 2019; Soho House Amsterdam and White City House, London, 2018. **Press and Publications:** *The Times*, ongoing design column; *Harper's Bazaar Netherlands*, June 2020; *Dezeen*, June 2019; *Elle Decoration UK*, March 2019; *Wallpaper**, April 2018. **Clients include:** Soho House, Four Seasons Hotels and Resorts, Starwood Capital Group, Caprice Holdings, and Morgans Hotel Group. **Awards:** winner, Bar, Club, or Lounge and Hotel Newbuild, Ahead Europe Awards, 2019; Interior Designer of the Year, IDEA Awards, 2014.
lindaboronkay.com
@lindaboronkay

Martin Brudnizki Design Studio

Martin Brudnizki

Born 1966 in Stockholm. Based in London and New York. Established 2000. **Selected Commissions:** Annabel's, London, 2018; The Beekman, New York, 2015; The Ivy, London, 2015; Soho Beach House, Miami, 2010; Scott's, London, 2006. **Clients include:** The Birley Group, Caprice Holdings, Soho House, Sydell Group, and the Royal Academy of Arts. **Awards:** AD100; *Elle Decor* A-list; Top 100 Interior Designers, *House & Garden*, 2019.
mbds.com
@m_b_d_s_ / @martinbrudnizki

Martyn Lawrence Bullard

Born 1967 in Bromley, UK. Based in Los Angeles. Established 1993. **Selected Commissions:** Capard House, County Laois, Ireland, 2020; Four Seasons Private Residences, Los Angeles, 2019; Hotel Californian, Santa Barbara, California, 2018; The Residences at Seafire, Grand Cayman, Caribbean, 2017; Castello di Santa Eurasia, Perugia, Italy, 2013. **Press and Publications:** *Veranda*, June 2020; *Elle Decoration UK*, March 2020; *AD*, February 2020; *Design & Decoration* (Rizzoli, 2016); *Live, Love & Decorate* (Rizzoli, 2011). **Clients include:** Kylie Jenner, Cindy Crawford, Tommy Hilfiger, RuPaul, and Cher. **Awards:** AD100; *Elle Decor* A-List; Design Icon 2020, Las Vegas Market; Top 25 Most Influential Interior Designers, *Hollywood Reporter*, 2012; International Interior Designer of the Year, Andrew Martin, 2010.
martynlawrencebullard.com
@martynbullard

Rafael de Cárdenas

Born 1974 in New York, where the firm is also based. Established 2006. **Selected Commissions:** MAC Cosmetics Store, concept design, global application, 2020; Glossier Headquarters, New York, 2018; Au Pont Rouge, St. Petersburg, Russia, 2015; Baccarat Flagship, New York, 2013; Wynwood Building Exterior Mural, Miami, Florida, 2011; and numerous private residences. **Press and Publications:** *AD*, May 2019; *Elle Decor*, February 2019; *T: The New York Times Style Magazine*, September 2017; *Rafael de Cárdenas: Architecture at Large* (Rizzoli, 2017); *Powershop 5: New Retail Design* (Frame, 2016). **Clients include:** Nike, Kenzo, Baccarat, Glossier, and Nordstrom. **Awards:** AD 100; Designer of the Year, Maison&Objet Americas, 2016.
rafaeldecardenas.com
@rafaeldecardenas.ltd

Darryl Carter

Born 1961 in Washington, D.C., where the firm is also based. Established 1998. **Selected Commissions:** Métier, Washington, D.C., 2016; Kinship, Washington, D.C., 2015; and numerous private residences. **Press and Publications:** *Milieu*, Spring 2018; *AD*, March 2017; *Elle Decor*, September 2014; *Veranda*, April 2014; *House Beautiful*, February 2014. **Clients include:** numerous private clients. **Awards:** AD100; *Elle Decor* A-List.
darrylcarter.com
@darrylcarterdesign

Cristina Celestino

Born 1980 in San Vito al Tagliamento, Italy. Based in Milan. Established 2013. **Selected Commissions:** Palazzo Avino, Ravello, Italy, 2020; 28 Posti, Milan, 2020; Experimental Cocktail Club, Venice, 2019; Fornace Brioni Headquarters, Gonzaga, Italy, 2019; The Pink Closet, Ravello, Italy, 2019. **Press and Publications:** *Elle Decoration UK*, June 2020; *AD Italy*, April 2020; *Vogue Living Australia*, February 2020; *Elle Decoration France*, February 2020; *Wallpaper**, January 2020. **Clients include:** Fendi, Palazzo Avino, Sergio Rossi, Experimental Group, and cc-tapis. **Awards:** AD100; winner, Wall Covering, Elle Deco International Design Awards, 2020; winner, Red Dot Design Award, 2020; shortlist, *Wallpaper** Design Awards, 2020.
cristinacelestino.com
@cristinacelestino

Champalimaud Design

Alexandra Champalimaud

Born 1952 in Lisbon, Portugal. Based in New York. Established 1981. **Selected Commissions:** Raffles Singapore, 2019; Beverly Hills Hotel Bungalows, 2019; Su Casa at Dorado Beach, Ritz-Carlton Reserve, Dorado, Puerto Rico, 2019; Fairmont Gold, Fairmont Royal York, 2019; Halekulani Okinawa, 2019. **Press and Publications:** *Forbes*, August 2020; *Sleeper* (no. 91), July 2020; *AD Russia*, June 2020; *Condé Nast Traveler*, May 2020; *Elle Decoration Country* (no. 14), Spring/Summer 2019. **Clients include:** Dorchester Collection and YTL Hotels. **Awards:** *Elle Decor* A-List; Hot List, *Condé Nast Traveler*, 2020; Best Suite, Ahead Americas Awards, 2020; Lawrence Israel Prize, Fashion Institute of Technology, 2019; Best Hotel Design, Pinnacle Awards, *Hotelier*, 2019; Hospitality Giant, *Interior Design*, 2019.
champalimaud.design
@champalimauddesign / @alexandrachampalimaud

CHZON

Dorothée Meilichzon

Born 1982 in Boulogne-Billancourt, France. Based in Paris. Established 2009. **Selected Commissions:** Il Palazzo Experimental, Venice, 2019; Menorca Experimental, Menorca, Spain, 2018; Hotel des Grands Boulevards, Paris, 2018; Balagan, Paris, 2017; Hotel Bachaumont, Paris, 2015. **Press and Publications:** *Wohn!Design*, July 2020; *House & Garden*, March 2020; *Arquitectura y Diseño*, January 2020; *AD Mexico*, November 2019. **Clients include:** Experimental Group, Gregory Marchand, Samy Marciano, Liberté, and Vitra. **Awards:** AD100; Le FD100; Designer of the Year, Maison&Objet, 2015.
chzon.com
@dorotheemeilichzon

Commune Design

Roman Alonso and Steven Johanknecht

Alonso born 1966 in Caracas, Venezuela; Johanknecht born 1958 in Long Island, New York. Established 2004. **Selected Commissions:** Ace Hotel Kyoto, Japan, 2020; Breadblok, Santa Monica, California, 2020; National Park Cabin, Angeles National Forest, California, 2019; Santa Monica Apartment, Santa Monica, California, 2018; Los Feliz Spanish Colonial, Los Angeles, 2015. **Press and Publications:** *Design Commune* (Abrams, 2020); *AD*, November 2020; *AD Spain*, September 2020; *Monocle*, July/August 2020; *Telegraph*, June 2020; *Commune: Designed in California* (Abrams, 2010). **Clients include:** Atelier Ace, Chez Panisse Foundation, Google, Goop, LACMA, and Tartine. **Awards:** AD100; *Elle Decor* A-List; winner, Interior Design, National Design Awards, Cooper Hewitt, Smithsonian Design Museum, 2015; Best New Hotel, *Wallpaper** Design Awards, 2015.
communedesign.com
@communedesign

Vincenzo De Cotiis

Born 1958 in Gonzaga, Italy. Based in Milan. Established 1997. **Selected Commissions:** numerous private residences. **Press and Publications:** *Vogue Living Australia*, July/August 2020; *T: The New York Times Style Magazine*, April 2020; *AD*, April 2020; *Cultured Magazine*, March 2020; *Vincenzo De Cotiis: Works* (Rizzoli Electa, 2019); *The Touch: Spaces Designed for the Senses* (Gestalten, 2019); *Interiors: The Greatest Rooms of the Century* (Phaidon, 2019). **Clients include:** numerous private clients. **Exhibitions:** *Book 1. Works*, Vincenzo De Cotiis Gallery, Milan, 2019–20; *Éternal*, Carpenters Workshop Gallery, Paris, 2019; *En Plein Air*, Vincenzo De Cotiis Gallery, Milan, and Carpenters Workshop Gallery, London and San Francisco, 2018–19.
decotiis.it
@vdecotiis

Design Research Studio

Tom Dixon

Born 1959 in Sfax, Tunisia. Based in London. Established 2002 (Design Research Studio, established 2007). **Selected Commissions:** The Manzoni, Milan, 2019; Gardening Will Save the World, RHS Chelsea Flower Show, London, 2019; Pullman Paris Centre-Bercy, 2019; The Coal Office, London, 2018; IKEA Delaktig furniture collection, 2018. **Press and Publications:** *Financial Times: How To Spend It*, June 2020; *Dezeen*, June 2020; *Wallpaper**, November 2019; *Elle Decoration UK*, December 2018; *Dixonary: Illuminations, Revelations and Post-rationalizations from a Chaotic Mind* (Violette, 2013). **Clients include:** IKEA, Harry's, and Native Union. **Awards:** winner, Elle Decoration British Design Awards, 2019; winner, London Design Medal, British Land Celebration of Design Awards, 2019; silver medalist, RHS Chelsea Flower, 2019; Designer of the Year, Maison&Objet, 2014; OBE for services to British Design, 2001.
tomdixon.net
@tomdixonstudio

Dimorestudio

Britt Moran and Emiliano Salci

Moran born 1973 in North Carolina, USA; Salci born 1972 in Arezzo, Italy. Based in Milan. Established 2003. **Selected Commissions:** Dior, St. Tropez, 2019; Fendi, London, 2017, and Monte Carlo, 2018; Leo's, The Arts Club, London, 2017; Palazzo Privé Fendi, Rome, 2015. **Press and Publications:** *AD France*, January/February 2019; *AD*, January 2019; *The Design City: Milan: Extraordinary Lab* (Forma, 2018); *Kinfolk* (no. 23), February 2017; *Financial Times: Superior Interiors*, October 2016. **Clients include:** Dior, Fendi, The Arts Club, Aesop, and Grupo Habita. **Awards and Events:** AD100; Salone del Mobile, Milan, 2019; PAD London, 2019; Miart, Milan, 2019; Design Miami/Basel, Switzerland, 2016.
dimorestudio.eu
@dimorestudio

Joseph Dirand

Born 1974 in Paris, where the firm is also based. Established 2000. **Selected Commissions:** Le Jardinier, New York, 2019; Shun, New York, 2019; Girafe, Paris, 2018; Four Seasons, The Surf Club, Miami, 2017. **Press and Publications:** *Vogue Living Australia*, September 2020; *AD France*, May/June 2020; *AD*, April 2020; *M Le magazine du Monde*, October 2018. **Clients include:** Groupe Malafosse, J. M. Weston, Four Seasons Hotels and Resorts, Le Jardinier, and Rosewood Hotels & Resorts. **Awards:** AD100
josephdirand.com

dix design+architecture

Sean Dix
Born 1974 in Kansas City, Missouri. Based in Hong Kong and Milan. Established 1999. **Selected Commissions:** Crown Super Deluxe, 2020; Yardbird, 2018; Carbone, 2014; Ho Lee Fook, 2014; Ronin, 2013 (all projects located in Hong Kong). **Press and Publications:** *Esquire Hong Kong*, January 2020; Michelin Guide Hong Kong, 2019 and 2020; Asia's 50 Best Restaurants, 2019; *Vogue Hong Kong*, July 2019; *New York Times*, February 2019. **Clients include:** Black Sheep Restaurants, Yardbird, Wink Hotels, Moschino, and Furla.
seandix.com
@seandixdesigns

Doherty Design Studio

Mardi Doherty
Born 1972 in Melbourne, Australia, where the firm is also based. Established 2014. **Selected Commissions:** Malvern Residence, 2019; Marquise Flagship Store, 2019; Church Residence, 2018; St Kilda Residence, 2018 (all projects located in Melbourne); Thornton Residence, Thornton, Australia, 2018. **Press and Publications:** *Elle Decoration UK*, November 2020; *Denizen Modern Living*, August 2020; *Design Lives Here: Australian Interiors, Furniture and Lighting* (Thames & Hudson, 2020); *Vogue Living Australia*, October 2018. **Clients include:** Marquis, Paul & Joe, Gewürzhaus, Empire Apartments, and numerous private clients. **Awards:** finalist, Belle Interior Design Awards, 2020; finalist, Australian Interior Design Awards, 2020; finalist, The Design Files Awards, 2020; winner, IDEA Awards, 2018.
dohertydesignstudio.com.au
@dohertydesignstudio

Sophie Dries Architect

Sophie Dries
Born 1986 in Dijon, France. Based in Paris and Milan. Established 2014. **Selected Commissions:** Michel Vivien Flagship, Paris, 2020; Arturo Arita, Paris, 2019; and numerous private residences and commercial projects. **Press and Publications:** *Louis Vuitton Paris City Guide* (Louis Vuitton, upcoming in 2021); *T: The New York Times Style Magazine*, June 2020; *M Le magazine du Monde*, January 2020; *Wallpaper**, April 2019; *Domus*, March 2019; *Surface*, February 2019; *Vases: 250 State-of-Art Designs* (Thames & Hudson, 2019); *Cosy Interiors: Slow Living Inspirations* (Booq Publishing, 2017). **Clients include:** View Hotels, Michel Vivien, Arturo Arita, Amiri, and Collectible design fair, Brussels. **Awards and Exhibitions:** shortlist, Emerging Interior Designer of the Year, *Dezeen*, 2020; winner, Best of Milan Design Week, *Milk Decoration*, 2019; winner, Best Shop Design, *AD France*, 2019; *Architects' Furniture, 1960–2020*, Cité De L'architecture & Du Patrimoine, Paris, 2019.
sophiedries.com
@sophiedriesarchitect

Bernard Dubois Architects

Bernard Dubois
Born 1979 in Brussels. Based in Brussels and Paris. Established 2014. **Selected Commissions:** Tangible Abstraction, limited edition furniture collection for Maniera gallery, Brussels, 2020; PNY restaurants, Paris, 2019 and 2020; Athletic Propulsion Lab Flagship, Los Angeles, 2019; ICICLE, Paris, 2019; Aesop, Brussels, 2018. **Press and Publications:** *A+*, June/July 2020; *Ark Journal* (no. 3), March 2020; *PIN–UP* (no. 26), Spring/ Summer 2020; *Air France*, April 2019. **Clients include:** Aesop, ICICLE, PNY, Zadig&Voltaire, and APL. **Awards and Exhibitions:** AD 100; *Tangible Abstraction*, Maniera, Brussels, 2020; *Ligne 102*, curated by *PIN–UP* for NYC× Design, New York, 2019; Belgian Pavilion, 14th International Architecture Exhibition, Venice Biennale, 2014.
bernarddubois.com
@bernard_dubois

André Fu Studio

André Fu
Born 1975 in Hong Kong, where the firm is also based. Established 2000. **Selected Commissions:** Hotel The Mitsui, Kyoto, 2020; St. Regis, Hong Kong, 2019; Waldorf Astoria, Bangkok, Thailand, 2018; Villa La Coste, Aix-en-Provence, France, 2017; The Upper House, Hong Kong, 2009. **Press and Publications:** *André Fu: Crossing Cultures with Design* (Thames & Hudson, 2020); *Departures*, April 2020; *Elle Decor*, September 2019; *Elle Decoration China*, July, 2019; *André Fu* (Assouline, 2015). **Clients include:** Swire Hotels, Maybourne Hotel Group, Four Seasons Hotels and Resorts, Capella Hotel Group, and St. Regis Hotels & Resorts. **Awards and Events:** winner, Top 25 Hotels in Asia, TripAdvisor, 2020; Interior Designer of the Year, *Elle Decoration China*, 2019; *Louis Vuitton Objets Nomades*, Salone del Mobile, Milan, 2018; Designer of the Year, Maison&Objet Asia, 2016.
andrefustudio.com
@andrefustudio

Ken Fulk

Born 1965 in Virginia, USA. Based in San Francisco and New York. Established 1997. **Selected Commissions:** Commodore Perry Estate, Austin, Texas, 2020; Loomis Lodge, Lake Tahoe, California, 2019; Saint Joseph's Arts Society, San Francisco, 2018; Henry Hall and Legacy Records, New York, 2017–18; The Battery, San Francisco, 2013. **Press and Publications:** *New York Times*, July 2020; *Vogue*, December 2019; *AD*, November 2019 (cover feature); *Elle Decor*, May 2019; *Mr. Ken Fulk's Magical World* (Abrams, 2016). **Clients include:** Kevin Systrom, Sean Parker, and Pharrell Williams. **Awards:** AD100; *Elle Decor* A-List; nominee, Outstanding Restaurant Design, James Beard Award, 2017 and 2020.
kenfulk.com
@kenfulk

Fawn Galli

Born 1969 in California. Based in New York. Established 2005. **Selected Commissions:** Short Hills Residence, Short Hills, New Jersey, 2017; Upper East Side Residence, New York, 2017; Upper West Side Residence, New York, 2017; Washington Square Park Residence, New York, 2015. **Press and Publications:** *Magical Rooms: Elements of Interior Design* (Rizzoli, 2019); *House Beautiful*, April 2019; *AD*, October 2017; *Elle Decor*, October 2015; *Domino*, April 2008. **Clients include:** numerous private clients.
fawngalli.com
@fawngalliinteriors

GOLDEN

Kylie Dorotic and Alicia McKimm
Dorotic and McKimm born in Melbourne, Australia, where the firm is also based. Established 2013. **Selected Commissions:** Buff Nail Studios, 2020; Brighton Residence, 2019; Laurent Kew, 2019; Lake View Penthouse, 2019 (all projects located in Melbourne); Viktoria & Woods, Sydney, 2019. **Press and Publications:** *Denizen*, September 2020; *Belle*, August/September 2020; *Mansion, The Australian*, July 2020; *Vogue Living Australia*, October 2018; *Smart Spaces: Creative Homes That Do More With Less* (Bauer Media, 2018). **Clients include:** Viktoria & Woods, Laurent Bakery, Seen Skin, Warrior One, and Buff Nail Studios. **Awards:** commendation, Residential Decoration, Australian Interior Design Awards, 2018 and 2019; winner, Best Café and Leisure Venue, World Interior News Awards, 2018; winner, Best Overall Restaurant, Restaurant & Bar Design Awards, 2017.
designbygolden.com.au
@designbygolden

Grisanti & Cussen

Hugo Grisanti and Kana Cussen
Grisanti born 1973 in Santiago, Chile; Cussen born 1982 in Santiago, where the firm is also based. Established 2007. **Selected Commissions:** Hotel Bidasoa, 2018; Polvo Bar De Vinos, 2018 (both projects located in Santiago). **Press and Publications:** *AD Mexico and Latin America*, June 2020; *Ministerio de Diseño Uruguay*, June 2020; *Revista Casas Peru*, September 2019; *Luxury Defined*, March 2019; ArchDaily, March 2019. **Clients include:** Sur Diseño, Hotel Bidasoa, Mallplaza, DS Automobiles, and Fundación La Fuente. **Awards:** Best Use of Color, Casa FOA Chile, 2018; Best Chilean Interior Designer, *ED*, 2015; Best Commercial Space, Casa FOA Chile, 2013; Best Interior Designer Space, CasaCor Chile, 2012.
grisanticussen.com
@grisanticussen

Luca Guadagnino

Born 1971 in Palermo, Italy. Based in Milan. Established 2016. **Selected Commissions:** Redemption, New York, 2019; Aesop Piccadilly, London, 2019; Aesop Rome, 2018; House on Lake Como, Lake Como, Italy, 2018. **Press and Publications:** *AD Germany*, December 2020; *T: The New York Times Style Magazine*, September 2018. **Clients include:** Aesop, Redemption, and numerous private clients. **Exhibitions and Events:** *You Got to Burn to Shine*, Galleria Nazionale d'Arte Moderna e Contemporanea, Rome, 2019; art direction for Porzellan Manufaktur Nymphenburg, Salone del Mobile, Milan, 2018.
@studiolucaguadagnino

Halden Interiors

Kesha Franklin
Born 1974 in Brooklyn. Based in Green Brook, New Jersey. Established 2010. **Selected Commissions:** Hudson River Project, Weehawken, New Jersey, 2020; Harlem Duplex Project, New York, 2017; San Jose Estate, San Jose, California, 2015; W Hotel Residence, New York, 2014; Tribeca Penthouse, New York, 2012. **Press and Publications:** *House & Garden South Africa*, November 2020; *Business of Home*, August 2020; *AD PRO*, June 2019; *ARRAY Magazine*, Spring 2019; *Elle Decor*, January 2018. **Clients include:** Colin Kaepernick, Amar'e Stoudemire, Doman Group, and Viacom. **Awards and Events:** Stars on the Rise Award, Decoration & Design Building, 2019; Dining by Design, DIFFA, event collaboration with the Black Artists + Designers Guild,

2019; Design on a Dime, 2018 and 2019; Emerging Designers to Watch, Black Interior Designers Network, 2016 and 2017.
haldeninteriors.com
@haldeninteriors

Hare + Klein
Meryl Hare
Born in Johannesburg, South Africa. Based in Sydney, Australia. Established 1989. **Selected Commissions:** numerous private residences. **Press and Publications:** *Hare + Klein: Interior* (Thames & Hudson, 2020); *Hare + Klein: Texture Colour Comfort* (Thames & Hudson, 2018); *Andrew Martin Interior Design Review* (teNeues, multiple volumes); *Beautiful Australian Homes* (no. 1 and 2) (Bauer Media, 2015 and 2017). **Clients include:** numerous private clients. **Awards:** winner, Hall of Fame and Best Residential Kitchen Design, Belle Coco Republic Interior Design Awards, 2020; Hall of Fame, *House & Garden Australia*, 2018; shortlist, Residential Single, IDEA Awards, 2017; Hall of Fame, Design Institute of Australia, 2011; winner, Australian Interior Design Awards, multiple years.
hareklein.com.au
@hareklein

Hecker Guthrie
Paul Hecker and Hamish Guthrie
Hecker born 1964 in Adelaide, Australia; Guthrie born 1970 in Melbourne, Australia. Based in Melbourne. Established 2001. **Selected Commissions:** Mitchelton Hotel and Winery, Nagambie, Australia, 2018; Vasse Felix Winery, Margaret River, Australia, 2018; Piccolina Gelateria, Melbourne, 2017; Elwood House Apartments, Melbourne, 2017; Ivy Penthouses and Entertainment Complex, Sydney, Australia, 2008. **Press and Publications:** *Design Anthology*, December 2019; *AD Spain*, May 2019; *Dezeen*, October 2018; *Resident Dog: Incredible Homes and the Dogs That Live There* (Thames & Hudson, 2018); *Take a Bath: Interior Design for Bathrooms* (Gestalten, 2017). **Clients include:** Piccolo Developments, Kookai, Merivale, Hyatt, and Heytesbury. **Awards:** winner, Rigg Design Prize, National Gallery of Victoria, 2019; winner (Hecker), Design Icon Award, Design Institute of Australia SA/NT Awards, 2018; Interior Designer of the Year, Belle Coco Republic Interior Design Awards, 2013; Gold Medal, IDEA Awards, 2012.
heckerguthrie.com
@heckerguthrie

Shawn Henderson
Born 1971 in Albany, New York. Based in New York. Established 2003. **Selected Commissions:** numerous private residences. **Press and Publications:** *Departures*, May 2020; *Elle Decor*, October and June 2020. **Clients include:** Sam Rockwell, Octavia Spencer, and Jimmie Johnson.
shawnhenderson.com
@shawnhendersonnyc

Beata Heuman
Born 1983 in Sireköpinge, Sweden. Based in London. Established 2013. **Selected Commissions:** Nantucket, Massachusetts, USA, 2019; Sussex Cottage, Sussex, 2018; Decorex VIP Lounge, London, 2018; Paddington Pied à Terre, London, 2017; Farm Girl Notting Hill, London, 2015. **Press and Publications:** *Every Room Should Sing* (Rizzoli, due in 2021). **Clients include:** numerous private clients. **Awards:** AD100; *Elle Decor* A-List; Finest 50 Interior Designers, *Country & Townhouse*, 2019; Top 100 Interior Designers, *House*

& Garden, 2019; Interior Designer of the Year, *House & Garden*, 2018.
beataheuman.com
@beataheuman

Fran Hickman
Born 1983 in London, where the firm is also based. Established 2014. **Selected Commissions:** Locket's, London, 2019; Paintbox, New York, 2019; Farfetch, Tokyo, 2019; Chess Club, London, 2017; Emilia Wickstead, London, 2016. **Press and Publications:** *Introspective, The 1stDibs Magazine*, Fall/Winter 2019; *House & Garden*, June 2019; *Elle Decoration UK*, January 2019; *Design Anthology UK* (no. 1), December 2018; *T: The New York Times Style Magazine*, February 2017. **Clients include:** Experimental Group, Emilia Wickstead, Farfetch, Wilton Group, and Goop. **Awards:** Top 100 Interior Designers, *House & Garden*, 2019; Finest 50 Interior Designers, *Country & Townhouse*, 2019; Interior Designer of the Year, *Elle Decoration* British Design Awards, 2019; winner, International Property Awards, 2017.
franhickman.com
@franhickman

Laura Hodges Studio
Laura Hodges
Born 1979 in Manchester, England. Based in Catonsville, Maryland, USA. Established 2016. **Selected Commissions:** Rosewood, Catonsville, 2019; Green Branch, Phoenix, Maryland, 2019; Ridgedale, Baltimore, 2019; Chesapeake, Baltimore, Maryland, 2018. **Press and Publications:** *House Beautiful*, December 2019; *Traditional Home*, September/October 2019; *Home & Design*, Spring 2019. **Clients include:** numerous private clients. **Awards:** winner, Best of the Rest, Luxe Red Awards, 2020; named Sustainable Furnishings Council Brand Ambassador, 2020; The List: 20 Designers for 2020, Sotheby's Home, 2020; Next Wave Designer, *House Beautiful*, 2019; New Trads, *Traditional Home*, 2019.
laurahodgesstudio.com
@laurahodgesstudio

Suzy Hoodless
Born in London, where the firm is also based. Established 2000. **Selected Commissions:** AllBright Mayfair, London, 2019; The Helios, Television Centre, London, 2018; and numerous private residences. **Press and Publications:** *House & Garden*, February 2019; *The Times*, November 2018; *Financial Times: How To Spend It*, July 2018; *Telegraph: Luxury*, April 2016; *New York Times*, November 2015. **Clients include:** numerous private clients.
suzyhoodless.com
@suzyhoodless

Young Huh Interior Design
Young Huh
Born 1969 in Seoul, South Korea. Based in New York. Established 2007. **Selected Commissions:** Historic Tudor, Chicago, 2021; 520 Park Avenue Apartment, New York, 2020; Point Grace, Providenciales, Turks and Caicos, 2019; Ritz-Carton Residences, Philadelphia, 2019; Ski Residence, Jackson Hole, Wyoming, 2015. **Press and Publications:** *Andrew Martin Interior Design Review* (teNeues, 2020); *Departures*, Fall 2020; *New York Times*, June 2020; *Elle Decor*, March 2019; *House Beautiful*, January/February 2019; *On Style: Inspiration and Advice from the New Generation of Interior Design* (Rizzoli, 2019); *The Power of Pattern: Interiors and Inspiration: A Resource Guide* (Rizzoli, 2018). **Clients include:** numerous private clients. **Awards:** *Elle Decor* A-List; "5 Young Interior

Designers on the Rise," *Vogue*, March 2015; winner, Innovation in Design Awards, *Cottages & Gardens*, 2011.
younghuh.com
@younghuh

Humbert & Poyet
Emil Humbert and Christophe Poyet
Humbert born 1980 in Paris; Poyet born 1982 in Monaco. Based in Monaco. Established 2008. **Selected Commissions:** Metamorphosis collection, in collaboration with Maison Pouenat, 2020; 26 Carré Or, Monaco, 2020; Villa Odaya, Cannes, France, 2019; Beefbar Paris, 2018; Turenne, Paris, 2018. **Press and Publications:** *AD Mexico*, August 2020 (cover feature); *AD Middle East*, June 2020; *AD*, May 2020; *Elle Decoration France*, May 2020 (cover feature). **Clients include:** The Hoxton, Beefbar, Alexis Mabille, Segond Group, and Shinsegae Group. **Awards and Events:** AD100; AD Intérieurs, Paris, 2018 and 2019.
humbertpoyet.com
@humbertetpoyet

Tamsin Johnson
Born 1985 in Melbourne, Australia. Based in Sydney, Australia. Established 2011. **Selected Commissions:** P. Johnson Showrooms, New York, London, Melbourne, and Sydney; Raes on Wategos Hotel and Sea Raes Yacht, Byron Bay, Australia, 2016–17; Playa by Lucy Folk, Bondi Beach, Australia, 2016; Frank Sinatra Office, Warner Brothers Studio, Los Angeles, 2015; and numerous private residences and commercial projects. **Press and Publications:** upcoming monograph (Rizzoli, due in 2021); *Vogue Living Australia*, September 2020 (cover feature); *Financial Times: How To Spend It*, November 2019; *Belle*, November 2019 (cover feature) and November 2018; *Cereal*, June 2019.
tamsinjohnson.com
@tamsinjohnson

Kit Kemp
Born in Southampton, UK. Based in London. Established 1985. **Selected Commissions:** founder and creative director of Firmdale Hotels, including Ham Yard Hotel, Soho Hotel, and Charlotte Street Hotel, London; and Crosby Street Hotel and The Whitby Hotel, New York. **Press and Publications:** *AD*, June 2020; *Homes & Gardens*, May 2020; *World of Interiors*, May 2019; *Belle*, May 2019; *Design Thread* (Hardie Grant, 2019); *Every Room Tells a Story* (Hardie Grant, 2015); *A Living Space* (Hardie Grant, 2012). **Clients include:** Wedgwood, Wilton Carpets, Andrew Martin, Anthropologie, and Christopher Farr. **Awards:** Urban Business Award, Crown Estate, 2017; winner, Hot List, *Condé Nast Traveller UK*, 2015; Hotel Designer of the Year, *House & Garden*, 2008; International Interior Designer of the Year, Andrew Martin, 2008.
kitkemp.com / firmdalehotels.com
@kitkempdesignthread

Rita Konig
Born 1973 in London, where the firm is also based. Established 2004. **Selected Commissions:** Beach House, Martha's Vineyard, Massachusetts, due for completion in 2022; San Vicente Bungalows, West Hollywood, 2018; North Farm, Teesdale, UK, 2018; Notting Hill Townhouse, London, 2018; Mill Valley, California, 2016. **Press and Publications:** *House & Garden*, March 2020, June 2018, and October 2016; *Elle Decor*, May 2019 and April 2016. **Events:** curated Christie's Collector sales, November 2019.
ritakonig.com
@ritakonig

Kråkvik & D'Orazio

Jannicke Kråkvik and Alessandro D'Orazio
Kråkvik born 1977 in Oslo; D'Orazio born 1965 in Rome.
Based in Oslo. Established 2003. **Selected Commissions:**
Fogia (interior styling), Stockholm, 2019; Territoriet,
Oslo, 2014; Jotun (color trend forecasting and interior
styling), ongoing. **Press and Publications:** *Nytt Rom*,
2019; *Sight Unseen*, November 2018; *Share, Case Studies
by Frama, Vol. 01* (New Heroes & Pioneers, 2018);
T: The New York Times Style Magazine, March 2017;
Residence, August 2017; *The Kinfolk Entrepreneur: Ideas
for Meaningful Work* (Kinfolk, 2017); *Wallpaper**, April
2016. **Clients include:** Jotun, Fogia, Kasthall, Fjordfiesta,
and Norwegian Presence. **Exhibitions:** *Designed to Last*,
ArkDes, Stockholm, 2017; *A Colour Composition – New
Norwegian Design*, Norwegian Embassy, Stockholm, 2017;
Structure, Milan Design Week, 2016.
krakvikdorazio.no
@kraakvikdorazio

Joanna Laajisto

Born 1977 in Helsinki, Finland, where the firm is also
based. Established 2010. **Selected Commissions:** Hotel
Torni, Helsinki, and Runo Hotel, Porvoo, Finland, 2021;
SushiBar + Wine, Oslo, Norway (two locations), 2020;
Institut Finlandais, Paris, 2018; Way Bakery and Winebar,
Helsinki, Finland, 2018. **Press and Publications:** *Dezeen*,
April 2020; *Out of the Woods: Architecture and Interiors
Built from Wood* (Gestalten, 2020); *AD Germany*, April
2019; *Monocle*, April 2019; *Northern Comfort: The Nordic
Art of Creative Living* (Gestalten, 2018); *Milk Decoration*,
December 2017. **Clients include:** Nanso, Vitra, We
Are Group, Sokotel, and Finnish Design Shop. **Awards:**
Interior Architect of the Year, Finnish Association
of Interior Architects, 2018.
joannalaajisto.com
@joannalaajisto / @studiojoannalaajisto

LH.Designs

Linda Hayslett
Born 1977 in Baltimore. Based in Los Angeles.
Established 2010. **Selected Commissions:** numerous
private residences. **Press and Publications:** *House
Beautiful*, October 2020; *Interiors*, August/September
2020; *Wall Street Journal*, July 2020; *Elle Decor*, June
2020; *California Home+Design*, November 2019. **Awards:**
Next Wave Designer, *House Beautiful*, 2019.
lhdesigned.com
@lhdesigned

Linehouse

Alex Mok and Briar Hickling
Mok born 1981 in Västerhaninge, Sweden. Based in
Shanghai; Hickling born 1983 in Gisborne, New Zealand.
Based in Hong Kong. Established 2013. **Selected
Commissions:** Pastry Store, W Osaka, Japan, 2021;
Booking.com restaurant, Amsterdam, the Netherlands,
2021; BaseHall, Hong Kong, 2020; John Anthony, Hong
Kong, 2018; WeWork Weihai Lu, Shanghai, China, 2016.
Press and Publications: *RIBA Journal*, April 2020;
Hemispheres, August 2019; *AD China*, May 2019; *Design
Anthology*, January 2019; *Elle Decoration China*, January
2019. **Clients include:** Booking.com, Sekisui House,
Kerry Properties, Herschel Supply, and WeWork. **Awards:**
AD100; Emerging Interior Designer of the Year, *Dezeen*
Awards, 2019; gold winner, Hospitality: Restaurants, WIN
Awards, 2019; highly commended, Bars & Restaurants,
INSIDE World Festival of Interiors, 2019.
linehousedesign.com
@line___house

Isabel López-Quesada

Born 1962 in Madrid, where the firm is also based.
Established 1983. **Selected Commissions:** Spanish
Embassies in Tokyo; Dakar, Senegal; and Doha, Qatar;
Torre Espacio Headquarters, Madrid, 2008; Acciona
Headquarters, Madrid, 2005; and numerous private
residences. **Press and Publications:** *Telva*, July 2020;
AD Spain, March 2020; *Elle Decor Spain*, July 2019; *Elle
Decor*, June 2019; *Interiors: The Greatest Rooms of the
Century* (Phaidon, 2019); *Isabel López-Quesada: At Home*
(Vendome, 2018). **Clients include:** numerous private
clients. **Awards:** AD100; *Elle Decor* A-List.
isabellopezquesada.com
@isabellopezquesada

Fiona Lynch

Born 1973 in Melbourne, Australia, where the firm
is also based. Established 2013. **Selected Commissions:**
Ace Hotel Sydney, Australia, 2021; CicciaBella, Sydney,
2020; 80 Collins, Melbourne, 2020; TarraWarra Museum
of Art, Tarrawarra, Australia, 2019; Lee Mathews,
Brisbane, 2018. **Press and Publications:** *Belle*, November
2020; *AD Russia*, September 2020; *Artichoke* (no. 72),
September 2020; Design Anthology Podcast, July 2020;
Elle Decor Spain, June 2020. **Clients include:** Atelier
Ace, TarraWarra Museum of Art, QICGRE/Universal
Design Studio, DEXUS, and Time & Place. **Awards and
Events:** AD100; Melbourne Design Week, 2019 and
2020; Designer of the Year, *Belle*, 2017; Work Shop,
curatorial exhibition series, ongoing.
fionalynch.com.au
@fionalynchoffice

Maison Vincent Darré

Vincent Darré
Born in Paris, where the firm is also based. Established
2008. **Selected Commissions:** Maison Vincent Darré,
Paris, 2020; Serpent à Plume, Paris, 2018; La Boutique,
Villa Noailles, Hyères, France, 2018; Hotel Montana, Paris,
2015; Schiaparelli showroom, Paris, 2012. **Press and
Publications:** *Cabana*, October 2020; *Purple*, October
2020; *AD France*, June 2020; *AD China*, April 2020; *Vincent
Darré: Surreal Interiors of Paris* (Rizzoli, 2018). **Clients
include:** Dior, Fred Paris, Eric Bompard, OKA, and Pierre
Frey. **Events:** scenography for La Biennale Paris,
2019; scenography for the Ritz Paris furniture auction,
Artcurial, 2018; scenography for Luxury Living
Group Showroom, Paris, 2017; AD Intérieurs, Paris,
multiple years.
maisondarre.com
@vincent_darre

Mlinaric, Henry and Zervudachi

Tino Zervudachi
Born 1963. Based in London, New York, and Paris.
Established 1964. **Selected Commissions:** House in
Washington, D.C., 2017; House in Rio, Rio de Janeiro,
2016; Huber Store, Vaduz, Liechtenstein, 2016; Chalet
in Rougemont, Rougemont, Switzerland, 2011; House
in Tokyo, 2010. **Press and Publications:** *World of Interiors*,
January 2019; *Boat*, September 2018; *House & Garden*,
December 2017; *AD*, January 2017; *Tino Zervudachi:
A Portfolio* (Pointed Leaf, 2012); *Mlinaric on Decorating*
(Frances Lincoln, 2008). **Clients include:** National
Portrait Gallery, London; Victoria & Albert Museum,
London; Regent Hotels & Resorts; and numerous
private commissions. **Awards:** AD100; Top 100 Interior
Designers, *House & Garden*, 2020.
mhzlondon.com

Greg Natale

Born 1974 in Sydney, Australia, where the firm is also
based. Established 2001. **Selected Commissions:**
Darlinghurst Apartment III, Sydney, 2019; Barwon
River House, Sydney, 2018; Inner West House, Sydney,
2018; Midtown Apartment, New York, 2017; Oklahoma
House, Oklahoma, 2017. **Press and Publications:** *Living
Etc*, September 2020; *AD Russia*, July/August 2020;
Wallpaper*, April 2020; *Elle Decoration France*, February/
March 2020; *The Patterned Interior* (Rizzoli, 2018). **Clients
include:** Snaidero, Cotton On Group, Farage, Kirkton Park
Hotel, and James Said. **Awards:** Top 50 Rooms, Best
Use of Colour, *House & Garden Australia*, 2019; Readers'
Choice Award, Best Residential Interior, *Belle*, 2018;
Luxury International Designer of the Year, High Point
Market, 2016; Interior Designer of the Year, *Belle*,
2011 and 2014.
gregnatale.com
@gregnatale

Paola Navone / Studio OTTO

Paola Navone
Born 1950 in Turin, Italy. Based in Milan. Established
2000. **Selected Commissions:** 25hours Hotel Piazza
San Paolino, Florence, Italy, 2021; COMO Castello del
Nero, Tavarnelle Val di Pesa, Italy, 2019; COMO Dempsey,
Singapore, 2017; COMO Metropolitan Miami Beach,
2014; COMO Point Yamu, Phuket, Thailand, 2013.
Press and Publications: *AD Italy*, September 2020; *Elle
Decor Italy*, August 2020; *Côté Sud*, December 2019;
Interni, April 2019; *Frame*, January/February 2019.
Clients include: COMO Hotels and Resorts, 25hours
Hotels, Gervasoni, Baxter, and Crate and Barrel.
Awards: jury member, *Dezeen* Awards, Archiproducts
Design Awards, and Frame Awards, 2019; winner,
Outdoor Seating, NYC×Design Awards, 2016; Interior
Design Hall of Fame, 2014; winner, Resort, Best of the
Year, *Interior Design*, 2014
paolanavone.it
@paola.navone

Neri&Hu

Lyndon Neri and Rossana Hu
Neri born 1965 in Ozamiz City, Philippines; Hu born
1968 in Kaohsiung City, Taiwan. Based in Shanghai.
Established 2004. **Selected Commissions:** Aranya Art
Center, Qinhuangdao, China, 2019; Tsingpu Yangzhou
Retreat, Yangzhou, China, 2017; Suzhou Chapel, Suzhou,
China, 2016; Rethinking the Split House, Shanghai,
2012; The Waterhouse at South Bund, Shanghai, 2010.
Press and Publications: *Azure*, May 2020; *AD Mexico*,
April 2020; *Telegraph*, March 2020; *Wallpaper**, February
2020; *Dezeen*, January 2020; *Neri&Hu Design and
Research Office: Works and Projects 2004–2014* (Park
Books, 2017); *Persistence of Vision: Shanghai Architects
in Dialogue* (MCCM Creations, 2007). **Awards:** winner,
Madrid Design Festival Awards, 2020; winner, Blueprint
Award for Design, 2019; winner, Hospitality, The Plan
Award, 2018; Interior Designer of the Year, Iconic Awards,
2017; Asia Designers of the Year, Maison&Objet, 2015.
neriandhu.com/en
@neriandhu

David Netto Design

David Netto
Born 1969 in New York. Based in Los Angeles.
Established 2000. **Selected Commissions:** numerous
private residences. **Press and Publications:** *Summer
to Summer: Houses by the Sea* (Vendome, 2020); *Veranda*,
July/August 2020; *Elle Decor*, February 2020; *Town &*

Country, March 2019; *City of Angels: Houses and Gardens of Los Angeles* (Vendome, 2018); *New York Living: Re-Inventing Home* (Rizzoli, 2017); *AD*, May 2016; *Vogue*, January 2008.
davidnettodesign.com
@davidnettosays

Norm Architects
Jonas Bjerre-Poulsen and Kasper Rønn Von Lotzbeck
Bjerre-Poulsen and Rønn Von Lotzbeck born 1976 in Copenhagen, where the firm is also based. Established 2008. **Selected Commissions:** Kinuta Terrace, Tokyo, 2019; The Audo, Copenhagen, 2019; Sticks'n'Sushi, London, 2018; K House, Kottegoda, Southern Province, Sri Lanka, 2018; Gjøvik House, Gjøvik, Norway, 2017.
normcph.com
@normarchitects

Note Design Studio
Cristiano Pigazzini and Johannes Karlström
Pigazzini born 1970 in Lecco, Italy; Karlström born 1976 in Östersund, Sweden. Based in Stockholm. Established 2008. **Selected Commissions:** Summit House, London, 2019; Grow Hotel, Stockholm, 2019; Hidden Tints, Stockholm, 2017; Sulla Bocca di Tutti, Stockholm, 2017. **Press and Publications:** *Metropolis*, March 2020; *Wallpaper**, November 2019; *Monocle*, November 2019; *Blueprint*, May 2019; *Elle Decoration Sweden*, April 2019. **Clients include:** Tagehus, Stockholm Furniture Fair, The Office Group, and numerous private clients. **Awards:** Designer of the Year, Frame Awards, 2020; winner, Salone del Mobile.Milano Award, in collaboration with Magis, 2018; Designer of the Year, *Elle Decoration Sweden*, 2016; and a number of different awards from *Dezeen* and *Wallpaper**.
notedesignstudio.se
@notedesignstudio

Marie-Anne Oudejans
Born 1964 in The Hague, the Netherlands. Based in Jaipur, India. Established in 2015. **Selected Commissions:** Aquazzura Boutique, Capri, Italy, 2020; Gem Palace, Mumbai, India, 2017; Bar and Caffé Palladio, Jaipur, India, 2013. **Press and Publications:** *Financial Times*, September 2020; *AD Middle East*, November 2019; *AD India*, March 2018; *AD*, March 2017; *World of Interiors*, June 2016; *The Floral Patterns of India* (Thames & Hudson, 2016). **Clients include:** Barbara Miolini, Siddharth Kasliwal, Alape Kaur, Debonnaire von Bismarck, and Aquazzura.
cargocollective.com/Marie-Anne_Oudejans
@m.a.jaipur

Stéphane Parmentier
Born 1966 in Nice, France. Based in Paris. Established 2003. **Selected Commissions:** The Webster, Montecito, California, and Toronto, 2020; AD Intérieurs, Paris, 2018 and 2019; Mauritius Villa, Bel Ombre, Mauritius, 2017; Paris 9th District, 2017. **Press and Publications:** *Elle Decoration France*, September 2020; *Artravel*, Summer 2019; *T: The New York Times Magazine*, March 2019; *Wallpaper**, June 2018; *Elle Decor*, July/August 2016. **Clients include:** Hermès, The Webster, Orange, Christofle, Giobagnara, Domaine des Etangs, and numerous private clients. **Awards and Events:** AD100; AD200 (influencers); Maison&Objet, Paris, 2011 and 2020; *Wallpaper** Design Awards, 2012 and 2018, *AD France* "Collections", 2015 and 2017, *Wallpaper* Handmade*, Salone del Mobile, Milan, 2014 and 2016.
stephaneparmentier.com
@stephaneparmentier

Ben Pentreath
Born 1971 in Dorchester, UK. Based in London. Established 2004. **Selected Commissions:** Sustainable Scottish Town, Tornagrain, Scotland, UK, ongoing; Private Waterside Residence, New Forest, UK, ongoing; Waterside Small Town, Fawley, UK, due for completion in 2036; Cornwall Castle, Cornwall, UK, phase 1 completed in 2021; Prague Apartment, Prague, 2021. **Press and Publications:** *English Decoration: Timeless Inspiration for the Contemporary Home* (Ryland Peters & Small, 2019); *English Houses: Inspirational Interiors from City Apartments to Country Manor Houses* (Ryland Peters & Small, 2016); *Three Classicists* (Bardwell Press, 2010); *Get Your House Right: Architectural Elements to Use and Avoid* (Sterling, 2007); Pentreath also writes regularly for the *Financial Times*. **Clients include:** Lime Wood Hotel, Duchy of Cornwall, Moray Estates, and Hackett. **Exhibitions:** *Three Classicists*, Royal Institute of British Architects, London, 2010.
benpentreath.com
@benpentreath

Perspective Studio
Robin Klang
Born 1987 in Uddevalla, Sweden. Based in Stockholm. Established 2016. **Selected Commissions:** Effective Communication, Stockholm, Sweden, 2019; Doctor_K, Stockholm, Sweden, 2018; and numerous private residences. **Press and Publications:** *Urban Mansions and Apartments* (Beta Plus, 2020); *My Residence* (no. 4), 2019; *RUM*, September 2020; *AD Spain*, March 2018; *Elle Decoration Sweden*, March 2017. **Clients include:** Doctor_K, Effective Communication, Quickbit, Fabrique Bakery, and Rute Stenugnsbageri.
perspectivestudio.se
@perspectivestudio

Emmanuel Picault
Born 1962 in Normandy, France. Based in Mexico City. Established 2001. **Selected Commissions:** Private Residence, La Paz, Mexico, 2020; Private Residence, Peña de Bernal, Mexico, 2019; Xucú Hacienda, Yucatan, Mexico, 2014; M. N. Roy, Mexico City, 2011; Nüba, Paris, France, 2010. **Press and Publications:** *Milk Decoration*, June 2018; *Corriere della Sera Living*, October 2017; *Elle Decor Spain*, October 2017; *World of Interiors*, August 2013; *Chic by Accident* (Fogra, 2011); *Chic by Accident* (Landucci, 2007). **Awards:** Best Bar Design, *Wallpaper** Design Awards, 2007.
chic-by-accident.com
@chicbyaccident

Reath Design
Frances Merrill
Born 1978 in New York. Based in Los Angeles. Established 2009. **Selected Commissions:** Altadena Residence and Franklin Hills Residence, Los Angeles, 2019; Georgina Residence, Santa Monica, California, 2018; Little Holmby Residence and The Oaks Residence, Los Angeles, 2018. **Press and Publications:** *Harper's Bazaar Germany*, June/July 2020; *AD Germany*, June 2020 (cover feature); *Elle Decoration UK*, April 2020; *Wall Street Journal*, January 2020; *AD*, February 2020 (cover feature).
reathdesign.com
@reathdesign

Redd Kaihoi
Miles Redd and David Kaihoi
Redd born 1969 in Atlanta; Kaihoi born 1977 in Willmar, Minnesota. Based in New York. Established 1998.

Selected Commissions: Monte Carlo Apartment, 2021; Los Angeles Residence, 2020; Houston Attic, 2019; Texas Farmhouse, Bellville, Texas, 2018; Bay Area Home, San Francisco, 2017; fabric and wallcovering collections, Schumacher, ongoing collaboration. **Press and Publications:** *Town & Country*, March 2020; *Veranda*, July 2019; *AD*, January 2019; *House Beautiful*, December 2018; *Elle Decor*, May 2018; *The Big Book of Chic* (Assouline, 2012). **Clients include:** numerous private clients. **Awards:** AD100; *Elle Decor* A-List.
reddkaihoi.com
@reddkaihoi / @milesredd / @davidkaihoi

Retrouvius
Maria Speake
Born 1970 in Oxford, UK. Based in London. Established 1993. **Selected Commissions:** Historical Apartment, Paris, 2021; Arts and Crafts Manor and 16th-century Old Mill, Dartmoor, UK, 2020; Regency Townhouse, London, 2020; New Build, London, 2020; Tobacco Farm, rural Umbria, Italy, 2019. **Press and Publications:** *House & Garden*, January 2021; *World of Interiors*, October 2020; *AD Spain*, March 2020; *Elle Decoration UK*, March 2020; *Reclaiming Style: Using Salvaged Materials to Create an Elegant Home* (Ryland Peters & Small, 2012 and 2019). **Clients include:** Bella Freud, Sam Roddick, and Lyn Harris. **Awards and Events:** AD100; AD200 (influencers); Interior Designer of the Year, *House & Garden*, 2019; guest speaker at *AD Germany*'s Design Summit, 2019.
retrouvius.com
@retrouvius

Richards Stanisich
Jonathan Richards and Kirsten Stanisich
Richards born 1972 in London; Stanisich born 1968 in Melbourne, Australia. Based in Sydney, Australia. Established 2018. **Selected Commissions:** Hotel Rose Bay, Beach House, 12-Micron, and Darlinghurst Residence, 2017; Paspaley Pearls, 2014 (all projects located in Sydney). **Press and Publications:** *The Local Project* (no. 3), 2020; *Interior Design*, July 2019; *Elle Decor Spain*, June 2019; *Vogue Living Australia*, Special Collector's Issue, March 2019; *Elle Decoration Denmark*, February 2019. **Clients include:** AMP Capital, Lendlease, Paspaley Pearls, The Wood Room, and the National Gallery of Victoria. **Awards:** Interior Architecture Award, NSW Architecture Awards, 2020; winner, Rigg Design Prize, National Gallery of Victoria, 2019; Interior Designer of the Year, Belle Coco Republic Interior Design Awards, 2017; Interior Designer of the Year, IDEA Awards, 2017.
richardsstanisich.com.au
@richards_stanisich

Right Meets Left Interior Design
Courtney McLeod
Born 1974 in New Orleans. Based in New York. Established 2012. **Selected Commissions:** Noho Loft, New York, 2020; Soho Duplex Apartment, New York, 2020; Private Home, Washington, D.C., 2020; Tech Company Offices, Hudson Yards, New York, 2018; Sands Point Family Home, Sands Point, New York, 2017. **Press and Publications:** *Veranda*, Sept/Oct 2020; *House Beautiful*, Jan/Feb 2020; *Modern Luxury*, March 2019; *Luxe Interiors + Design*, January 2019; *Aspire Design and Home*, Spring 2016 (cover feature). **Clients include:** numerous private clients. **Awards:** Style Spotter, High Point Market, 2019; Emerging Designer, *Luxe Interiors + Design*, 2019.
rmlid.com
@rightmeetsleftinteriordesign

Rockwell Group
David Rockwell
Born 1956 in Chicago. Based in New York, Los Angeles, and Madrid. Established 1984. **Selected Commissions:** Waterline Club, New York, 2020; Warner Music Group, Los Angeles, 2019; Hayes Theater, New York, 2018; Gran Hotel Inglés, Madrid, 2018; Equinox Hotel, New York, 2019. **Press and Publications:** *New Yorker*, October 2020; *Designboom*, September 2020; *Bloomberg Businessweek*, August 2020; *New York Times*, March 2020; *WSJ. Magazine*, October 2019. **Clients include:** José Andrés, Robert De Niro, Nobu Matsuhisa, Danny Meyer, and Cédric and Ochi Vongerichten. **Awards and Exhibitions:** *Lawn*, National Building Museum Summer Block Party, Washington, D.C., 2019; Tony Award, Best Scenic Design in a Musical, *She Loves Me*, 2016; President's Award, American Institute of Architecture, New York, 2015; Outstanding Achievement in Interior Design, National Design Awards, Cooper Hewitt, Smithsonian Design Museum, 2008.
rockwellgroup.com
@rockwellgroup

Roman and Williams
Robin Standefer and Stephen Alesch
Based in New York. Established 2002. **Selected Commissions:** The British Galleries, Metropolitan Museum of Art, New York, 2020; Verōnika, Fotografiska, New York, 2020; La Mercerie, The Guild Outdoor Dining, New York, 2020. **Press and Publications:** *Icon Sweden*, Fall 2020 (cover feature); *AD*, March 2020; *WSJ. Magazine*, March 2020; *T: The New York Times Style Magazine*, September 2019; *New York Magazine*, May 2018. **Clients include:** Gwyneth Paltrow, The Metropolitan Museum of Art, Fotografiska, David and Monica Zwirner, and Jean-Georges Vongerichten. **Awards:** AD100; *Elle Decor* A-List
romanandwilliams.com
@roman_and_williams_

Romanek Design Studio
Brigette Romanek
Born in Chicago. Based in Los Angeles. Established 2018. **Selected Commissions:** Allbright, West Hollywood, 2019; Delilah Club, West Hollywood, 2016; Petit Trois, Los Angeles, 2014; and numerous private residences. **Press and Publications:** *House Beautiful*, June 2020; *Elle Decor*, February 2020; *AD*, November 2019; *Vogue*, March 2018. **Clients include:** Beyoncé, Joe Jonas, Demi Moore, Gwyneth Paltrow, and Kelly Rowland. **Awards:** AD100; *Elle Decor* A-List.
romanekdesignstudio.com
@romanek.design.studio

Daniel Romualdez
Born in Manila, Philippines. Based in New York. Established 1993. **Selected Commissions:** numerous private residences. **Press and Publications:** *AD*, December 2019; *Elle Decor*, October 2019; *Vanity Fair*, July 2017; *T: The New York Times Style Magazine*, December 2013; *Vogue*, October 2012. **Clients include:** Aerin Lauder, Tory Burch, Daphne Guinness, Vito Schnabel, and Lauren Santo Domingo. **Awards:** AD100; *Elle Decor* A-List.

RP Miller
Rodman Primack
Born 1975 in Laguna Beach, California. Based in New York; Aspen, Colorado; and Mexico City. Established 2004. **Selected Commissions:** Bella Vista Ranch, Ojai, California, 2021; SFA Advisory, New York, 2019; Kentucky Farmhouse Retreat, Louisville, Kentucky, 2018; Las Tortugas, Kona, Hawaii, 2012; Basset Road, London, 2010. **Press and Publications:** *House & Garden*, September 2020; *Casa Vogue Brazil*, April 2020; *AD*, January 2018; *Elle Decor Italy*, May 2017; *T: The New York Times Style Magazine*, December 2014. **Clients include:** Stephen Reily and Emily Bingham, Anne Crawford and Dudley Dezonia, Lisa Schiff, Alison and Jonathan Green, and Whitney Wolfe Herd and Michael Herd. **Awards and Events:** AD100; AGO Projects pop-up, Aspen 2020; Roman Molds Fendi collection, in collaboration with Kueng Caputo, Design Miami/Basel, Switzerland, 2019; The 1stDibs 50, 2019.
rpmillerdesign.com
@rpmillerdesign / @rodmanprimack

Achille Salvagni
Born 1970 in Rome. Based in Rome, London, and New York. Established in 2002. **Selected Commissions:** Mansion, Mumbai, India, 2021; The Benson, New York, 2020; Town House, New York, 2020; Waterfront Villa, Miami, 2020; Achille Salvagni Atelier (new gallery), London, 2020. **Press and Publications:** *Where Architects Sleep: The Most Stylish Hotels in the World* (Phaidon, 2020); *Splendor of Marble: Marvelous Spaces by the World's Top Architects and Designers* (Rizzoli, 2020); *Achille Salvagni* (Rizzoli, 2019). **Clients include:** Azimut Benetti, Rossinavi, Naftali Group, Oceanco, and Baglietto. **Awards and Exhibitions:** AD100; *Elle Decor* A-List; *Achille Salvagni: Five Years of Creation*, Maison Gerard, New York, 2017; *Sharpness and Transparency*, Giustini / Stagetti, Rome, 2017.
achillesalvagni.com / salvagniarchitetti.com
@achillesalvagni / @achillesalvagniatelier

Tom Scheerer
Based in New York. Established 1995. **Selected Commissions:** NYC Apartment, New York, 2019; East Hampton Beach House, East Hampton, New York, 2017; Zanzibar, The Abacos, Bahamas, 2016; House in the Tropics, Mill Reef Club, Antigua, 2016; Georgian House in Highland Park, Dallas, Texas, 2015. **Press and Publications:** *Elle Decor*, October 2020; *AD*, July 2019; *House Beautiful*, June 2019; *Tom Scheerer: More Decorating* (Vendome, 2019), *T: The New York Times Style Magazine*, August 2013; *Tom Scheerer Decorates* (Vendome, 2013). **Clients include:** numerous private clients. **Awards:** AD100; *Elle Decor* A-List.
tomscheerer.com
@tomscheerer

Glenn Sestig Architects
Glenn Sestig
Born 1968 in Ghent, Belgium. Based in Deurle, Belgium. Established 1999. **Selected Commissions:** Pavilion Sestig, Deurle, Belgium, 2019; Penthouse Mulier, Antwerp, Belgium, 2016; Penthouse Tuymans-Arocha, Antwerp, Belgium, 2016; Hieronymus, Zurich, 2014. **Press and Publications:** *Wallpaper**, February 2020; *AD Germany*, June 2016; *AD France* "Collector", 2016; *System*, Fall/Winter, 2015; *Elle Decor Italy*, February 2004. **Clients include:** Raf Simons, Luc Tuymans, Pieter Mulier, Soulwax, 2manydjs, and Olivier Theyskens. **Other:** Townhouse Sestig featured in the movie *Spider in the Web*, starring Monica Bellucci and Ben Kingsley, 2019; scenography for *Olivier Theyskens – She Walks in Beauty*, MoMu, Antwerp, Belgium, 2017–18; scenography for several fashion shows, Villa Eugénie, Brussels, Belgium.
glennsestigarchitects.com
@glenn.sestig

SevilPeach
Sevil Peach and Gary Turnbull
Peach born 1949 in Istanbul, Turkey; Turnbull born 1954 in Edinburgh, Scotland, UK. Based in London. Established 1994. **Selected Commissions:** Kvadrat Headquarters, Denmark, 2018; Swiss Re Headquarters, Zurich, 2017; Vitra Offices, Weil am Rhein, 2010, and Birsfelden, 2015; Novartis Campuses, Basel, 2002, and Shanghai, 2014; Microsoft Headquarters, Amsterdam, 2008. **Press and Publications:** *Neue Zürcher Zeitung*, May 2020; *Hiatus*, November 2017; *Vitra*, October 2017; *De Architect*, September 2015; *Interwoven*, September 2013; *Novartis Campus: A Contemporary Work Environment: Premises, Elements, Perspectives* (Hatje Cantz, 2009). **Clients include:** Vitra, Kvadrat, Microsoft, Novartis, and Swiss Re. **Awards:** Interior Designer of the Year, *Dezeen* Awards, 2019; Lifetime Achievement Award, Frame Awards, 2018; winner, Best Medium Office, FX Awards, 2000.
sevilpeach.co.uk
@sevilpeach

SheltonMindel
Lee F. Mindel
Born in New Jersey. Based in New York. Established 1978. **Selected Commissions:** Salesforce Transit Center competition winner, in collaboration with Pelli Clarke Pelli Architects, Hines, Goldman Sachs, and the Mark Company, San Francisco, ongoing; Sag Harbor Residence, New York, 2020; Manhattan Triplex, New York, 2018; West Village Think Tank, New York, 2018; Southampton Residence, New York, 2015. **Press and Publications:** *Galerie*, September 2020; *AD*, July 2020; *Cultured*, July 2020; *Interior Design Homes*, Winter 2019; *Elle Decor*, September 2019. **Clients include:** Sting and Trudie Styler, Kevin Warsh and Jane Lauder, Laurie Tisch, Jane Hudis, and Ceruzzi Properties. **Awards:** AD100; *Elle Decor* A-List; winner, Apartment, NYC×Design Awards, 2020; winner, Large Apartment and Small Corporate Office, *Interior Design* Best of Year Awards, 2019; Design Award of Honor, SARA NY Design Awards, 2018.
sheltonmindel.com
@sheltonmindel

Space Copenhagen
Signe Bindslev Henriksen and Peter Bundgaard Rützou. Henriksen born 1973 in Copenhagen; Rützou born 1966 in Copenhagen. Based in Copenhagen. Established 2005. **Selected Commissions:** Le Pristine, Antwerp, 2020; The Stratford, London, 2019; Geist, Copenhagen, 2019; 11 Howard, New York, 2016; Noma, Copenhagen, 2012. **Clients include:** Aby Rosen, Harry Handelsman, Mori Building Corporation, Noma, and Sergio Herman. **Awards:** shortlist, Best New Hotel, *Wallpaper** Design Awards, 2020; winner, Hotel Renovation & Restoration, Ahead Global Awards, 2019.
spacecph.com
@spacecopenhagen

The Stella Collective
Hana Hakim
Born 1979 in London. Based in Melbourne, Australia. Established 2015. **Selected Commissions:** Hazel, Melbourne, 2019; Artedomus, Sydney, 2017, and Brisbane, 2019; Zoobibi, Melbourne, 2018; Blacksmith, Lake Mulwala, Australia, 2018; Memocorp, Sydney, 2016. **Press and Publications:** *Vogue Living Australia*, September 2019; *Frame*, August 2019; *Australian Financial Review*, March 2019; *Grand Designs Australia* (no. 7.4), August 2018. **Clients include:** Tony Zoobi,

Blacksmith, The Mulberry Group, Phil Brenton/ Artedomus, and Memocorp. **Awards:** winner, Best Retail, Australian Interior Design Awards, 2020; winner, Best Bar, Eat Drink Design Awards, 2019; Best Emerging Practice, WIN Awards, 2019; People's Choice, Frame Awards, 2018.
thestellacollective.co
@thestellacollective

Robert Stilin
Born 1965 in Ashland, Wisconsin. Based in New York. Established 1989. **Selected Commissions:** Shingle Style Country House, East Hampton, New York, due for completion in 2022; Oceanfront Bermuda Style Family Estate, Palm Beach, Florida, 2021; Bucolic Family Estate, Louisville, Kentucky, 2018; Duplex Penthouse Overlooking Central Park, New York, 2012; Oceanfront Beach House, Sagaponack, New York, 2008. **Press and Publications:** *Departures*, June 2020; *Galerie*, Spring 2020; *AD*, April 2019; *Robert Stilin: Interiors* (Vendome, 2019); *Interiors: The Greatest Rooms of the Century* (Phaidon, 2019). **Clients include:** Howard and Sheri Schultz, Fernando Garcia, Susan Stroman, and numerous private clients. **Awards:** AD100; *Elle Decor* A-List.
robertstilin.com
@robertstilin

Studio Ashby
Sophie Ashby
Born 1988 in London, where the firm is also based. Established 2014. **Selected Commissions:** Floral Court, London, 2019; Holland Park Villas, London, 2019; Neo Bankside Penthouse, London, 2019; the Robertson Small Hotel, Western Cape, South Africa, 2017; TVC Apartment, London, 2016. **Press and Publications:** *Marie Claire Maison*, February 2020; *House & Garden*, June 2019; *Financial Times: How to Spend It*, April 2019; *Vogue*, January 2019; *Observer Magazine*, January 2019. **Clients include:** Battersea Power Station, Capco, Native Land, the Robertson Small Hotel, and Casely-Hayford. **Awards and Events:** AD100; shortlist, International Interior Designer of the Year, Andrew Martin, 2015–20; Top 100 Interior Designers, *House & Garden*, 2019; 50 Best Interior Designers, *Country & Townhouse*, 2019; Hot 150 Rising Star, *English Home*, 2018–19; Interior Designer of the Year, British Homes Awards, 2018 and 2019; United in Design, co-founder.
studioashby.com
@studioashby

Studio Daminato
Albano Daminato
Born 1966 in Adelaide, Australia. Based in Bangkok, Thailand, and Singapore. Established 2001. **Selected Commissions:** Lake Como Villa, Como, Italy, 2019; Arnalaya Bali, Indonesia, 2014; KH Residence, Singapore, 2014; MJ Residence, undisclosed location, 2010. **Press and Publications:** *AD Germany*, May 2020; *AD France*, evasion travel edition (no. 2), 2019; *Design Anthology*, Asia Edition (no. 23), 2019; *Corriere della Sera Living*, November 2019. **Clients include:** Rolf Harrison, Aman Resorts, Chanintr, and numerous private clients. **Awards:** AD100.
studiodaminato.com
@studiodaminato

Studio Jacques Garcia
Jacques Garcia
Born 1947 in Malakoff, France. Based in Paris. Established 1982. **Selected Commissions:** Hôtel Barrière

Le Fouquet's Paris, 2019; Six Senses Maxwell, Singapore, 2018; La Réserve Paris Hotel and Spa, 2015; Park Chinois, London, 2015; and numerous private residences. **Press and Publications:** *Elle Decoration France*, November 2019; *AD*, August 2019; *World of Interiors*, February 2019; *Condé Nast Traveller UK*, April 2019; *Jacques Garcia: Twenty Years of Passion, Château du Champ De Bataille* (Flammarion, 2013). **Clients include:** numerous private clients. **Awards:** Best Hotel, Reader's Choice, *Condé Nast Traveler*, 2017 and 2018.
studiojacquesgarcia.com
@jacquesgarciaofficiel

Studio KO
Olivier Marty and Karl Fournier
Marty born 1975 in Palaiseau, France; Fournier born 1970 in Saint-Raphaël, France. Based in Paris and Marrakech, Morocco. Established 2000. **Selected Commissions:** Flamingo Estate, Los Angeles, 2018; Musée Yves Saint Laurent, Marrakech, Morocco, 2017; Chiltern Firehouse, London, 2014; Villa K, Tagadert, Morocco, 2009. **Press and Publications:** *WSJ. Magazine*, November 2019 (cover feature); *AD France*, May/June 2019; *T: The New York Times Style Magazine*, September 2018; *AD*, September 2017; *Studio KO* (Rizzoli, 2017). **Clients include:** André Balazs, Francis Ford Coppola, Marella Agnelli, Richard Christiansen, and Cyril Lignac. **Awards and Events:** jury member, Design Parade Toulon, 5th International Festival of Interior Design, Toulon, France, 2020; *WSJ. Magazine* Innovator Award, 2019; AFEX Grand Prix, 16th International Architecture Exhibition, Venice Biennale, 2018; Prix d'Encouragement, Académie des Beaux-Arts, 2018; Best Public Building, *Wallpaper** Design Awards, 2018.
studioko.com
@studioko

Studio Mumbai
Bijoy Jain
Born 1965 in Mumbai, India. Based in Mumbai and Milan. Established 1995. **Selected Commissions:** Château de Beaucastel Winery Extension, Courthézon, France, ongoing; LOG, Onomichi, Japan, 2018; Ganga Maki Textile Studio, Dehradun, India, 2017; Saath Rasta, Mumbai, 2016; Copper House II, Chondi, India, 2012. **Press and Publications:** *Studio Mumbai: 2012–2019* (El Croquis, 2019); *Studio Mumbai: Inspiration and Process in Architecture* (Moleskine, 2013); *Studio Mumbai: Praxis* (Toto, 2012); *Studio Mumbai: 2003–2011* (El Croquis, 2011); *Work-Place: Studio Mumbai* (Archizoom, 2011). **Clients include:** Chiaki Maki, Discover Link Setouchi, Famille Perrin, Anissa Khanna, and Mahindra's. **Awards:** winner, Alvar Aalto Medal, 2020; International Fellow, Royal Institute of British Architects, 2017; Honorary Doctorate, University of Hasselt, Belgium, 2014; Grande Medaille d'Or, L'Académie d'architecture, Paris, 2014; Special Mention, 12th International Architecture Exhibition, Venice Biennale, 2010; finalist, Aga Khan Award for Architecture, 2010. **Exhibitions:** *Maniera 06*, Brussels, Belgium, 2019; *Nature Rules: Dreaming of Earth Project*, Hara Museum of Contemporary Art, Tokyo, 2019; *The Hypostatic Transformation*, Nature Morte, New Delhi, India, 2019.
studiomumbai.com

Studio Peregalli
Roberto Peregalli and Laura Sartori Rimini
Peregalli born 1961 in Milan; Sartori Rimini born 1964 in Padua, Italy. Based in Milan. Established 1990s. **Selected Commissions:** Tegernsee Pavilion, Tegernsee,

Germany, 2017; Art Collector Apartment, Milan, 2016; Capri Retreat, Capri, Italy, 2016; Apartment in a Hôtel Particulier, Paris, 2015; Hampstead Mansion, London, 2015; 19th-Century Building in S-Chanf, Switzerland, 2012; Medina Riad, Tangier, Morocco, 2007. **Press and Publications:** *AD Germany*, October 2020; *Elle Decor*, April 2020; *AD*, January 2020 (cover feature); *Vogue*, June 2018; *Grand Tour: The Worldly Projects of Studio Peregalli* (Rizzoli, 2018); *The Invention of the Past: Interior Design and Architecture of Studio Peregalli* (Rizzoli, 2011). **Clients include:** numerous private clients. **Awards and Events:** AD100; Architectural Studio of the Year, Foodcommunity Awards, 2018; set design for *War and Peace* by Prokofiev, Spoleto Festival, Italy, 1999; set design for several exhibitions, Palazzo Reale, Milan.

Studio Shamshiri
Pamela and Ramin Shamshiri
Both born in Tehran, Iran. Based in Los Angeles. Established 2016. **Selected Commissions:** Maison de la Luz, New Orleans, 2019; Sonia Boyajian Jewelry Studio and Showroom, Los Angeles, 2019; and numerous private residences. **Press and Publications:** *The Most Beautiful Rooms in the World: A Curated Selection by the International Editors of AD* (Rizzoli, 2020); *AD Germany*, February 2020; *AD*, January 2020; *AD France*, January 2020. **Clients include:** numerous private clients. **Awards:** AD100.
studioshamshiri.com
@studioshamshiri / @pamelashamshiri

Studio Sofield
William Sofield
Born 1961 in Perth Amboy, New Jersey. Based in New York. Established 1996. **Selected Commissions:** 111 West 57th Street, New York, 2020; Beckford House and Beckford Tower, 2019; 135 East 79th Street, New York, 2014. **Press and Publications:** *Elle Decor*, October 2019; *AD*, September 2019; *New York Design at Home* (Abrams, 2019); *Interiors: The Greatest Rooms of the Century* (Phaidon, 2019); *Life Along the Hudson: The Historic Country Estates of the Livingston Family* (Rizzoli, 2018). **Clients include:** Tom Ford, Helen and Brice Marden, Ricky and Ralph Lauren, and Kelly Ripa and Mark Consuelos. **Awards:** AD100; *Elle Decor* A-List; Architectural Design Award, Architectural Commission of Beverly Hills, 1999, 2003, and 2015; Interior Design Hall of Fame, 30th Anniversary Award, 2014; winner, Interior Design, National Design Awards, Cooper Hewitt, Smithsonian Design Museum, 2010.
studiosofield.com

Studioilse
Ilse Crawford
Born in London, where the firm is also based. Established 2001. **Selected Commissions:** Savoy, Helsinki, 2020; Swedish Summer House, southern Sweden, 2019; Private Home, Stockholm, 2017; Ett Hem Stockholm, 2012. **Press and Publications:** *A Frame for Life: The Designs of Studioilse* (Rizzoli, 2014); *Home Is Where the Heart Is?* (Quadrille, 2009); *Sensual Home: Liberate Your Senses and Change Your Life* (Rizzoli, 1998). **Clients include:** Cathay Pacific, Aesop, IKEA, Ett Hem Stockholm, and Soho House. **Awards:** Crawford was awarded an MBE for services to interior design in 2014.
studioilse.com
@studioilse_

Takenouchi Webb
Marc Webb and Naoko Takenouchi
Webb born 1969 in Liverpool, England; Takenouchi born 1974 in Aichi, Japan. Based in Singapore. Established 2006. **Selected Commissions:** CapitaSpring, Singapore, 2021; Shang Social, Singapore, 2019; Straits Clan, Singapore, 2018; Esora, Singapore, 2018; The Katamama, Bali, Indonesia, 2016. **Press and Publications:** *Tatler Homes Singapore*, March 2019; *Design Anthology*, June 2018; *Cubes*, September 2018; *Monocle*, April 2018; *Appetizer: New Interiors for Restaurants and Cafés* (Gestalten, 2017). **Clients include:** Shangri-La Group, Four Seasons Hotels and Resorts, the Lo & Behold Group, Capitaland, and PTT Family/Potato Head. **Awards:** Design Project of the Year, *Tatler Design Awards*, 2019; Top Female Designer (Takenouchi), Design Anthology Awards, 2019.
takenouchiwebb.com
@takenouchiwebb

David Thulstrup
Born 1978 in Copenhagen, where the firm is also based. Established 2009. **Selected Commissions:** Vester Voldgade, Copenhagen, 2020; David Thulstrup's Apartment, Copenhagen, 2019; Collage Men, Aarhus, Denmark, 2019; Mark Kenly Domino Tan, Copenhagen, 2018; Noma, Copenhagen, 2018. **Press and Publications:** *AD*, October 2020; *Est*, September 2020; *ARK Journal*, March 2020; *Surface*, July 2019; *WSJ. Magazine*, March 2018. **Clients include:** Noma, J.Lindeberg, Royal Copenhagen, Georg Jensen, and Mark Kenly Domino Tan. **Awards:** AD200 (influencers); winner, Design of the Year and Space of the Year, *Bo Bedre* Design Awards, 2020; Best New Restaurant, *Wallpaper** Design Awards, 2019; winner, Furniture of the Year and Interior Designer of the Year *Bo Bedre* Design Awards, 2018.
studiodavidthulstrup.com
@studiodavidthulstrup

Faye Toogood
Born 1977. Based in London. Established 2008. **Selected Commissions:** Casa Paloma, Private Residence, Ibiza, 2018; Mulberry Regent Street, London, 2018; North Hill, London, 2018; Carhartt WIP Kings Cross, London, 2017; Tapestry Penthouse, London, 2017. **Press and Publications:** *Vogue*, October 2020; *AD*, September 2020; *T: The New York Times Style Magazine*, March 2020; *WSJ. Magazine*, April 2017; *Financial Times: How To Spend It*, January 2015. **Clients include:** Mulberry, Carhartt, Hermès, and Tiina the Store. **Awards and Exhibitions:** AD100; AD200 (influencers); *Downtime: Daylight, Candlelight, Moonlight*, NGV Triennial, Melbourne, Australia, 2020; *Assemblage 6: Unlearning*, Friedman Benda, New York, 2020; *Useful/Beautiful: Why Craft Matters*, Harewood Biennial, Leeds, UK, 2019; *I Draw*, D Museum, Seoul, South Korea, 2019; Designer of the Year, Frame Awards, 2019.
t-o-o-g-o-o-d.com / fayetoogood.com
@t_o_o_g_o_o_d

Virginia Tupker Interiors
Virginia Tupker
Born 1978 in London. Based in Darien, Connecticut, USA. Established 2009. **Selected Commissions:** Upper East Side Brownstone, New York, 2020; Upper East Side Apartment, New York, 2018; Bridgehampton Beach House, Bridgehampton, New York, 2018; Southampton Estate, Southampton, New York, 2018; Chelsea Townhouse, New York, 2011. **Press and Publications:** *Vogue*, January 2012 and September 2019; *AD*, March 2019; *Elle Decor*, May 2016. **Clients include:** Lauren Santo Domingo, Tabitha Simmons, and Derek Blasberg. **Awards:** AD100; *Elle Decor* A-List; Stars on the Rise Award, Decoration & Design Building, 2017.
virginiatupker.com
@virginiatupker

Vincent Van Duysen
Born 1962 in Lokeren, Belgium. Based in Antwerp, Belgium. Established 1989. **Selected Commissions:** JNcQUOI Comporta, Portugal, ongoing; EK Residence, Los Angeles, 2020; Central: The Original Store, Bangkok, Thailand, 2020; Casa M, Melides, Portugal, 2019; August, Antwerp, Belgium, 2019; HBH Residence, Southampton, New York, 2018. **Press and Publications:** *Casabella*, June 2020; *T: The New York Times Style Magazine*, March 2020; *Wallpaper**, September 2019; *Vincent Van Duysen: Works 2009–2018* (Thames & Hudson, 2018); *Vincent Van Duysen: Complete Works* (Thames & Hudson, 2010). **Clients include:** Central Group, Kanye West and Kim Kardashian West, José Caireta, Jenni Kayne, Loro Piana, and Paula Amorim and Miguel Guedes de Sousa. **Awards:** AD100; *Elle Decor* A-List; Interior Designer of the Year, EDIDA, 2020; Lifetime Achievement Award, Henry van de Velde, 2019; Designer of the Year, Biennale Interieur, Belgium, 2016. **Other:** Molteni&C | Dada, creative director, 2016–present.
vincentvanduysen.com
@vincentvanduysenarchitects / @vincentvanduysen

Gert Voorjans
Born 1962 in Leut, Belgium. Based in Antwerp, Belgium. Established 1997. **Selected Commissions:** DIVA Antwerp Home of Diamonds, Antwerp, 2017; Manila House Private Members' Club, 2016; Joyce, Hong Kong, 2007; Dries Van Noten, global locations, 2005–10. **Press and Publications:** *AD Spain*, April 2019; *Vogue Hong Kong*, March 2019; *Galerie*, Spring 2019; *Vogue Russia*, August 2018; *Tatler Philippines*, August 2018. **Clients include:** Dries Van Noten, DIVA, Manila House, Joyce, and Shangri-La Hotels and Resorts. **Events:** Art Basel, Hong Kong, 2019; SEVVA, Hong Kong, 2019; SANSIRI x Gert Voorjans, Bangkok, 2019; AD Intérieurs, Paris, 2016 and 2017.
gertvoorjans.com
@gertvoorjans

Joyce Wang
Born 1982 in Hawaii. Based in London and Hong Kong. Established 2011. **Selected Commissions:** Mott 32 Singapore, 2019; Oscuro Lounge and Kyubi Restaurant, The Arts Club, London, 2019; Mandarin Oriental Hyde Park, London, 2019; Equinox Hudson Yards Club and Spa, New York, 2019; Ichu, Hong Kong, 2018. **Press and Publications:** *Vogue Hong Kong*, February 2020; *South China Morning Post*, February 2020; *Tatler Hong Kong*, March 2019; *Wallpaper**, November 2019; *Barrons*, October 2019. **Clients include:** Mandarin Oriental, Mott 32, Equinox Hotels, The Arts Club, and Ichu. **Awards and Events:** jury member, *Dezeen* Awards 2020; Designer of the Year, Hospitality Design, 2020; Vanguard, Design Anthology Awards, 2019; scenography for *Louis Vuitton Objets Nomades*, Art Basel, Hong Kong, 2019; World Interior of the Year, INSIDE: World Festival of Interiors, 2014.
joycewang.com
@joycewangstudio

Kelly Wearstler
Born 1967 in Myrtle Beach, South Carolina. Based in Los Angeles. Established mid-1990s. **Selected Commissions:** Austin Proper, Austin, Texas, 2019; Santa Monica Proper, Santa Monica, California, 2019; Four Seasons Resort Anguilla, West End, Anguilla, 2016. **Press and Publications:** *AD France*, May/June 2020; *AD*, May 2020; *Elle Decoration UK*, May 2020; *Vogue Living Australia*, May/June 2019; *Kelly Wearstler: Evocative Style* (Rizzoli, 2019). **Clients include:** Bergdorf Goodman, Viceroy Hotels & Resorts, Westfield Century City, Tides Miami, and Four Seasons Hotels and Resorts. **Awards and Events:** in 2020, Wearstler was the first interior designer to teach a MasterClass series; AD100; *Elle Decor* A-List; Top International Designer, *AD Spain*, 2016; Top 20 Interior Designers, *Wallpaper**, 2015; The Style & Design 100, *Time*, 2007.
kellywearstler.com
@kellywearstler

Bunny Williams
Bunny Williams and Elizabeth Lawrence
Williams born 1944 in Charlottesville, Virginia; Lawrence born 1978 in Wilmington, Delaware. Based in New York. Established 1988. **Selected Commissions:** Mexico Office, Mexico City, 2019; House in Provence, France, 2018; Southampton Estate, Southampton, New York, 2018; Aspen Vacation Ski Home, 2017; New York City Penthouse, 2011. **Clients include:** numerous private clients. **Awards and Events:** Rising Star Award (Lawrence), New York School of Interior Design, 2020 AD100; *Elle Decor* A-List; Giants of Design, *House Beautiful*, 2006; Hall of Fame, *Interior Design*, 1995; chair of Kips Bay Decorator Show House since 2012.
bunnywilliams.com
@bunnywilliams_interiordesign

Woodson & Rummerfield's House of Design
Ron Woodson and Jaime Rummerfield
Woodson born in Los Angeles; Rummerfield born in Long Beach, California. Based in Los Angeles. Established 2004. **Selected Commissions:** Ritz-Carlton Residences, Los Angeles, 2016; Richard Neutra, Los Angeles, 2012; La Collina, Beverly Hills, 2010; Doheny Road, Beverly Hills, 2010; Donald Wexler, Palms Springs, 2008. **Press and Publications:** *House Beautiful*, January 2018; *Elle Decor*, February 2018; *Luxe Interiors + Design*, May 2017; *AD Italy*, December 2015; *High Style* (Chronicle Books, 2008). **Clients include:** Courtney Love, Christina Aguilera, John Travolta and Kelly Preston, Nick Cannon, and Versace. **Awards:** California's Top 50 Tastemakers and Influencers, *Angeleno*, 2020; Best Interior Design, City of West Hollywood Awards, 2019; Interior Designers of the Year, ARTS Awards, Dallas Market Center, 2017; Top 20 Interior Designers in Los Angeles, *Hollywood Reporter*, 2017; Top 25 African American Interior Designers (Woodson), Black Interior Designers Network, 2012–present. **Other:** founders, Save Iconic Architecture.
wandrdesign.com
@woodson_rummerfields / @jrummerfield / @rwwoodson

Yabu Pushelberg
George Yabu and Glenn Pushelberg
Yabu born in Toronto; Pushelberg born in Toronto. Based in Toronto and New York. Established 1980. **Selected Commissions:** La Samaritaine, Paris, 2020; Four Seasons Kuwait, 2019; Arbor, Hong Kong, 2018; Las Alcobas Napa Valley, California, 2017; London EDITION, 2013. **Press and Publications:** *WWD*, May 2020; *Vogue Hong Kong*, March 2020; *AD Pro*, April 2019; *New York Times*, April 2019; *Forbes*, March 2017; *New York Times*, July 2013. **Clients include:** Aman, Bergdorf Goodman, EDITION Hotels, LVMH, Raffles Sentosa Island. **Awards:** *Elle Decor* A-List; BoF 500; Interior Designer of The Year, *Elle Decor*

Japan, 2019; Travel Designer of The Year, *Surface*, 2019; Most Admired Firm, *Interior Design*, 2018 and 2019.
yabupushelberg.com
@yabupushelberg

Teo Yang Studio
Teo Yang
Born in Seoul, South Korea, where the firm is also based. Established 2009. **Selected Commissions:** Wellness K and Restaurant, Kukje Gallery, Seoul, 2020; Vacheron Constantin Collaboration, Hong Kong, 2019; Café Aalto by Mealdo, Seoul, 2018; VIP Reception, Korean Cultural Center, Beijing, 2017; Lotte World Tower 123rd Floor, Sky Premium Lounge, Seoul, 2017. **Press and Publications:** *Galerie*, Summer 2020; *Cereal*, Spring 2020; *Wallpaper**, January 2019; *Elle Decor China*, July 2018; *Design Anthology*, June 2018. **Clients include:** Lotte Group, ROK Ministry of Culture, Sports & Tourism, Samsung, Kukje Gallery, and Vacheron Constantin.
Awards and Exhibitions: Topawards Asia, 2020; *Wallpaper* Handmade*, Salone del Mobile, Milan, 2019; YEOL Heritage Foundation Furniture Exhibition, 2019; *One of Not Many*, exhibition for Vacheron Constantin, Hong Kong, 2019; Award of Merits, Korea Expressway Corporation, 2016.
teoyangstudio.com
@teoyang

Pierre Yovanovitch
Born 1965 in Nice, France. Based in Paris and New York. Established 2001. **Selected Commissions:** XI Penthouses, New York, 2021; Private residences, London, Paris, and the Hamptons, New York, 2020; Le Coucou, Méribel, France, 2019; Hélène Darroze, The Connaught Hotel, London, 2019; LOVE furniture collection, 2019; Tour Maubourg, Paris, 2019. **Press and Publications:** *AD*, August 2020; *Elle Decor*, June 2020; *AD France*, May 2020; *Financial Times*, December 2019; *Pierre Yovanovitch: Interior Architecture* (Rizzoli, 2019). **Clients include:** Kering Group, Maisons Pariente Hotel Group, HFZ Capital Group, Vignobles Austruy, and Kamel Mennour Gallery. **Awards and Events:** AD100; *Elle Decor* A-List; jury member, *Dezeen* Awards, 2020; Designer of the Year, *Wallpaper**, 2019; jury member and exhibition curator, Design Parade Toulon, 3rd International Festival of Interior Design, Toulon, France, 2018; AD Intérieurs, Paris, multiple years.
pierreyovanovitch.com
@pierre.yovanovitch

INDEX

Page numbers in *italics* refer to illustrations

11 Howard *238*
25th Street 151, *151*
28th Street *150*, 151
56 Leonard, Indoor/Outdoor Sculpture Garden *232*
432 Park Avenue *37*

A

Aalto, Alvar 223, 229
The Abacos, Bahamas, Zanzibar 225, *225*
Acuna, James 14–17, 312
AD Intérieurs *287*
Aesop 87, *87*, 265
    Aesop (London) *101*
    Aesop (Rome) *101*
Agnes Studio 219
Alesch, Stephen 210–11, 318
Allbright Mayfair 127, *127*
Allegra, The Stratford *236*
Alonso, Roman 64–5, 313
Altadena 193, *193*
Amagansett, New York, USA, Amagansett House 175, *175*
Amélie Maison d'art 23, *23*
Amenia, New York, USA, Troutbeck 57, *57*
Ampeer *52*, 53
Amsterdam, Cecconi's, Soho House Amsterdam 43, *43*
Anderson, Wes 9, 117, 175
André Fu Studio 88–9, 314
Annabel's Private Members' Club 47, *47*
Antwerp, Belgium
    August 281, *283*
    Jim Thompson *286*
    Penthouse Mulier *227*
    VVD II Attic 281, *281*
    VVD II Residence 281, *281*
Apartment 48 18–19, 312
Apartment Jean Goujon *252*
Apollo, Achille Salvagni Atelier 223, *223*
Arctander, Philip 137
Arlington, Roger 93
Arnalaya Bali 249, *249*
Arp, Jean 175
Art Basel Hong Kong 289
Art Collector Pied-à-Terre *82*, *83*
Artedomus Sydney 241, *241*
Artek 229
    Artek HQ *228*, 229
Arturo Arita 83, *83*
ASH 9, 20–1, 312
Ashby, Sophie 244–7, 319

Aspen, Colorado, USA, Aspen Home *112*, 113, *113*
Associazione Chianti *78*
Attico Design 55
The Audo *176*, 177, *177*
Audoux-Minet 137
August 281, *283*
Aups, France, Château de Fabrègues *309*, *309*
Australian Interior Design Awards 97
Aux Abris 205

B

Back Home, Milan Design Week *54*, 55
Les Bains 21
Bali, Indonesia, Arnalaya Bali 249, *249*
Baltimore, Maryland, USA, Chesapeake 123, *124*
Bangkok, Thailand, Peacock Alley, Waldorf Astoria Bangkok *88*, 89
Bankowsky, Marc 161
Bar and Caffé Palladio *182*, 183, *183*
Bar Marilou, Maison de la Luz 259, *260*
Barcelona, Spain, Wellbeing Collection, Nanimarquina Textile Collection 265, *265*, *266*
Barragán, Luis 23, 191
Barrière-Desseigne, Diane 251
Barwon River House *164*, 165, *165*
Basquiat, Jean-Michel 49, 87
Batiik Studio 9, 22–3, 312
Baur's Restaurant 47
Bay Area Home *194*, 195, *195*
Beach House 203, *203*
Beefbar Paris *134–5*
The Beekman Hotel 47, *47*
Behun, Kelly 9, 24–7, 312
Bel Ombre, Mauritius, Mauritius Villa 185, *185*
Bella's Home *198*, 199, *199*
Bellville, Texas, Texas Farmhouse 195, *196–7*
Benichou, Rebecca 22–3, 312
BENSLEY 28–31, 312
Bensley, Bill 28–31, 312
Bergamin, Sig 32–5, 312
Bergdorf Goodman 303
Berke, Deborah 36–7, 312
Berkus, Nate 9, 38–41, 312
Bernard Dubois Architects 86–7, 314
Berners Tavern, London EDITION 303, *304–5*
Bethesda Residence 53, *53*
Beverly Hills, California, USA
Beverly Hills Residence *292*, 293, *293*
Tom Ford 263, *263*

Big Sky, Montana, USA, Montana Ski House *114–15*
Birch Castle 91, *91*
Bjerre-Poulsen, Jonas 176–7, 317
Blasberg, Derek 279
Bloomsbury Group 141
BoConcept 99
Boozer, Rayman 18–19, 312
Boronkay, Linda 42–5, 312
Borsani, Osvaldo 73
Bottura, Massimo 265
Bowen, Andrew 20–21, 312
Boyajian, Sonia 259, *259*
Brâncuși, Constantin 39
Brent, Jeremiah 39
Bridgehampton, New York, USA, Bridgehampton Beach House 279
Brigette's Home 213, *213*, *214*, *215*
Brighton Residence 97, *97*
Brooklyn, New York, USA, Private Brooklyn Brownstone *204*, 205
Brudnizki, Martin 43, 46–7, 313
Brussels, Belgium
    Aesop 87, *87*
    Ixelles *308*, *309*
Bryan, Katherine 257
The Bu *212*, 213, *213*
Bullard, Martyn Lawrence 48–9, 313
Buxbaum Gordon, Lauren 39, 312
Byron Bay, New South Wales, Australia, Raes on Wategos *136*, 137

C

California, USA, National Park Cabin 65
Callidus Guild 25
Cambridge, Duchess of 187
Campbell, Nina 145
Candlenut, COMO Dempsey *168*, 169
Candy Bar, The Siren Hotel 21, *21*
Cannes, France, Villa Odaya *132*, 133, *133*
Capella Ubud 29, *29*
Carbone *90*, 91
Cárdenas, Rafael de 50–1, 313
Cardin, Pierre 309
Carhartt 275
    Carhartt WIP Kings Cross *275*
Carlton North Residence 109, *109*
Carré Or 133, *133*
Carter, Darryl 9, 52–3, 313
Casa Arrayan 99
Casa FOA 98
Casely-Hayford, Charlie 245
Catonsville, Maryland, USA, Rosewood *122*, 123
Cecconi's, Soho House Amsterdam 43, *43*

Celestino, Cristina 54–5, 313
Central Park West 93, *93*, 94
Chalet in Rougemont *162*
Champalimaud, Alexandra 56–9, 313
Champalimaud Design 56–9, 313
Chapo, Pierre 163
Charlotte Street Hotel 141, *143*
ChartierDalix 23
Château de Fabrègues *309*, *309*
Chelsea Apartment *186*, 187, *187*
Chesapeake 123, *124*
Chess Club *120*, 121
Chic by Accident 191
Chicago, Illinois, USA, Chicago Townhouse 39, *39*
Chimney House 271, *273*
Chondi, Maharashtra, India, Copper House II 255, *255*
CHZON 60–3, 313
Cibic, Aldo 281
Cliff Top House *104*, 105, *105*
Clockwork, Fairmont Royal York 207, *207*
The Coal Office 69, *69*
Coburg, Germany, Schloss Untersiemau *284*, 285
Cocktail Hour, Achille Salvagni Atelier *223*
Coed Darcy, Wales, UK, Welsh House *187*, 187
Commune Design 64–5, 259, 313
Como, Italy, Lake Como Villa 249, *249*
COMO Hotels and Resorts 169
    COMO Dempsey *168*, 169, *169*, *170–1*
Connecticut House 175, *175*
Conran Design Group 81
Contemplative Haussmanian Space *84*
Cooper, Will 20–1, 312
Cooper Hewitt National Design Award 233
Copenhagen, Denmark
    The Audo *176*, 177, *177*
    Chimney House 271, *273*
    Jotun Lady Catalogue Shoot *147*
    Noma *270*, 271, *271*
    Peter's House 271
    Restaurant 108 237, *239*
    Vester Voldgade 272
Copper House II 255, *255*
Cossé, Matthieu 309
Le Coucou 309, *310*, *311*
Coutume, Institut Finlandais Paris 149, *149*
Cox, Stephen 141
Crawford, Ilse 264–7, 320
Créac'h, Bertrand 133
Create Academy 145

Cumming, Rose 93
Cussen, Kana 98–9, 314

D

Daminato, Albano 248–9, 319
Darlinghurst Apartment *108*
Darlinghurst Apartment III *165*
Darlinghurst Residence 203, *203*
Darré, Vincent 160–1, 316
Dautresme, Maxime 10–13, 312
David Collins Studio 81
David Netto Design 9, 174–5, 316–17
De Cotiis, Vincenzo 66–7, 313
De Meyer, Paul 227
De Palma, Brian 233
de Sede 49
Deborah Berke Partners 36–7, 312
Dehradun, Uttarakhand, India, Ganga
    Maki Textile Studio *254*, 255, *255*
Delettrez, Delfina 51
Dempsey Cookhouse and Bar, COMO
    Dempsey 169, *170–1*
Design Institute of Australia 105
Design Research Studio 68–71, 313
Despont, Thierry 217
Desseigne, Dominique 251
Detroit, Michigan, USA
    Candy Bar, The Siren Hotel 21, *21*
    Junior League of Detroit Show
        House 205, *205*
    The Siren Hotel 21, *21*
Dimorestudio 72–5, 313
Dior 73
    Dior Dubai *73*
Dirand, Jacques 77
Dirand, Joseph 76–7, 314
Divine *22*, 23, *23*
Dix, Sean 78–9
dix design+architecture 78–9, 314
Dixon, Tom 43, 68–71, 313
Doherty, Mardi 80–1, 314
Doherty Design Studio 80–1, 314
D'Orazio, Alessandro 146–7, 316
Dorotic, Kylie 9, 96–7, 314
Dries, Sophie 82–5, 314
Dries Van Noten Tokyo 285, *285*
du Chalard, Amélie 23, *23*
Dubai, United Arab Emirates, Dior Dubai
    73
Dubois, Bernard 86–7, 314
Dufy, Raoul 127

E

East Hampton, New York, USA, East
    Hampton Beach House *224*, 225
East Melbourne Residence *109*
Ebeltoft, Denmark, Kvadrat HQ 229,
    229, *230*
Emilia Wickstead 121, *121*
Empress *268*, 269
Esora 269, *269*
Ett Hem Hotel Stockholm *264*, 265

Experimental Cocktail Club 55, *55*
Experimental Group 61

F

Farm Girl Chelsea 9, *116*, 117
Fendi 55, 73, 307
    Fendi Casa 55
    Fendi Sloane Street *73*
Finnish Association of Interior
    Architects 149
Firmdale Hotel 141
Fitzroy House 157, *157*, *158*
Flamingo Estate 253, *253*
Flatiron Loft *18*
Flavin, Dan 233
The Fleming 11, *11*
Floral Court 244, 245
Florence, Italy, Villa in Florence 73,
    74–5
Fogia 147
    Fogia 2019 Catalogue Shoot *146*
Foley, Marcus 11
Ford, Tom 99, 263, *263*
Four Seasons, The Surf Club 77, *77*
Fournier, Karl 252–3, 319
Frame 241
Franklin, Kesha 103, 314–15
Franklin Hills 193, *193*
Freud, Bella 199
Fu, André 9, 88–9, 314
Fulk, Ken 90–1, 314
Fundação Ricardo do Espirito Santo
    Silva 57
Furstenberg, Diane von 299

G

Galilée Apartment *86*
Galleguillos, Juan 99
Galli, Fawn 92–5, 314
Ganga Maki Textile Studio *254*, 255, *255*
Garcia, Jacques 250–1, 319
Garcia, Nina 285
Garraf, Little Beach House Barcelona
    43, *43*
Gates, Theaster 113
Geelong, Victoria, Australia, Barwon
    River House *164*, 165, *165*
Gensler Architects 149
Gillier, Thierry 87
Girafe *76*, 77
Givenchy 77, 185
Glen Ellen, California, USA, The Lake
    House *91*
Glenn Sestig Architects 226–7, 318
Goéritz, Mathias 191
GOLDEN 9, 96–7, 314
Green Branch *125*
Greenwich, Connecticut, USA,
    Connecticut House 175, *175*
Greenwich Village Penthouse 39, *39*, *40*
Greenwich Village Residence 50, *51*, *51*
Grisanti, Hugo 98–9, 314

Grisanti & Cussen 98–9, 314
Guadagnino, Luca 100–1, 314
Guarujá, Iporanga Beach House 33, *34–5*
Guthrie, Hamish 108–11, 315
Gyedong Hanok Residence *306*, 307

H

Hakim, Hana 240–1, 319
Halden Interiors 102–3, 314–15
Hall, Bridie 187
The Hamptons, New York, USA
    Hamptons Home *24*
    Hamptons Residence *130*
Hancock Park Residence *300*, *301*
Hare, Meryl 104–7, 315
Hare + Klein 9, 104–7, 315
Haring, Keith 165
Haslam, Nicky 9, 117
Hayslett, Linda 150–1, 316
Hecker, Paul 108–11, 315
Hecker Guthrie 108–11, 315
Heckman, Ari 20–1, 312
Heizer, Michael 255
Held, Al 175
Hélène Darroze 309
Helsinki, Finland
    Artek HQ *228*, 229
    Hotel Torni Helsinki *148*, 149
    The Savoy Helsinki *265*
Henderson, Shawn 112–15, 315
Henriksen, Signe Bindslev 237, 318–19
Hermès 11, 185
Hermosa Beach, California, USA
    25th Street 151, *151*
    28th Street *150*, 151
Heuman, Beata 9, 116–19, 315
HH Penthouse *280*
Hickling, Briar 152–3, 316
Hickman, Fran 120–1, 315
Hidden Tints 179, *179*, *180*
Hieronymus *226*, 227, *227*
Hills, Adam 198–201
Hillsdale, New York, USA, Hillsdale
    Home 113, *113*
Hjorth, Axel Einar 309
Ho Chi Minh City, Vietnam, Renkon 79, *79*
Hockney, David 253
Hodges, Laura 122–5, 315
Holland Park Villas 245, *245*
Hollywood, California, USA, Hollywood
    Residence *298*
Honbo at The Mills 15
Hong Kong
    Associazione Chianti 78
    The Fleming 11, *11*
    Honbo at The Mills 15
    Ichu *288*, 289
    John Anthony *152*, 153
    Louise Hong Kong 89
    Miss Lee Restaurant 15, *15*
    Nha Trang Vietnamese Canteen
        16–17

The Ocean 11, *12–13*
Osteria Marzia *10*, 11, *11*
St. Regis Hong Kong 89, *89*
Soho House Hong Kong 44–5
Tate Dining Room 14, 15
Yardbird 79, *79*
Hoodless, Suzy 126–9, 315
Hôtel Barrière Le Fouquet's Paris 251,
    251
Hotel Bel-Air 57, *59*
Hotel de la Coupole, MGallery 30–1
Hotel Rose Bay *202*
Hotel Torni Helsinki *148*, 149
House in Rio *163*
House in Tokyo *163*
House of Vincenzo and Claudia Rose De
    Cotiis 66, 67, *67*
Houshmand, John 207
Hoyt, Cody 25
Hu, Rossana 173, 316–17
Huanca, Donna 219
Hudson River Pied-à-Terre *103*
Hudson Yards 207
Huh, Young 130–1, 315
Humbert, Emil 132–5, 315
Humbert & Poyet 132–5, 315
Hunt, Holly 103
Hyde Park Gate 141, *142*
Hyères, France, La Boutique, Villa
    Noailles *160*

I

Ichu *288*, 289
ICICLE 87
IKEA 265
Il Palazzo Experimental 61, *62*
Inner West House *166–7*
Institut Finlandais 149, *149*
Interior Design Hall of Fame 57, 233
Interior Design Institute 149
Iporanga Beach House 33, *34–5*
Ippoh Tempura Bar, COMO Dempsey
    169, *169*
Ixelles *308*, 309

J

J. M. Weston 77
Jagger, Mick 163, 285
Jain, Bijoy 254–5, 319
Jaipur, India, Bar and Caffé Palladio
    182, 183, *183*
Jeanneret, Pierre 87, 133, 155, 185
Jim Thompson 286
JJ Acuna / Bespoke Studio 14–17, 312
Johanknecht, Steven 64–5, 313
John Anthony *152*, 153
Johnson, Tamsin 136–9, 315
Jotun 147
    Jotun Lady Catalogue Shoot *147*
Judd, Donald 303
Junior League of Detroit Show House
    205, *205*

K

Kaihoi, David 194–7, 317
Kaptensgatan I 189, *189*
Kaptensgatan II *188*
Karl Lagerfeld 161, 185
Katsuya Brickell 303, *303*
Keliki, Capella Ubud 29, *29*
Kelly Behun Studio 9, 24–7, 312
Kemp, Kit 140–3, 315
The Kent *56*
Kentucky Farmhouse Retreat *218*, 219, *219*
Klang, Robin 188–9, 317
Kollekted By 147
Konig, Rita 144–5, 316
Kortrijk, Belgium, VDC Residence *282*
Kråkvik, Jannicke 146–7, 316
Kråkvik & D'Orazio 146–7, 315
Kuma, Kengo 163
Kvadrat HQ 229, *229*, *230*
Kyoto, Achille Salvagni Atelier *222*

L

La Boutique, Villa Noailles *160*
Laajisto, Joanna 148–9, 316
Lagerfeld, Karl 55, 185
Lairesse, Gérard de 285
Lake Como Villa 249, *249*
The Lake House *91*
Landers, Sean 217
Lanvin 73, 185
Las Vegas, Nevada, USA, Carbone *90*, 91
Lau, Vicky 15
Laura Hodges Studio 122–5, 315
Laurent Kew 96
LaVerne, Philip and Kelvin 113
Lawrence, Elizabeth 297, 320
Le Corbusier 121, 191
LFM Loft *233*
LH.Designs 150–1, 316
Liaigre, Christian 83
Linehouse 152–3, 316
Little Beach House Barcelona 43, *43*
Little Holmby *192*, 193, *193*
London, UK
   Aesop *101*
   Allbright Mayfair 127, *127*
   Allegra, The Stratford *236*
   Annabel's Private Members' Club 47, *47*
   Apollo, Achille Salvagni Atelier 223, *223*
   Bella's Home *198*, 199, *199*
   Berners Tavern, London EDITION 303, *304–5*
   Carhartt WIP Kings Cross *275*
   Charlotte Street Hotel 141, *143*
   Chelsea Apartment *186*, 187, *187*
   Chess Club *120*, 121
   The Coal Office 69, *69*
   Cocktail Hour, Achille Salvagni Atelier *223*
   Emilia Wickstead 121, *121*
   Farm Girl Chelsea 9, *116*, 117
   Fendi Sloane Street *73*
   Floral Court *244*, 245
   Holland Park Villas 245, *245*
   Hyde Park Gate 141, *142*
   Kyoto, Achille Salvagni Atelier *222*
   London EDITION *302*, 303
   London Residence 257, *257*
   London Residence with Garden *174*, 175
   London Townhouse *233*
   The Lounge, The Stratford *237*
   Mandarin Oriental Hyde Park 289, *289*
   Martha's Home *199*, *200*
   Mezzanine Cocktail Bar *237*
   Mulberry Regent Street *276–7*
   North Hill *274*
   Paddington Pied-à-Terre 117, *117*
   Sam's Home 199, *201*
   Sea Containers London 68, 69, *70–1*
   A Sophisticated Townhouse *126*
   Steeles Road *231*
   Sticks'n'Sushi 177, *177*
   Summit House *178*, 179, *179*
   Suzy's Own Home *128*, 129
   Tapestry Penthouse 275, *275*
   TVC Apartment *246–7*
   West London Townhouse 117, *118*, *119*
Long Beach, California, USA, Palo Verde *151*
Long Island Home 25, *25*, *26*
Loos, Adolf 289
López-Quesada, Isabel 154–5, 316
Los Altos *258*
Los Angeles, California, USA
   Altadena 193, *193*
   Brigette's Home 213, *213*, *214*, *215*
   Flamingo Estate 253, *253*
   Franklin Hills 193, *193*
   Hancock Park Residence *300*, 301
   Hotel Bel-Air 57, *59*
   Little Holmby *192*, 193, *193*
   Los Angeles Residence *299*
   Los Feliz Spanish Colonial 64, 65
   Romualdez Residence 217, *217*
   Sonia Boyajian Jewelry Studio *259*
Louise Hong Kong 89
Louisville, Kentucky, USA, Kentucky Farmhouse Retreat *218*, 219, *219*
The Lounge, The Stratford *237*
Lynch, Fiona 156–9, 316

M

M. N. Roy *191*
McIntyre, Peter 81
McKimm, Alicia 9, 96–7, 314
McLeod, Courtney 204–5, 318
McNaughton, James 49
Madison Avenue 293, *294*
Madrid, Spain, Madrid House *155*
Mahoney, Monica C. 219
Maison&Objet 61
Maison de la Luz 259, *260*, *261*
Maison Vincent Darré 160–1, *161*, 316
Maki, Chiaki 255
Malibu, California, USA
   The Bu *212*, 213, *213*
   Malibu Residence *293*
Mallet-Stevens, Robert 161
Malvern Residence *81*
Mandarin Oriental Hyde Park 289, *289*
Manhattan Triplex 233, *234*, *235*
Mantoloking, New Jersey, Mantoloking Residence *131*
Marino, Peter 93, 271
Marquise *81*
Martha's Home *199*, *200*
Martin Brudnizki Design Studio 46–7, 313
Marty, Olivier 252–3, 319
Matégot, Mathieu 93
Mauritius Villa 185, *185*
Mayor, Julian 39
Meacham Nockles McQualter 137
Medina, Seattle Home 41
Meilichzon, Dorothée 9, 55, 60–3, 313
Melbourne, Victoria, Australia 96
   Brighton Residence 97, *97*
   Carlton North Residence 109, *109*
   East Melbourne Residence *109*
   Fitzroy House 157, *157*, *158*
   Malvern Residence *81*
   Ottawa House *159*
   Piccolina Collingwood *110–11*
   St Kilda Residence *80*
   South Yarra House *156*, 157, *157*
   Wattle House 97, *97*
   Zoobibi *240*, 241, *241*
Memphis Group 169, 219
Menorca, Spain, Menorca Experimental 60, 61, *61*
Méribel, France, Le Coucou 309, *310*, *311*
Merrill, Frances 192–3, 317
Mexico City, Mexico, Mexico City Residence *220–1*
Mezzanine Cocktail Bar *237*
Miami, Florida, USA
   Four Seasons, The Surf Club 77, *77*
   Katsuya Brickell 303, *303*
Michaux, Florian 11
Midtown Penthouse *26*, 27
Milan, Italy
   Back Home, Milan Design Week 54, 55
   House of Vincenzo and Claudia Rose De Cotiis 66, 67, *67*
Milan Design Week 55, 147
Mindel, Lee F. 232–5, 318
Minkoff, Jonathan 20–1, 312
Miolini, Barbara 183
Mirò, Joan 61
Miss, Mary 255
Miss Lee Restaurant 15, *15*
MJ Residence *248*
Mlinaric, David 162–3
Mlinaric, Henry and Zervudachi 162–3, 316
Moda Operandi 121, 279
Mok, Alex 152–3, 316
Mollino, Carlo 121
Monaco, Carré Or 133, *133*
Mongiardino, Lorenzo 279
Montana Ski House *114–15*
Moran, Britt 73, 313
Morris, William 187
Mott 32 Singapore 289, *290–1*
Mulberry 275
   Mulberry Regent Street *276–7*
Mumbai, Soho House Mumbai 42, *43*
Musée d'Orsay 83
Museum of Modern Art, New York 9, 69

N

Nanimarquina 265, *265*, *266*
Natale, Greg 164–7, 316
Nate Berkus Associates 9, 38–41, 312
National Park Cabin 65
Navone, Paola 168–71, 316
Neri, Lyndon 172–3, 316–17
Neri&Hu 8, 153, 172–3, 316
Netto, David 9, 174–5, 316–17
Neutra, Richard 175
New Orleans, Louisiana, USA
   Bar Marilou, Maison de la Luz 259, *260*
   Maison de la Luz 259, *260*, *261*
New York City, New York, USA
   11 Howard *238*
   56 Leonard, Indoor/Outdoor Sculpture Garden *232*
   432 Park Avenue *37*
   The Beekman Hotel 47, *47*
   Central Park West 93, *93*, *94*
   Flatiron Loft *18*
   Greenwich Village Penthouse 39, *39*, *40*
   Greenwich Village Residence 50, *51*, *51*
   HH Penthouse *280*
   Hudson Yards *207*
   The Kent *56*
   LFM Loft *233*
   Madison Avenue 293, *294*
   Manhattan Triplex 233, *234*, *235*
   Midtown Penthouse *26*, 27
   New York City Pied-à-Terre *296*, 297
   Nobu Downtown *206*, 207, *208–9*
   Noho Residence 19, *19*
   Paradise Club, Times Square EDITION 303, *303*
   Redemption *100*

Roman and Williams Guild 211, *211*
Roush *216*
Tom Ford 263, *263*
Tribeca Residence 243, *243*
Upper East Side Apartment *278, 279*
Upper East Side Residence (ASH) *20*
Upper East Side Residence (Robert Stilin) *242, 243, 243*
Upper East Side Townhouse 37, *37*
Verõnika *210*, 211, *211*
Washington Square Park 93, *95*
West Chelsea Apartment *36*, 37
West Eleventh Street Residence *51*
The Whitby Hotel *140*, 141, *141*
Nha Trang Vietnamese Canteen *16–17*
Nobu Downtown *206, 207, 208–9*
Noho Residence 19, *19*
Noma 237, *270, 271, 271*
Norm Architects 176–7, 317
Norobata, Grow Hotel *181*
North Farm *144*, 145, *145*
North Hill *274*
Note Design Studio 178–81, 317
Nouvel, Jean 271
NXTHVN 37
NYC×DESIGN 233

O
Obumex 227
The Ocean 11, *12–13*
Offices Paris Champs-Élysées *185*
Ogunbanwo, Lakin 245
O'Keeffe, Georgia 259
Old Furniture Factory *105, 106*
Olivetti 55
Oppenheim, Meret 55, 73
Osteria Marzia *10*, 11, *11*
Ottawa House *159*
Oudejans, Marie-Anne 182–3, 317

P
Paddington Pied-à-Terre 117, *117*
Palazzo Privé Fendi VIP Apartment Store *72*, 73
Palm Beach, Florida, USA
    Palm Beach I *262*
    Palm Beach Residence 297, *297*
Palm Springs, California, USA
    Palm Springs Residence *299*
    Villa Grigio 48, *49, 49*
Palo Verde 151, *151*
Paradise Club, Times Square EDITION 303, *303*
Paris, France
    AD Intérieurs *287*
    Amélie Maison d'art 23, *23*
    Apartment Jean Goujon *252*
    Art Collector Pied-à-Terre *82, 83*
    Arturo Arita 83, *83*
    Beefbar Paris *134–5*

Contemplative Haussmanian Space *84*
Coutume, Institut Finlandais Paris 149, *149*
Divine 22, *23, 23*
Galilée Apartment *86*
Girafe *76, 77*
Hôtel Barrière Le Fouquet's Paris 251, *251*
ICICLE *87*
J. M. Weston *77*
Offices Paris Champs-Élysées *185*
Paris 9th District *184*, 185
Paris Apartment *154, 155, 155*
Paris Residence *256, 257, 257*
La Réserve Paris Hotel and Spa *250*, 251
Street Art Collector *85*
Parmentier, Stéphane 184–5, 317
Peach, Sevil 228–31, 318
Peacock Alley, Waldorf Astoria Bangkok *88, 89*
Peduzzi, Rocco 249
Penthouse Mulier *227*
Pentreath, Ben 186–7, 317
Pentreath & Hall 187
Peregalli, Roberto 256–7, 319
Perriand, Charlotte 87
Perspective Studio 188–9, 317
Peter's House *271*
Phoenix, Maryland, USA, Green Branch *125*
Picasso, Pablo 61, 87, 133
Picault, Emmanuel 9, 190–1, 317
Piccolina Collingwood *110–11*
Platner, Warren 77
Ponti, Gio 67
Porter Teleo 205
Poyet, Christophe 132–5, 315
Primack, Rodman 218–21, 318
Private Brooklyn Brownstone *204*, 205
Private Home Sweden *267*
Pushelberg, Glenn 302–5, 321
Putman, Andrée 25

R
Raes on Wategos *136*, 137
Raffles Singapore 57, *57, 58*, 169
Ralph Lauren 233, 263, 279
Reath Design 192–3, 317
Redd, Miles 194–7, 317
Redd Kaihoi 194–7, 317
Redemption *100*
Redzepi, René 271
Rengthong, Jirachai 29
Renkon 79, *79*
La Réserve Paris Hotel and Spa 250, 251
Restaurant 108 237, *239*
Retrouvius 198–201, 317
Richards, Jonathan 202–3, 317
Richards Stanisich 202–3, 317

Right Meets Left Interior Design 204–5, 317
Rijavec, Ivan 157
Riksbyggen 99, *99*
Rio de Janeiro, Brazil, House in Rio *163*
Ristorante Adriatica 63
The Robertson Small Hotel 245, *245*
Rockwell, David 206–9, 318
Rockwell Group 206–9, 318
Roddick, Sam 199
Roman and Williams 210–11, 318
Roman and Williams Guild 211, *211*
Romanek, Brigette 212–15, 318
Romanek Design Studio 212–15, 318
Rome, Italy
    Aesop *101*
    Palazzo Privé Fendi VIP Apartment 72, 73
Romualdez, Daniel 216–17, 318
Romualdez Residence 217, *217*
Rønn Von Lotzbeck, Kasper 176–7, 317
Rose, Claudia 67
Rosewood *122, 123*
Rosewood Hotels 11, 29
Rougemont, Switzerland, Chalet in Rougemont *162*
Roush *216*
Royère, Jean 121, 163
RP Miller 218–21, 318
Ruby, Sterling 285
Rummerfield, Jaime 298–9, 320
Rützou, Peter Bundgaard 237, 318–19

S
Saarinen, Eero 225
Saddle River, New Jersey, USA, Saddle River Residence *19*
St Kilda Residence *80*
St. Regis Hong Kong 89, *89*
Salci, Emiliano 73, 313
Salvagni, Achille 222–3, 318
Sam's Home 199, *201*
Samseong-dong Residence 307, *307*
San Diego, California, USA, Los Altos *258*
San Francisco, California, USA
    Bay Area Home *194*, 195, *195*
    Birch Castle 91, *91*
San Jose, California, San Jose Estate 102, *103, 103*
Sands Point, New York, USA, Sands Point Family Home *205*
Santa Catarina House *191*
Santa Monica, California, USA
    Santa Monica Apartment *65*
    Santa Monica Proper 293, *295*
Santiago, Chile
    Casa Arrayan *99*
    Casa FOA *98*
Santo Domingo, Lauren 279
São Paulo, Tropical House 8, *32, 33, 33*

Sapa, Hotel de la Coupole, MGallery *30–1*
Sartori Rimini, Laura 257, 319
The Savoy Helsinki *265*
Scarpa, Carlo 55, 67, 289
Scheerer, Tom 224–5, 318
Schindler, Rudolph 259
Schloss Untersiemau *284, 285*
Schrager, Ian 25
Sea Containers London 68, 69, *70–1*
Seattle Home *41*
Segal, Walter 275
Seoul, South Korea
    Gyedong Hanok Residence *306*, 307
    Samseong-dong Residence 307, *307*
    Sulwhasoo Flagship *173*
    Wellness K, Kukje Gallery *307*
Sestig, Glenn 226–7, 318
SevilPeach 228–31, 318
Shamshiri, Pamela and Ramin 259, 319
Shanghai, China, Tingtai Teahouse 153, *153*
Shelton, Peter L. 233
SheltonMindel 232–5, 318
Shinta Mani Hotel Group 29
    Shinta Mani Siem Reap *28*, 29
Short Hills, New Jersey, USA, Short Hills *92*, 93, *93*
SIA Projects 299
Siem Reap, Shinta Mani Siem Reap *28*, 29
Simons, Raf 227
Singapore
    Candlenut, COMO Dempsey *168*, 169
    Dempsey Cookhouse and Bar, COMO Dempsey 169, *170–1*
    Empress *268*, 269
    Esora 269, *269*
    Ippoh Tempura Bar, COMO Dempsey 169, *169*
    Mott 32 Singapore 289, *290–1*
    Raffles Singapore 57, *57, 58*
    Tiffin Room, Raffles Singapore 57, *57*
    Whitegrass *269*
The Siren Hotel 21, *21*
Smithson, Robert 255
Sofield, William 262–3, 319
Soho House 43
    Soho House Hong Kong *44–5*
    Soho House Mumbai *42*, 43
    Soho House New York *265*
Sonia Boyajian Jewelry Studio *259*
Sophie Dries Architect 82–5, 314
A Sophisticated Townhouse *126*
South Australian Design Institute of Australia 109
South Yarra House *156*, 157, *157*
Southampton, New York, Long Island Home 25, *25, 26*
Space Copenhagen 236–9, 318
Speake, Maria 198–201, 317

Standefer, Robin 211, 318
Stanisich, Kirsten 202–3, 317
Starck, Philippe 25
Steeles Road 231
The Stella Collective 240–1, 318–19
Stern, Robert A. M. 93
Sticks'n'Sushi 177, 177
Stilin, Robert 242–3, 319
Sting 233
Stockholm, Sweden
   Ett Hem Hotel Stockholm 264, 265
   Fogia 2019 Catalogue Shoot 146
   Hidden Tints 179, 179, 180
   Kaptensgatan I 189, 189
   Kaptensgatan II 188
   Norobata, Grow Hotel 181
   Private Home Sweden 267
   Torsgatan 189, 189
The Stratford 236, 237, 237
Street Art Collector 85
Studio Alchimia 169
Studio Ashby 244–7, 319
Studio Daminato 248–9, 319
Studio Geiger Architecture 65
Studio Jacques Garcia 250–1, 319
Studio KO 252–3, 319
Studio Mumbai 254–5, 319
Studio OTTO 168–71, 316
Studio Peregalli 256–7, 319
Studio Shamshiri 258–61, 319
Studio Sofield 262–3, 319
Studioilse 264–7, 319
Styler, Trudie 233
Stynen, Léon 227
Sulwhasoo Flagship 173
Summit House 178, 179, 179
Sussex, UK, Sussex Cottage 117
Suzhou, Jiangsu Province, China,
   Suzhou Chapel 8, 173, 173
Suzy's Own Home 128, 129
Swarovski 289
Swedish Summer House 265
Switzerland, Baur's Restaurant 47
Sydney, New South Wales, Australia
   Artedomus Sydney 241, 241
   Beach House 203, 203
   Cliff Top House 104, 105, 105
   Darlinghurst Apartment 108
   Darlinghurst Apartment III 165
   Darlinghurst Residence 203, 203
   Hotel Rose Bay 202
   Inner West House 166–7
   Old Furniture Factory 105, 106
   Palm Beach Residence 139
   Tamarama Residence 137, 137, 138
   Woollahra Valley 107

T
Takenouchi, Naoko 268–9, 320
Takenouchi Webb 268–9, 320
Tamarama Residence 137, 137, 138
Tapestry Penthouse 275, 275

Tate Dining Room 14, 15
Teesdale, UK, North Farm 144, 145, 145
Teo Yang Studio 306–7, 321
Tepoztlán, Morelos, Mexico, Santa
   Catarina House 191
Texas Farmhouse 195, 196–7
Thulstrup, David 270–3, 320
Tiffin Room, Raffles Singapore 57, 57
Tingtai Teahouse 153, 153
Tino Zervudachi & Associés 163
Tocca 183
Tokyo, Japan
   Dries Van Noten Tokyo 285, 285
   House in Tokyo 163
Tom Ford (Beverly Hills) 263, 263
Tom Ford (New York City) 263, 263
Toogood, Faye 274–7, 320
Toronto, Ontario, Canada, Clockwork,
   Fairmont Royal York 207, 207
Torsgatan 189, 189
Tribeca Residence 243, 243
Tropical House 8, 32, 33, 33
Troutbeck 57, 57
Tsingpu Yangzhou Retreat 172, 173
Tupker, Virginia 278–9, 320
Turnbull, Gary 229, 318
Turrell, James 233
TVC Apartment 246–7
Twombly, Cy 175
Tynell, Paavo 309

U
Ubaldini, Benedetta Mori 233
Upper East Side Apartment 278, 279
Upper East Side Residence (ASH) 20
Upper East Side Residence (Robert
   Stilin) 242, 243, 243
Upper East Side Townhouse 37, 37
Uppsala, Sweden, Riksbyggen 99, 99
Urquijo, Inés 155

V
Vacheron Constantin 307
Van Duysen, Vincent 265, 280–3, 320
Van Noten, Dries 285, 285
VDC Residence 282
Venice, Italy
   Experimental Cocktail Club 55, 55
   Il Palazzo Experimental 61, 62
   Ristorante Adriatica 63
Verõnika 210, 211, 211
Vester Voldgade 272
Villa in Florence 73, 74–5
Villa Grigio 48, 49, 49
Villa Odaya 132, 133, 133
VIPP 271
Virginia Tupker Interiors 278–9, 320
Vistosi, Luciano 61
Vitra 229
Voorjans, Gert 9, 284–7, 320
VVD II Attic 281, 281
VVD II Residence 281, 281

W
Wang, Joyce 288–91, 320
Warhol, Andy 49, 165, 299
Washington, D.C., USA
   Ampeer 52, 53
   Bethesda Residence 53, 53
   Washington Square Park 93, 95
Wattle House 97, 97
Wearstler, Kelly 292–5, 320
Webb, Marc 268–9, 320
Weehawken, New Jersey, Hudson River
   Pied-à-Terre 103
Wegner, Hans 213
Wellbeing Collection, Nanimarquina
   Textile Collection 265, 265, 266
Wellness K, Kukje Gallery 307
Welsh House 187, 187
West Chelsea Apartment 36, 37
West Eleventh Street Residence 51
West Hollywood, West Hollywood
   Residence 38
West London Townhouse 117, 118, 119
Western Cape, South Africa, The
   Robertson Small Hotel 245, 245
The Whitby Hotel 140, 141, 141
White, Stanford 53
Whitegrass 269
Wickstead, Emilia 121, 121
Williams, Bunny 296–7, 320
Woodson, Ron 298–9, 320
Woodson & Rummerfield's House of
   Design 298–301, 320
Woollahra Valley 107
A Work of Substance 10–13, 312
Wright, Frank Lloyd 191

X
Xucú, Yucatán, Mexico, Xucú Hacienda
   190, 191, 191

Y
Yabu, George 302–5, 321
Yabu Pushelberg 302–5, 320–1
Yang, Teo 306–7, 321
Yangzhou, Jiangsu Province, China,
   Tsingpu Yangzhou Retreat 172, 173
Yardbird 79, 79
Young Huh Interior Design 130–1, 315
Yovanovitch, Pierre 83, 308–11, 321
Yves Saint Laurent 161, 253, 263

Z
Zanzibar 225, 225
Zervudachi, Tino 163, 316
Zoobibi 240, 241, 241
Zurich, Switzerland, Hieronymus 226,
   227, 227

PICTURE CREDITS

Cover Images:

Wallpaper (front and back): Simon Brown, Courtesy of Firmdale Hotels; blue curtain (front, back, and spine): Tuomas Uusheimo, Courtesy of SevilPeach; corrugated surface (front, lower half): Jovian Lim, Courtesy of Takenouchi Webb; terrazo (back): Dzek Marmoreal tile designed by Max Lamb, Courtesy of Dzek; tiles (front, center): Karel Balas, Courtesy of CHZON.

Interior Images:

(t) = top
(c) = center
(b) = bottom

Aaron Pocock, Courtesy of Studio Daminato: 249(b); Adam Kuehl, Courtesy of JJ Acuna / Bespoke Studio: 15(b), 16–17; Adrian Gaut, Courtesy of Roman and Williams: 210, 211(t); Adrien Dirand: 76–77; Aesop / Romain Laprade, Courtesy of Bernard Dubois Architects: 87(t); Albert Font, Courtesy of Studioilse: 265(b), 266; Alexander James, Courtesy of Studio Ashby: 246–7; Alfredo Gildemeister, Courtesy of Grisanti & Cussen: 98; Amanda Kho, Courtesy of Linda Boronkay: 44–45; Ana María López, Courtesy of Grisanti & Cussen: 99(b); Andrea Ferrari, Courtesy of Dimorestudio: 72, 73(b), 74–75; Andreas von Einsiedel / Getty Images: 162; Andy Liffner, Courtesy of Perspective Studio: 188–9; Annabel Elston, Courtesy of Fran Hickman Design & Interiors: 120–1; Anson Smart: 136–9; Anson Smart, Courtesy of Greg Natale: 164–7; Anthony Crolla, Courtesy of Suzy Hoodless: 126; Anton Sucksdorf, Courtesy of Studioilse: 265(c); Ben Rahn / A-Frame: 207(b); BENSLEY: 29(t); BENSLEY / Björn Teufel: 28; BENSLEY / Krishna Adithya: 29(b), 30–31; Bertrand Fompeyrine / BCDF studio, Courtesy of Batiik Studio: 23(b); Björn Wallander / OTTO Archive: 50–51; Björn Wallander, Courtesy of Sig Bergamin: 32–35; Björn Wallander, Courtesy of Tom Scheerer: 225; Black Sheep Restaurants, Courtesy of dix design+architecture: 78; Brittany Ambridge / OTTO Archive: 103(b); Bycastel, Courtesy of Sophie Dries: 83(b); Chris Cooper, Courtesy of Deborah Berke Partners: 37(t); Christian Harder: 20–21; Christopher Dibble, Courtesy of Nate Berkus Associates: 38, 41; Christopher Stark: 102, 103(t); Costas Picadas, Courtesy of Fawn Galli: 95; Courtesy of Roman and Williams: 211(b); Courtesy of Studio OTTO: 168–71; Daici Ano / FWD, Courtesy of Gert Voorjans: 285(b); Daniel Kukla, Courtesy of Kelly Behun: 25(t); Dennis Lo, Courtesy of A Work of Substance: 10–13; DePasquale+Maffini: 190, 191(b); Derek Swalwell: 80–81; Derek Swalwell, Courtesy of The Stella Collective: 241(b); Dirk Weiblen, Courtesy of Linehouse: 153; Douglas Friedman / Trunk Archive: 90–91; Douglas Friedman, Courtesy of Martyn Lawrence Bullard: 48–49; Douglas Friedman, Courtesy of Romanek Design Studio: 213–15; Dylan Chandler: 279(t); EDITION Hotels, Courtesy of Yabu Pushelberg: 302, 303(b), 304–5; Edmon Leong, Courtesy of Joyce Wang Studio: 290–1; Emily Andrews, Courtesy of Design Research Studio: 68, 70–71; Eric Laignel / Rockwell Group: 206, 208–9; Evan Joseph, Courtesy of Champalimaud Design: 56; Fabrice Fouillet, Courtesy of Daniel Romualdez Architects: 217; Fabrice Rambert, Courtesy of Studio Jacques Garcia: 251; Felix Forest, Courtesy of Richards Stanisich: 202–3; Felix Odell, Courtesy of Studioilse: 265(t); Francesco Lagnese / OTTO Archive: 175(t); Francesco Lagnese, Courtesy of Bunny Williams Inc: 297; Francesco Lagnese, Courtesy of Tom

Scheerer: 224; Francis Amiand, Courtesy of Humbert & Poyet: 132–5; François Halard, Courtesy of Kelly Wearstler: 293(b); François Halard, Courtesy of Vincent Van Duysen: 280, 282; Frederik Vercruysse, Courtesy of Studio Daminato: 249(t); French+Tye: 275(b), 276–7; Gaëlle Le Boulicaut: 253; Giaime Meloni, Courtesy of Batiik Studio: 22, 23(t); Gieves Anderson: 278, 279(b); Gilbert McCarragher, Courtesy of SevilPeach: 229–31; Giovanni Hänninen: 254; Giulio Ghirardi: 100–1; Gordon Beall, Courtesy of Darryl Carter: 52; Grégoire Gardette, Courtesy of Studio Jacques Garcia: 250; Heather Talbert, Courtesy of Nate Berkus Associates: 39(t); Helen Cathcart, Courtesy of Studioilse: 267; Helen Norman: 123(b), 124; Hélène Binet: 255(b); Henry Bourne, Courtesy of Toogood: 274; Henry Wilson, Courtesy of Marie-Anne Oudejans: 182–3; Hur In Young (Studio Hur), Courtesy of Teo Yang Studio: 306; Idha Lindhag, Courtesy of Grisanti & Cussen: 99(t); Irina Boersma, Courtesy of David Thulstrup: 270, 271(b), 272–3; Iwan Baan: 255(t); James John Jetel, Courtesy of JJ Acuna / Bespoke Studio: 14; James McDonald, Courtesy of Joyce Wang Studio: 289; James McDonald, Courtesy of Martin Brudnizki Design Studio: 46–47; Jason Ingram: 186, 187(t); Jean Pierre Vaillancourt, Courtesy of Stéphane Parmentier: 185(t); Jean-Pierre Gabriel Lebailly: 226–7; Jean-François Jaussaud / Lux Productions: 184, 185(b); Jen Wilding, Courtesy of Hare + Klein: 104, 105(t); Jennifer Hughes: 122, 123(t), 125; Jérôme Galland: 309(b), 310–11; Joachim Wichmann, Courtesy of Vincenzo De Cotiis: 66–67; John Bessler, Courtesy of Young Huh: 131; John Dolan Photography, Courtesy of Right Meets Left Interior Design: 204; John Neitzel / Digital Destinations, Courtesy of Right Meets Left Interior Design: 205; Jonas Bjerre-Poulsen / Fogia: 146; Jonas Bjerre-Poulsen, Courtesy of Norm Architects: 176–7; Jonas Lindström, Courtesy of Note Design Studio: 181; Jonathan Leijonhufvud, Courtesy of Linehouse: 152; Julie Holder, Courtesy of Nate Berkus Associates: 39(b), 40; Justin Coit, Courtesy of Romanek Design Studio: 212; Joe Fletcher, Courtesy of Studio Daminato: 248; Jose Manuel Alorda: 308, 309(t); Jovian Lim, Courtesy of Takenouchi Webb: 269; Karel Balas, Courtesy of CHZON: 60–63; Karel Balas, Courtesy of Cristina Celestino: 55(b); Karyn Millet: 299–301; Kasia Gatkowska, Courtesy of Vincent Van Duysen: 281(b); Kelly Marshall, Courtesy of Apartment 48: 19(t); Kris Tamburello, Courtesy of Yabu Pushelberg: 303(t); Laure Joliet / This Represents: 192–3; Lauren Pressey: 150–1; Leon Liang Xu / Frontality, Courtesy of JJ Acuna / Bespoke Studio: 15(t); Leonardo Costa: 163(b); Line Klein / Jotun: 147; Lit Ma, Courtesy of Joyce Wang Studio: 288; Lykke Foged: 201; Magnus Marding, Courtesy of Studioilse: 264; Marcel Lennartz, Courtesy of Gert Voorjans: 286–7; Marco Ricca, Courtesy of Apartment 48: 19(b); Margaret Stepien, Courtesy of Linda Boronkay: 43(b); Mark Seelen, Courtesy of Linda Boronkay: 43(t); Mary E. Nichols: 298; Masano Kawana, Courtesy of AFSO: 88; Melanie Acevedo, Courtesy of Kelly Wearstler: 294; Michael Moran / OTTO Archive: 232–5; Michael Mundy, Courtesy of Daniel Romualdez Architects: 216; Michael Sinclair: 198–200; Michael Sinclair, Courtesy of Note Design Studio: 178, 179(t); Michael Weber, Courtesy of AFSO: 89(t); Michael Weber, Courtesy of Champalimaud Design: 59; Mickey Hoyle, Courtesy of Studio Ashby: 245(t); Miguel Flores-Vianna / The Interior Archive: 53; Mike Palumbo, Courtesy of dix design+architecture: 79(t), 79(c); Mikko Ryhänen, Courtesy of Studio Joanna Laajisto: 148–9; Miles and Miles, Courtesy of Champalimaud: 57(t); Mirjam Bleeker: 191(t); Mitchell Geng, Courtesy of AFSO: 89(b); Ngoc Minh Ngo, Courtesy of Young Huh: 130;

Nicholas Calcott, Courtesy of Kelly Behun: 24; Nick Parisse, Courtesy of Apartment 48: 18; Nobuaki Nakagawa, Courtesy of Mlinaric, Henry & Zervudachi: 163(t); Note Design Studio: 179(b), 180; Omar Sartor, Courtesy of Cristina Celestino: 54, 55(t); Paola Pansini, Courtesy of Dimorestudio: 73(t); Paolo Petrignani, Courtesy of Achille Salvagni Atelier: 222, 223(b); Pascal Chevallier / WiB Agency: 256, 257(t); Pascale Beroujon, Courtesy of Maison Darré: 160; Paul Costello, Courtesy of Bunny Williams Inc: 296; Paul Massey / House & Garden ©The Condé Nast Publications Ltd: 128; Paul Massey, Courtesy of Suzy Hoodless: 129; Pedro Pegenaute: 172–3; Peer Lindgreen, Courtesy of Design Research Studio: 69; Peter Krasilnikoff, Courtesy of David Thulstrup: 273(t); Philip Durrant, Courtesy of Studio Ashby: 245(b): 244; Philippe Kliot, Courtesy of Achille Salvagni Atelier: 223(t); Raffles / Ralf Tooten, Courtesy of Champalimaud Design: 57(b), 58; Ricardo Labougle: 154–5; Richard Powers: 64; Richard Powers, Courtesy of Fawn Galli: 92–94; Richard Powers, Courtesy of Kelly Behun: 26(b), 27; Rishad Mistri: 175(b); Robert Rieger, Courtesy of Vincent Van Duysen: 283; Romain Laprade, Courtesy of Bernard Dubois Architects: 86, 87(b); Scott Frances / OTTO Archive: 207(t), 262; Scott Frances, Courtesy of Deborah Berke Partners: 37(b); Sean Fennessy, Courtesy of Fiona Lynch: 159; Sean Fennessy, Courtesy of The Stella Collective: 240, 241(t); Shannon McGrath, Courtesy of Hare + Klein: 105(b), 106–7; Shannon McGrath, Courtesy of Hecker Guthrie: 108–11; Sharyn Cairns: 96–97, 156–8; Shim Yun Suk (Studio Sim), Courtesy of Teo Yang Studio: 307; Simon Bevan: 187(b); Simon Brown / The Interior Archive: 144–5; Simon Brown, Courtesy of Beata Heuman: 116–19; Simon Brown, Courtesy of Firmdale Hotels: 140–3; Simon Brown, Courtesy of Linda Boronkay: 42; Simon Upton / The Interior Archive: 174, 257(b); Siu Yan Fung & Kenji Chim, Courtesy of dix design+architecture: 79(b); Stephan Julliard, Courtesy of Sophie Dries: 82, 83(t), 84–85; Stephen Busken: 259; Stephen Kent Johnson / OTTO Archive: 65, 112–15, 218–21, 242–3; Stephen Kent Johnson, Courtesy of Studio Shamshiri: 260–1; Taran Wilkhu, Courtesy of Suzy Hoodless: 127; Tawan Cochonnet, Courtesy of Takenouchi Webb: 268; The Ingalls, Courtesy of Kelly Wearstler: 292, 293(t), 295; Thomas Seear-Budd, Courtesy of Vincent Van Duysen: 281(t); Tim Van de Velde, Courtesy of Gert Voorjans: 284, 285(t); Tobias Harvey: 275(t); Tom Ford International / Christian Horan: 263(t); Tom Ford International / Ted Morrison: 263(b); Trevor Tondro / OTTO Archive: 194–7; Tuomas Uusheimo, Courtesy of SevilPeach: 228; Vincent Desailly, Courtesy of Maison Darré: 161; wichmann+ bendtsen, Courtesy of Space Copenhagen: 236–9; William Waldron, Courtesy of Deborah Berke Partners: 36; William Waldron, Courtesy of Kelly Behun: 25(b), 26(t); Yann Deret: 252; Yoshihiro Makino, Courtesy of Studio Shamshiri: 258.

Every reasonable effort has been made to acknowledge the ownership of copyright for photographs included in this volume. Any errors that may have occurred are inadvertent, and will be corrected in subsequent editions provided notification is sent in writing to the publisher.

Phaidon Press Limited
2 Cooperage Yard
London E15 2QR

Phaidon Press Inc.
65 Bleecker Street
New York, NY 10012

phaidon.com

First published 2021
© 2021 Phaidon Press Limited

ISBN 978 1 83866 187 8

A CIP catalogue record for this book is
available from the British Library and the
Library of Congress.

Commissioning Editor: Virginia McLeod
Project Editor: Robyn Taylor
Production Controller: Jane Harman
Design: Melanie Mues, Mues Design, London
Artworker: Chris Lacy

Printed in Italy

CONTRIBUTOR BIOGRAPHIES

Camilla Frances is a journalist and editor
with more than a decade's experience writing
news and features for leading magazines
and newspapers. After graduating from
Cambridge University with a degree in
archaeology and anthropology, she went
on to study journalism at London's City
University. She is currently deputy editor of
the *London List*, a digital publication covering
art, architecture, and design.

Rachel Giles is a writer and editor working
in art, architecture, and design. Her previous
projects with Phaidon include *The Design Book*
(2020), *Living on Vacation* (2020), *Interiors:
The Greatest Rooms of the Century* (2019), and
the *Atlas of Brutalist Architecture* (2018).

Vera Kean lives in New York, where she writes
about art, film, and design.

Adelle Mills is a writer and artist living in
Melbourne (Narrm), Australia. Her doctorate
explored visual and human histories of the
instant message.

Pip Usher is a journalist known for her
cultural pieces and long-form profiles.
She has written for titles that include the
Economist, *Financial Times*, and *Vogue*. As a
lead writer for *Kinfolk*, Usher has interviewed
leading names in the art and design world,
and contributed extensively to *Kinfolk
Entrepreneur*, a collection of interviews with
today's creative class. After living in London,
New York, Beirut, and Bangkok, Usher has
made Jerusalem her home—for now.

PUBLISHER'S ACKNOWLEDGMENTS

The publisher would like to extend special
thanks to Caitlin Arnell Argles, Theresa
Bebbington, Jenny Florence, Jane Harman,
Chris Lacy, Virginia McLeod, João Mota,
Melanie Mues, William Norwich, Angelika
Pirkl, Isabella Ritchie, Hans Stofregen,
and Elizabeth White, as well as the wider
Phaidon team, for their support, enthusiasm,
and insight during the making of this book.
In addition, we would like to thank all the
nominators, designers, and writers for their
invaluable contributions—we are indebted to
you for your expertise and creativity.

CONTRIBUTOR CREDITS

Camilla Frances: A Work of Substance 10;
Apartment 48 18; Batiik Studio 22; BENSLEY
28; CHZON 60; Joseph Dirand 76; Sophie Dries
Architect 82; Bernard Dubois Architects 86;
André Fu Studio 88; Fran Hickman 120; Suzy
Hoodless 126; Tamsin Johnson 136; Joanna
Laajisto 148; Linehouse 152; Fiona Lynch 156;
Maison Vincent Darré 160; Mlinaric, Henry and
Zervudachi 162; Greg Natale 164; Neri&Hu 172;
Marie-Anne Oudejans 182; Stéphane Parmentier
184; Ben Pentreath 186; Emmanuel Picault
190; Glenn Sestig Architects 226; SevilPeach
228; Space Copenhagen 236; Studio Daminato
248; Studio Jacques Garcia 250; Studio KO 252;
Studio Mumbai 254; Studioilse 264; Virginia
Tupker Interiors 278; Vincent Van Duysen 280;
Pierre Yovanovitch 308.

Rachel Giles: Cristina Celestino 54; Vincenzo De
Cotiis 66; Dimorestudio 72; Luca Guadagnino
100; Humbert & Poyet 132; Isabel López-
Quesada 154; Paola Navone / Studio OTTO 168;
Rockwell Group 206; Daniel Romualdez 216;
Achille Salvagni 222; Robert Stilin 242; Studio
Peregalli 256; Studio Sofield 262; Gert Voorjans
284; Bunny Williams 296.

Vera Kean: Kelly Behun 24; Sig Bergamin 32;
Nate Berkus Associates 38; Martyn Lawrence
Bullard 48; Rafael de Cárdenas 50; Darryl Carter
52; Commune Design 64; Ken Fulk 90; Grisanti &
Cussen 98; Halden Interiors 102; Shawn
Henderson 112; Laura Hodges Studio 122; Young
Huh Interior Design 130; LH.Designs 150; David
Netto Design 174; Reath Design 192; Redd Kaihoi
194; Right Meets Left Interior Design 204; Roman
and Williams 210; Romanek Design Studio
212; RP Miller 218; Tom Scheerer 224; Studio
Shamshiri 258; Kelly Wearstler 292; Woodson &
Rummerfield's House of Design 298; Yabu
Pushelberg 302.

Adelle Mills: ASH 20; Deborah Berke Partners
36; Champalimaud Design 56; Fawn Galli 92;
SheltonMindel 232.

Pip Usher: JJ Acuna / Bespoke Studio 14;
Linda Boronkay 42; Martin Brudnizki Design
Studio 46; Design Research Studio 68; dix
design+architecture 78; Doherty Design Studio
80; GOLDEN 96; Hare + Klein 104; Hecker
Guthrie 108; Beata Heuman 116; Kit Kemp
140; Rita Konig 144; Kråkvik & D'Orazio 146;
Norm Architects 176; Note Design Studio 178;
Perspective Studio 188; Retrouvius 198;
Richards Stanisich 202; The Stella Collective
240; Studio Ashby 244; Takenouchi Webb 268;
David Thulstrup 270; Faye Toogood 274; Joyce
Wang 288; Teo Yang Studio 306.